Persistent Inequality

The children of undocumented migrants in the U.S. are trapped at the intersection of two systems in crisis: the public education system and the immigration law system. Based on a long tradition of scholarship in Latino education and on newer critical race theory ideas, *Persistent Inequality* answers burning questions about how educational policy has to rise to meet the unique challenges of undocumented students' lives as well as those which face nearly all Latinos in the U.S. educational system. How solid is the Supreme Court precedent, *Plyler v. Doe,* that allows undocumented children the opportunity to attend public K-12 school free of charge? What would happen if the Supreme Court overruled it? What is the DREAM Act and how would this proposed federal law affect the lives of undocumented students? How have immigration raids affected public-school children and school administrators? To shed some light on these vital questions, the authors provide a critical analysis of the various legal and policy aspects of the U.S. educational system, asserting that both the legal and educational systems in this country need to address the living and working conditions of undocumented Latino students and remove the obstacles to educational achievement which these students struggle with daily.

María Pabón López is a Professor of Law at Indiana University School of Law, Indianapolis.

Gerardo R. López is an Associate Professor of Education in the Department of Educational Leadership and Policy Studies at Indiana University, Bloomington.

The Critical Educator
Edited by Richard Delgado and Jean Stefancic

Persistent Inequality

Contemporary Realities in the
Education of Undocumented
Latina/o Students

María Pabón López ◆ **Gerardo R. López**

Routledge
Taylor & Francis Group

NEW YORK AND LONDON

First published 2010
by Routledge
270 Madison Ave, New York NY 10016

Simultaneously published in the UK
by Routledge
2 Park Square, Milton Park, Abingdon, Oxon, OX14 4RN

Routledge is an imprint of the Taylor & Francis Group, an informa business

Transferred to Digital Printing 2010

Typeset in Minion by Swales & Willis Ltd, Exeter, Devon

Library of Congress Cataloging in Publication Data
López, María Pabón.
Persistent inequality : contemporary realities in the education of undocumented
Latina/o students / María Pabón López and Gerardo R. López.
p. cm. — (The critical educator)
Includes bibliographical references and index.
1. Latin Americans—Education—United States. 2. Latin American students—
United States—Social conditions. I. López, Gerardo R. II. Title.
LC2670.3.L66 2009
371.829'68073—dc22
2009024314

ISBN 10: (hbk) 0–415–95793–1
ISBN 10: (pbk) 0–415–95794–X
ISBN 10: (ebk) 0–203–86513–8

ISBN 13: (hbk) 978–0–415–95793–9
ISBN 13: (pbk) 978–0–415–95794–6
ISBN 13: (ebk) 978–0–203–86513–2

Dedication

This book is a labor of love which we dedicate to our families. It is for our parents, both present and absent: Esteban and Leticia López; Luis and Naida Pabón. We appreciate all you have done for us. We also dedicate this book to our daughters Marina Nayar and Cora Lucía, who give inspiration and meaning to all we do. When Lucía found out we were writing a book about the education of children of immigrants, she cheerfully asked: "Can I help you?" Their help has consisted of being their wonderful young selves, keeping their parents grounded during the writing of this book. It is our sincere hope that their future—like that of the undocumented students about whom we write in this book—will be one bright with promise and possibility.

Contents

Acknowledgments

We thank Richard Delgado and Jean Stefancic for the opportunity to become part of the Critical Educator series. The kindness and patience of our editor Catherine Bernard is much appreciated as well. The following research assistants are commended for their indefatigable work on the different phases of this project: Diomedes Tsitouras, Blake Howell, Matthew Galasso, Patricia Chen, Rebecca Haven, Yan Kyoung (Lou) Nam, Stephanie Sicker, Magdalena Josipowicz, Stephen Leclere, Micah Vincent, Michelle Marie Polanco, Marisa Aguilar and Melody Goldberg. Indiana University School of Law—Indianapolis and the Grimes Trust provided generous funding to assist in the research for this book. We appreciate the superb research support of Miriam Murphy, Associate Director of the Ruth Lilly Law Library of the Indiana University School of Law, Indianapolis, and Dragomir Cosanici, then Head of Reference of the Ruth Lilly Law Library of the Indiana University School of Law, Indianapolis. The invaluable administrative support of Kyle Galster is much appreciated, as is the assistance of April Bruce, Angela Greene, April Meade, and Erin White. The authors also thank Richard Delgado, Kevin R. Johnson, Victor C. Romero, R. George Wright, Karen E. Bravo, Shawn M. Boyne, and Jennifer Chacón for reading earlier drafts of the chapters. Ediberto Román provided valuable insights, for which we grateful.

Introduction: Undocumented Students in the United States

An Educational and Critical Overview

More than a quarter century ago, the Supreme Court of the United States ruled that the children of persons who are unlawfully present in this country should be allowed to attend public schools. This case, *Plyler v. Doe*, marks the point of departure of this book. In this book, we highlight the current situation of Latino undocumented students—their social, legal, and political realities—while identifying the structures that disempower them. Using census and other available government data, we calculate the number of undocumented Latino students currently in U.S. schools and set forth a picture of their educational status and attainment. We will also review the challenges that stand in the way of educational achievement for Latino undocumented students, and paint a portrait of their life in schools.

But what exactly are the obstacles facing this young and vulnerable population? What are the daily lives of these students like? This introduction contextualizes the plight of Latina/o undocumented students in the United States, providing demographic and school enrollment information, explanations for migration and settlement patterns, and descriptions of the multiple challenges confronting schools in educating undocumented Latino students.

Undocumented Students at a Crossroads

The children of undocumented migrants in the United States are trapped at the intersection of two systems in crisis: the public education system and the immigration law system. These young people, who have come to the U.S. "through no fault of their own,"[1] are caught in the crossfire of the harsh law, policy, and rhetoric that currently pervade these two systems. Undocumented students also face legal uncertainties peculiar to them, and other uncertain identical to those facing other minority youth of low socioeconomic status. They also bear the brunt of the failure of the political process to secure comprehensive immigration reform.

These students suffer the inequities of high-stakes testing under the No Child Left Behind Act (NCLB),[2] as well as the daily challenge of resegregated

1

schools and recent U.S. Supreme Court precedent striking down voluntary integration plans.[3] The failure of schools to effectively meet their multifaceted educational and linguistic needs has created an educational crisis that leaves little room for optimism.[4]

Harsh immigration enforcement has brought nationwide workplace and predawn home raids and created a climate of fear among undocumented families worried about sending their children to school because of the danger of raids there.[5] Other children are left alone without an adult caretaker when their parents are seized and deported in these raids. Family members who have come to this country and eke out a living are now treated as criminal offenders and made part of the criminal law system. For example, in Iowa in May of 2008, following the largest immigration workplace raid in history, federal prosecutors charged 400 undocumented workers with aggravated identity theft and Social Security fraud, rather than the milder immigration violations which they would have been charged with in the past.[6]

In the midst of this maelstrom are the children of unauthorized migrants, who come to this country when their parents are pushed out of their countries by poverty or oppressive regimes. Pulled to the United States by the possibility of work and the opportunity of a decent life in a democracy, these parents break civil immigration law because they have no alternatives. The quotas for yearly admission established by Congress are extremely limited, and most working-class immigrants cannot qualify for employment-based immigration categories. The conditions these families typically find in the United States are often nearly as challenging as the ones they left in their home country: having to work in deplorable conditions to make ends meet, living in substandard housing, and having to endure hostile attitudes and constant threat of deportation.

A Note on Terminology

In this book we use "undocumented" or "unauthorized" to denote a person who is not a U.S. citizen and who is present in this country without legal authorization. We do not use the term "illegal," which is not an immigration law term. Furthermore, we use the term "noncitizen" in lieu of the term "alien," which is the immigration law term defining those who are not U.S. citizens.[7] This usage follows the practice of immigration law scholars who consider the term "alien" needlessly pejorative with connotations of otherness or lack of humanity.[8]

The children of undocumented migrants who are present in the country without authorization—as well as undocumented migrant children who are in this country without their parents or caregivers—may attend public schools under the *Plyler v. Doe* Supreme Court decision. We refer to this group collectively as "undocumented students." Those students who are born in the United States to undocumented parents are U.S. citizens by operation of the Fourteenth Amendment. Even so, some state policies fall heavily on them because of their parents' status. For example, in Indiana, authorities denied higher education assistance to U.S. citizens and legal permanent resident children whose parents were undocumented.[9] The Indiana scholarship program is a very successful one, having helped over 25,000 students, and is funded to the tune of $19 million a year.[10] A lawsuit recently allowed the children of undocumented parents to participate in the program; otherwise, the progeny of 75,000 people believed to be undocumented would have been excluded.

Despite these successes, proposed state legislation punishes U.S. citizen children for their parents' undocumented status. California voters will soon consider an initiative which will

> require all parents of newborns in California to prove U.S. citizenship or legal residency in order to receive their baby's birth certificate. Those who could not w[ill] have to pay a $75 fee for a certificate noting the child's "Birth to a Foreign Parent." The U.S. Department of Homeland Security would be alerted to the discrepancy."[11]

Thus, it is evident that the parent's unlawful status is being attributed to the children, even if they are U.S. citizens at birth.

The term "immigrant" is often used to identify the population of those present without legal authorization in the United States. However, this is incorrect usage under U.S. immigration law. Immigrants are noncitizens lawfully admitted to stay in the United States on a permanent basis. Thus, the undocumented population is not properly termed "immigrant." Thus, this book rejects that terminology. Finally, the term Latino or Latina is used to denote those coming from Latin American countries, as well as Chicano or Chicana, a term used to denote second-generation Mexican Americans.[12]

With this terminology in mind, let us address the obstacles daily confronting undocumented students in the United States.

Challenges Facing Undocumented Students

Numerous challenges face undocumented students despite *Plyler v. Doe*.[13] In *Plyler*, the Court held that undocumented children are entitled to a state-funded primary and secondary education. Yet undocumented students—the majority of them Latinos, mostly of Mexican origin—remain hostages to the anti-immigrant backlash, notwithstanding *Plyler*'s guarantee of a free public education. Although these students should be the heirs to a legacy of educational equality rooted in two earlier Mexican American school desegregation cases,[14] as well as the full-scale desegregation secured by *Brown v. Board of*

Education,[15] they nevertheless continue to find themselves enrolled in schools with high drop-out rates and low educational achievement.[16] Their future educational outlook is bleak, with educational success negatively correlated with time spent in the U.S.[17] As Rubén Rumbaut has concluded, "All other things being equal ... [Americanization] may be counterproductive for educational achievement."[18]

If the educational legacy has failed to materialize for Latino undocumented students, the questions that need urgent answers in order to assure the educational future of these students in the United States are:

- What can we learn from *Plyler v. Doe*, the seminal case itself, in view of the current educational outcomes of undocumented students?
- What is the future of *Plyler* as legal precedent under the new Supreme Court headed by Chief Justice John Roberts?
- What have been the impediments to reaching the full potential of *Plyler*'s promise of educational equality for undocumented students?
- What is the significance of *Plyler* in the current discussion of race, equality and exclusion in contemporary United States society?

These are large questions that no single book can completely answer. In an attempt to shed some light on these vital queries, however, this book explores various legal and policy aspects of the United States educational system as related to Latino undocumented students to assess how they have fared post-*Plyler.*

What We Know about Latino and Noncitizen Students

The latest census data show that 10.5 million students in the United States are children of noncitizens, and one-fourth of these students are foreign-born.[19] More than one-third of the children of noncitizens hail from Mexico while one-fifth come from other Latin American countries.[20] The census data also show that over 11.4 million Latino children under the age of 18 reside in the United States.[21] This number represents 16 percent of all the children in the United States, even though only 14 percent of the overall population is Latino.[22]

The census also indicates that the Latino population increased by approximately ten million individuals between 1990 and 2000, accounting for 38 percent of the United States' population growth during that decade.[23] During the period 1993–2003, Latino students accounted for two of every three students added to U.S. public schools.[24] The Census Bureau projects that by the year 2050, Latinos in the United States will number ninety-eight million— more than three times their current number—representing about 25 percent of the total population.[25] Moreover, by 2020, more than one in five children under 18 in the United States will be of Latino origin.[26]

Persons who live in undocumented status in the U.S. are forced by their precarious immigration situation to be elusive. Because students are a sub-component of the larger undocumented population, it is difficult to estimate the number of such schoolchildren in the United States.[27] Undocumented parents are reluctant to come forward and identify themselves to census takers or other social service providers for fear of being reported to the Immigration and Customs Enforcement agency ("ICE"). Some estimates have shown that undocumented students comprise two out of every ten undocumented persons in the country.[28] The latest studies estimate that there are 1.8 million undocumented children of the 11.9 million undocumented persons in the United States.[29] According to the available data, 65,000 undocumented students nationwide graduate from high school every year, whereas an estimated 15,000 undocumented students nationwide drop out of high school.[30]

While the number of undocumented Latino students remains unknown, the data on Latino students as a whole are much more reliable. Recent government figures suggest that much of the increase in minority enrollment in elementary and secondary schools is attributable to Latinos. In 2004, 42.1 percent of public elementary and secondary school students nationwide were racial minorities.[31] Slightly under half of these, or 19.1 percent, of all U.S. public school K-12 students were Latino.[32] In terms of change over time, the overall percentage of minority students in public schools increased by 17 percent between 1972 and 2000.[33] Slightly more than 10 percent of that increase was attributable to Latinos, while the number of African American students increased by only 2 percent.[34] Yet, Latinos have higher dropout rates and lower high school completion rates than African American, Asian American or White-Anglo students.[35] The dropout rate for Latino students is 28 percent as compared with 7 percent for White-Anglo students and 13 percent for African American students.[36] Finally, aggregate national statistics document lower achievement levels for Latino students in several areas, including standardized testing.[37]

While in school, Latino and African American fourth- and eighth-graders score below Asians and whites in the National Assessment of Educational Progress (NAEP) reading assessment.[38] Of all racial/ethnic groups, Latino elementary and secondary students had the highest percentage of students who spoke a language other than English.[39] In fact, when one looks at the available data, it is apparent that the current influx of new immigrant groups—documented and undocumented alike—is directly correlated with increases in the number of students who enter U. S. schools with little or no English proficiency.[40] Between 1990 and 2000, the overall Limited English Proficient ("LEP") student population in the United States increased from 14 million to 21.3 million.[41] Moreover, the most recent census data show that two-thirds of all non-English-speaking families speak Spanish.[42]

The data further show that 1.8 million school-age children live in households in which no one age 14 or older speaks English "very well."[43] This number is sobering because English proficiency is directly related to school achievement.[44] In the absence of adequate bilingual education, language minority students in general—and noncitizen students specifically (who are disproportionately represented among LEP students)[45]—are at serious risk for failure in school.

Members of the mainstream in the U.S. often view Latinos as cultural "others," even among marginalized groups. They are perceived as problem minorities, largely because of their growing presence in the U.S. coupled with their supposed failure to effectively assimilate into the larger society. The rapid growth of the Latino population, especially in regions outside the Southwest, has also been a source of tension and concern. States like North Carolina, South Carolina, Georgia, Arkansas, Missouri, Iowa, and Nebraska, are rapidly becoming destinations where Latino "newcomers" are settling.[46] Drawn by U.S. businesses and the desire to provide a better livelihood for their children, Latinos are now invigorating local economies in areas that have not historically attracted Latino workers. Issues pertaining to identity, citizenship, and belonging intensify in these communities because current personnel in schools and other state agencies lack experience and first-hand knowledge in working with them. Many Latino newcomers face a hostile reception, as local residents often struggle with how to best accommodate this group.

Undocumented children face special challenges because of the added stress associated with the fear of deportation and separation from family members.[47] This fear can extend all the way to the school gate. For example, in Virginia,

> [p]ublic employees in higher education are *encouraged* to voluntarily disclose to the Immigration and Naturalization Service and to the Office of the Attorney General in Virginia factual information indicating that a student on campus is unlawfully present in the United States, or enrolled without proper authorization.[48]

While this official policy is in effect only for colleges and universities, some elementary school officials have called ICE when parents "appeared" to be undocumented as they attempted to register their children in school.[49] In some instances, authorities have arrested and deported parents while taking their children to school.[50] Thus, both parents and students have this fear of being removed from the United States while exercising their *Plyler*-protected school attendance.

This fear of deportation has increased in the wake of the federal government's invitation to local law enforcement agencies to enforce immigration laws.[51] For example, in Florida, state law enforcement entered into a Memorandum of Agreement with the federal government so state law enforcement agents receive training from immigration authorities and then work under federal supervision enforcing federal immigration law.[52] Other states, such as Alabama, Arizona and Tennessee have followed suit.[53] Thus, deportation for the undocumented student may only be as far away as a call to the local police.

While the fear of deportation is omnipresent, issues related to economic survival, access to proper health and dental care, access to adequate housing and quality schools, and the psychological toll of being displaced in a foreign land all place enhanced demands on the undocumented student and add to the overall stigma of being a migrant.[54] Add to this the recent rise in housing segregation patterns—made worse by the recent Supreme Court decisions limiting school desegregation and authorizing return to neighborhood schools[55]—and the educational outlook for Latinos/undocumented students does not look very promising.[56]

This resegregation trend disproportionately affects Latinos due to the rise of predominantly Latino neighborhood schools once school districts discontinued busing.[57] In fact, data cited by the Supreme Court for the year 2000–2001 show that 76.3 percent of Latino children attend schools where minorities made up a majority of the student body.[58] The increased segregation of Latino students is most apparent in the western part of the country, where 80 percent of Latino students attend predominantly minority schools—schools with 50–100 percent minority enrollment.[59] Between 1968 and 2001, the percentage of Latino students in intensely segregated schools—schools with 90–100 percent minority enrollment—more than tripled from 12 percent to 37 percent.[60] Thus, Latino undocumented students who live in urban areas are likely experiencing the resegregation of United States public schools,[61] along with the high dropout rates, less well-qualified teachers, and fewer educational opportunities that go along with it.[62]

The rapid resegregation of public schools is made worse by unequal school funding formulas that often rely on property values to fulfill their educational mission. As a result of *San Antonio v. Rodriguez*,[63] states are not required to fund school districts equally, so long as the property tax formula provides for a basic school education and bears a rational relationship to a legitimate state interest.[64] Unfortunately, minority students disproportionately reside in poorer school districts where they generally perform below average on standardized tests and where, in fact, schools are more expensive to operate.[65] Moreover, after *Rodriguez*, school-finance equity concerns may only be challenged via state constitutional provisions. In other words, if a state constitution does not specifically address educational equity in school financing, those challenging unequal school financing will probably be left without any recourse.

For all these reasons, persistent inequality haunts the education of Latino students. A recently published longitudinal study of 15,000 eighth-grade students in the United States shows that, on average, Latinos are overrepresented with respect to certain risk factors. Such figures evidence how unprepared these students are for postsecondary education.[66] The study found that Latinos are overrepresented in the following risk areas: having parents without a high school degree ("educational legacy"); having a low family income; having siblings who have dropped out of school; being held back in school; having a C or lower grade point average; changing schools; and having children while still in high school.[67] The report concludes that:

> At almost every level ... Latino youth face an upward struggle. The impact of these forces is to suppress the educational opportunity for these youth and lead them to a future that requires more effort to keep on current standing with other students, much less than trying to climb up the ladder of opportunity.[68]

Needless to say, if a student is both Latino *and* undocumented, these challenges are compounded.

This is all a relatively new phenomenon. The rise of the large numbers of undocumented students today is the product of the country's recent regime of heightened border security. The difficulties in crossing the U.S.–Mexico border mean that undocumented parents often bring their children with them on the first crossing. In the past, undocumented parents would leave their children back at home in the care of friends or relatives until they secured jobs, learned to speak English, found housing, and settled into their lives in the U.S. Then, they would send for the children.

Enhanced border enforcement has increased the price of clandestine border crossing. Each crossing is much more expensive than before—the "coyotes" are charging more than twice or three times their past rates, now in the thousands of dollars—to guide would-be migrants to the U.S.[69] Also, they now traverse more dangerous terrain which is less patrolled by U.S. Border Patrol agents. Thus, many parents are forced to bring their children with them the first time, so they can travel together safely. The children are then thrust into survival mode along with their parents, creating nearly insurmountable obstacles to the youths' assimilation.[70] Because the parents lack basic cultural information, such as where it is safe to go for services and where not, or in which schools it is safe to enroll the children, or which doctors will treat them and not hand them in to the immigration authorities, it is the children who have to mature at an earlier age to assist their parents.

These children find themselves with parents who are fearful of deportation and uncertain of their future, clearly not the most auspicious beginning of the parent–child relationship in their new home in the U.S. Because the children typically learn English faster than the adults, who are at work all day and have scarce availability of adult English classes, the adults fall into the practice of having the youths act as interpreters. This dynamic places the children in an unexpected position of being a cultural expert and language interpreter for their parents. These new and different challenges which face undocumented students as they navigate their new lives in the U.S. call for a deep analysis of their experiences. This book uses Critical Race Theory as a theoretical framework to analyze the undocumented student and his or her encounters with all aspects of U.S. society, particularly the educational and legal systems.

Critical Race Theory

Throughout our chapters, we will deploy elements of Critical Race Theory ("CRT") and highlight its influence in the field of education, as well as explain how this book intersects with the work of CRT scholars in both Law and Education. CRT is a framework used to examine and challenge the ways race and racism implicitly and explicitly shape social structures, practices, and discourses. CRT scholars begin with the premise that race is a social construct and that racism is permanent in U.S. society. Rather than focus on explicit acts or incidents of racism, CRT scholars instead focus on the subtle, hidden, and insidious forms that operate at a deeper, more systemic level. By focusing on the hidden and everyday forms of racism, CRT posits that racism has never waned; it has merely assumed a normality, and thus an invisibility, in our daily lives.[71]

CRT provides a unique tool to analyze race and racism in the United States with its hallmark themes of interest convergence and racial homeostasis.[72] Interest convergence means that the advances of racial minorities only come about when it is in the interest of the dominant white majority, while racial homeostasis acknowledges the permanence of racism in U.S. society.

Another hallmark CRT theme is intersectionality, with its recognition that the categorizing of individuals (or groups) according to a single attribute for purposes of critical analysis leaves out the interplay of the attributes themselves. Leading CRT theorists Richard Delgado and Jean Stefancic have noted that "'[i]ntersectionality' means the examination of race, sex, class, national origin, and sexual orientation, and how their combination plays out in various settings."[73] They inquire what the significance is for people when they "exist at an intersection of recognized sites of oppression."[74] Intersectionality is particularly useful for the critical analysis of the lives of undocumented students, whose existences daily straddle the line between race, class/socioeconomic status, national origin and immigration status and who may be subject to multiple oppressions based on a myriad combinations of these identities.

Education scholars Tara Yosso and Daniel Solorzano have identified five CRT tenets.[75] They are: (1) the intercentricity of race and racism, (2) the challenge to dominant ideology, (3) the commitment to social justice, (4) the centrality of experiential knowledge, and (5) the interdisciplinary perspective.[76]

CRT has spurred multiple offshoot movements, such as Latino Critical Race Theory ("LatCrit"), Critical Race Feminism (CRF), Asian American Legal Scholarship (AsianCrit), and Queer Legal Theory, just to name a few. LatCrit scholarship, in particular, works to bring racial problems into social consciousness by examining layers of ethnic and racial subordination affecting Latinos and Latinas.[77] In other words, LatCrit centers the richness of Latino identities and experiences in order to develop an activist-oriented discourse that promotes social justice for Latinas and Latinos. The centering of experiential knowledge has found a useful tool in counter-stories.

Counterstorytelling

One aspect of CRT is the deployment of stories and counterstories—particularly those of people of color. CRT scholars identify two differing accounts of reality: the dominant reality that "looks ordinary and natural"[78] to most individuals, and a racial reality[79] that society has not circulated. The counterstories of people of color are those stories that are not told, stories that are consciously and/or unconsciously ignored or downplayed because they highlight a vastly different account of racism and racial relations in the United States.

Counterstorytelling is a method of recounting the experiences and perspectives of racially and socially marginalized people. They reflect the experiences of people of color in order to raise social awareness of injustice.[80] Some counterstorytelling skeptics contend that the focus should be on class inequality and capitalism rather than on race.[81] Other critics believe that the stories are less than useful because the experiences are atypical, they overemphasize race, they lack clarity, or they distort the truth.[82] Despite the critics, many CRT-oriented scholars highlight the functions of counterstories. These functions include: building community where it is most needed, challenging perceived wisdoms of race and racism, nurturing community wealth, and facilitating a transformative agenda.[83]

In fact, counterstories have been applied to educational challenges to better understand how minorities experience and respond to racism in school settings. In doing so, CRT in education asks four critical questions:

1 How do racism, sexism, classism, and other forms of subordination shape the experiences of students in the U.S.?
2 How do institutions of education maintain race, gender, class and immigration status (alienage) discrimination?

3 How do students respond to racism, sexism, and classism and discrimination status?
4 How can education work as a tool to remedy these problems?[84]

This book seeks answers to these four fundamental questions, with specific attention to the Latino undocumented student. These counterstories will attempt to highlight the real life experiences of the undocumented students—their fears, concerns and their young lives marked by an uncertain status.

Outline of the Book

Each of the chapters in this book focuses on a particular aspect of the experiences of undocumented students in the United States, analyzed from a legal and policy perspective. Chapter 1 discusses how, although *Plyler v. Doe*, a 1982 United States Supreme Court opinion, guarantees undocumented children the right to a free public education, more than 25 years later we have not seen substantial improvement in their educational achievement. Thus, this chapter will examine the *Plyler* opinion, to uncover shortcomings in its drafting and legal analysis that weaken its precedential value for Latino undocumented students. This chapter will also assess *Plyler*'s rationale and its challenges, current validity and possible survival. Finally, this chapter will illustrate how school districts nationwide have complied with *Plyler* over the years as well as alternative bases for its holding and global educational practices for undocumented students.

Chapter 2 surveys the obstacles that undocumented students face in their quest for higher education and analyzes and updates recent access to higher education litigation in various states. The chapter also surveys state and federal legislative proposals, such as the Development, Relief and Education for Alien Mission (DREAM) Act, which aim to provide undocumented students access to higher education. Finally, this chapter analyzes the First Amendment freedom of expression of undocumented students who have recently organized movements and campaigns to advocate for the pursuit of higher education and lawful employment opportunities for undocumented students.

Chapter 3 traces the roots of language education policies, arguing that the current backlash against bilingual education is, at least in part, a product of those very same acts, court decisions, policies, and referenda that aim to promote the language rights of language minority students. This chapter argues that language rights policies, while enormously important, nevertheless reinforce a deficit perception of second-language learners by characterizing them as having a "language problem."

Chapter 4 discusses accountability under NCLB and its implications for undocumented students and other children of color. This chapter argues that

NCLB is a double-edged sword. On the one hand, it calls for increased accountability for all students, including those who are low-income, limited English proficient, Latino, African American, or enrolled in special education. The Act calls for 100 percent proficiency in Mathematics, Reading, and Science by the year 2014, by holding schools accountable for meeting Adequate Yearly Progress ("AYP") in state-level exams and by requiring that teachers and paraprofessionals be "highly qualified" in their content area. Although promising on the surface, NCLB is having a disproportionate impact on schools that serve linguistically and culturally diverse students, because those schools have to meet AYP for several different subgroups of students.

Given the high-stakes nature of these tests, many schools find themselves forced to take extreme measures to avoid sanctions under the AYP requirement. For example, many schools are increasingly pushing remedial programs for students who fail to pass the state test, while others are frenziedly revising classes to "teach to the test." Others are increasingly counseling failing students into alternative education or high school equivalency programs in order to avoid having these failing students as liabilities on their school rosters. In this race to meet AYP, the linguistically and culturally student disadvantage is the one who often gets left behind.

Chapter 5 addresses two potential dangers for undocumented students while attending school in the U.S. The first one resides in the so-called racial privacy initiatives, such as the one that went down to defeat in California in 2003. These initiatives would prohibit states from gathering and classifying information based on race or ethnicity; among other things, they would make scientific studies of race very difficult. The chapter examines the effect of such initiatives upon the educational opportunities of undocumented students. The chapter will also build upon the literature analyzing the constitutionality of these initiatives and explore whether they are good policy.

The chapter also explores the second potential danger in the schoolhouse, that is, the implications of potential immigration enforcement at public schools. These pose serious concerns for undocumented K-12 students who attend public schools under the mandate of *Plyler*. Some are afraid to attend school because they or their parents believe that immigration officials may raid the school building at any time. Most state laws require students below the age of 18 years to attend school, while *Plyler v. Doe* requires schools to provide educational services to all students living in their school districts. While particular policies in the immigration enforcement agencies may counsel against raiding schools, this new enforcement era may usher enhanced immigration enforcement on or near schools. The concerns are: (1) whether immigration agents can conduct school building raids and (2) whether school personnel can refuse to share student records with these officials. These are important concerns because school should be a safe environment conducive to learning. Students and their parents should be able to be confident that sending a child to school does not expose the family to deportation. Indeed, *Plyler* implies as much. This chapter examines the ability of *Plyler* to protect students from these raids. Furthermore it analyzes the ability of undocumented parents to participate in their children's education by coming to school meetings, attending field trips and being engaged in their children's education without fear of deportation at school or in a school-related activity.

The conclusion points to the persistent inequality of educational opportunities for undocumented Latino students. Despite the best efforts made in the litigation, legislation, and policy arena, unless immigration reform passes so that the undocumented students can regularize their immigration status, our educational system will only be producing highly educated undocumented persons whose job prospects are completely curtailed by their immigration status.

The conclusion also critiques immigration and educational laws and policies that aim to "fix" the problem of educating undocumented students, while highlighting a fundamental flaw, namely their failure to address the educational and living conditions of undocumented Latino students. Such conditions, unfortunately, may likely not be much different from those of the U.S. citizen and legal resident Latino children, many of whom live in marginalized communities and in mixed immigration status families. These students clearly are not reaching their full education potential and have very similar challenges to those of undocumented students, except for those which are immigration status-related. Thus, for undocumented students, their persistent inequality will continue, placing them in the middle of the immigration reform rhetoric and debate but also at the proverbial bottom of the barrel in educational achievement in the United States.

1

Examination of *Plyler v. Doe* and its Aftermath, Including Additional Bases for Undocumented Students' Access to Public Education

In *Plyler v. Doe*, the United States Supreme Court guaranteed undocumented children a free public education, yet more than twenty-five years later these students have not experienced substantial improvement in their educational achievement. Furthermore, scholars have found that *Plyler* "clearly is alive and well,"[1] but it has endured federal and state legislative challenges. Thus, although the Supreme Court decided *Plyler* more than a quarter century ago, granting the opportunity of public education to undocumented children, it still faces challenges to its authority.

The possibility of further legal challenges, including the potential overruling of *Plyler*, makes pertinent an exploration of alternative legal bases for the guarantee of public school attendance for undocumented children. These are found primarily in (1) the right to parent enunciated by the U.S. Supreme Court in federal constitutional case law and (2) the equal protection guarantees of state constitutional provisions.

How U.S. public schools have complied with the mandate of *Plyler* over the years and how to extend the reach of *Plyler* to free pre-primary education in the U.S are two topics which also warrant consideration. Furthermore, the practices around the world regarding the public education of undocumented students and concluding thoughts on the vitality of *Plyler* in a modern, globalized world are considered as well.

Plyler v. Doe: A Close Look at a Landmark Decision and its Early History

In order to fully understand the *Plyler v. Doe*[2] decision, it is necessary to be aware of the events that led to the case, as well as what has happened in the quarter century since the Supreme Court decision. While this decision dates from 1982, it is the pinnacle of a decades-long struggle for undocumented noncitizens, not only in Texas but in the United States as a whole.

Understanding *Plyler* from the Beginning

Prior to 1975, every child in Texas was able to attend public school, and the government provided funding to the schools based on the number of students enrolled in the school. However, in May of 1975, the state legislature amended the Texas Education Code to provide that only U.S. citizens or lawfully admitted noncitizens would be permitted to attend public schools.[3] School districts were allowed to decide whether to allow undocumented students on a tuition-paying basis, but these students would not be counted for financial aid purposes.[4] The act passed without debate, legislative history or other testimony or study.[5] In fact, in 1975, upon request by the State Commissioner of Education, the Texas Attorney General had issued an opinion regarding undocumented children in the schools.[6] In this opinion, the Attorney General found no basis in Texas law to deny education to any children in the state, including undocumented students, and that school boards could not create exceptions to the law.[7] Yet the Texas law authorizing school districts to treat undocumented children differently from U.S. citizen and lawfully admitted children passed anyway that same year.

Some school districts, such as the Independent School District of the city of Tyler, in west Texas, continued to admit undocumented students. However, this changed in 1977, when the Board of Trustees of the school district, fearing that Tyler would become a "haven" for illegal aliens, adopted the following policy, designed to implement the statute:[8]

> The Tyler Independent School District shall enroll all qualified students who are citizens of the United States or legally admitted aliens, and who are residents of this school district, free of tuition charge. Illegal alien children may enroll and attend schools in the Tyler Independent School District by payment of the full tuition fee.[9]

The Tyler school district thereupon required that all undocumented students —about 60 from a student body of 1,600—pay the $1,000 per year tuition.[10]

In September 1977, the Mexican American Legal Defense and Educational Fund (MALDEF) filed a class action on behalf of sixteen Mexican American undocumented students of the Tyler district. The suit called for a preliminary injunction to allow the students to attend school, as the plaintiffs contended that the Tyler school district's practice violated the Equal Protection Clause.[11] The district court granted a preliminary injunction and then a permanent injunction a year later, following extensive briefing and a lengthy hearing. The court found that:

> The predictable effects of depriving an undocumented child of an education are clear and undisputed. Already disadvantaged as a result of

poverty, lack of English-speaking ability, and undeniable racial preju-
dices, these children, without an education, will become permanently
locked into the lowest socioeconomic class. Furthermore, witnesses
from both sides testified that the illegal alien of today may well be the
legal alien of tomorrow.[12]

A telling fact about Tyler, Texas at the time of the *Plyler* litigation is that
around 60 percent of the legal immigrants were former undocumented
migrants. This is a fact the trial court recognized without more, as seen above,
because of the possibility that the undocumented student plaintiffs in the
case would become legal residents themselves. On the other hand, others at
the time viewed undocumented persons as a drain on the community. However, Judge William Wayne Justice found that undocumented persons,
including the parents of the plaintiff children, paid taxes and rent.[13]

The trial court found that the Texas law violated the Equal Protection
Clause of the Fourteenth Amendment of the U.S. Constitution, because it
amounted to a total deprivation of education without a rational basis.[14] The
court rejected the state's arguments regarding the cost of educating undocumented children, finding that the federal government largely subsidized the
additional costs that the education of these children entailed and that "it is
not sufficient justification that a law saves money."[15]

One argument the trial court rejected as not having been proven by the evidence was "in her opening statement, counsel for the state argued that (t)here
are cost factors which fall outside the average daily attendance costs in terms
of lost textbooks, problems you would not have with the average student."[16]
Was the state's lawyer contending that undocumented students had a higher
propensity to steal textbooks? Or could there have been an alternative coun-
terstory to the missing books, such as that these children are often migrants,
who move from state to state with their parents, who follow the harvesting of
crops for their daily subsistence? What if in a hurry to leave for the next field,
the family forgot to bring the textbooks? In any case, Judge Justice handily
dismissed the state's assertion, stating that "not a shred of evidence was ever
offered to substantiate the suggestion that undocumented children tend to
lose or 'remove' textbooks at a higher rate than their citizen or lawfully resident schoolmates."[17] By doing so, Judge Justice unknowingly applied the
Critical Race Theory hallmark theme of antiessentialism, rejecting the notion
of all Latinos having one identity, in this case as criminals.

Finally, the court found that federal law preempted the Texas legislation as
immigration law is federal law and the Texas law was inconsistent with "the
objectives of Congress."[18] Regarding the federal government's objectives,
the court found a "commitment to expanding educational opportunity," in
Article 47 of the Buenos Aires Protocol of the Organization of American
States, which states as follows:

The Member States will exert the greatest efforts, in accordance with
their constitutional processes, to ensure the effective exercise of the
right to education, on the following bases:

a) Elementary education, compulsory for children of school age,
shall also be offered to all others who can benefit from it. When provided by the State it shall be without charge[19]

The court also found that federal law preempted the Texas legislation. The
decision ultimately ended with the court's rejecting the suggestion of the
state's Latino undocumented students' criminality in the theft of textbooks.

However, this litigation only applied to the Tyler, Texas I.S.D., so that
plaintiffs in other Texas school districts filed similar cases challenging the
constitutionality of the Texas statute. These other cases were eventually all
consolidated under United States District Judge Woodrow B. Seals into the
case *In re Alien Children*.[20] While a different court heard the case, it reached
the same result: finding that the Texas statute was unconstitutional under the
Equal Protection Clause.[21] The main differences between the two opinions
were that Judge Seals in *Alien Children* subjected the Texas law to a higher
level of scrutiny before invalidating it under Equal Protection, and that he did
not find the statute to be preempted by federal law.[22] As part of his preemption analysis, Judge Seals also found Article 47 of the Buenos Aires Protocol
to be inapplicable to the case, since it was not a self-executing treaty capable
of invalidating an inconsistent state law.[23]

Texas appealed both cases to the United States Circuit Court of Appeals for
the Fifth Circuit, which affirmed the trial courts' decision on equal protection grounds.[24] The court agreed with Judge Seals, however, that federal law
did not preempt the Texas statute. The Fifth Circuit was not unsympathetic
to the state:

This Court is acutely aware that Texas is suffering the local effects of a
national problem. When national immigration laws are not or cannot be
enforced, it is the states, most particularly the border states, that bear the
heaviest burden. This court can readily understand the problems faced
by a state such as Texas. However, this Court cannot suspend the operation of the Constitution to aid a state to solve its political problems.[25]

Predictably, the state of Texas appealed to the United States Supreme
Court.

Plyler v. Doe at the Supreme Court

Between January, when the case was argued, and June of 1982, when it was
decided, the Supreme Court justices conferred about their thoughts about

Plyler v. Doe. Justice William J. Brennan, Jr., who was assigned the task of writing the Court's opinion, did not want to base the case solely on the status of the undocumented children.[26] Rather, he preferred that the decision be closely related to the state's policies concerning the undocumented population as a whole. Justice Brennan agreed with Judge Seals' approach in the *Alien Children* cases, and decided that the policies must be viewed under strict scrutiny. However, the use of strict scrutiny was not a unanimous view at the Court. *Plyler* presented two rather stark realities: (1) undocumented children who were thrust into their situation not of their own volition, and (2) the complete deprivation of a state benefit, education.[27] While Justice Brennan was keenly aware that the right to an education was not a fundamental one under the U.S. Constitution, to him it was a very important right. He found that

> the justifications offered by the State in support of § 21.031 do not approach the showing of compelling need required if a State is to deny to this discrete group of children the free public education it offers to every other child residing within its borders.[28]

Justice Lewis F. Powell, Jr., the apparent swing vote in the case, conceded that Brennan's draft was "impressive," but found that it swept too broadly.[29] Instead of strict scrutiny, Powell reasoned that intermediate scrutiny should be used, much like the scrutiny applied to governmental concerning gender and illegitimacy. Justice Harry A. Blackmun worked to resolve the dispute between Justices Powell and Brennan. In Justice Blackmun's view, the opinion should not turn on whether the undocumented children were suspect class. A "suspect class", as defined in *U.S. v. Carolene Products*, a case in which the Court interpreted the Fourteenth Amendment, is a class which has been "subjected to such a history of purposeful unequal treatment, or relegated to such a position of political powerlessness as to command extraordinary protection from the majoritarian political process."[30] Justice Blackmun believed that the Court should focus instead on the fundamental right to education. Justice Blackmun wrote that:

> In short, one could say that the reason education is fundamental is that it is preservative of other rights. The reason that it is fundamental to this group is that some of these children will be here permanently. And it is for the Federal Government, rather than the States to determine which children will be allowed to remain in the United States.[31]

However, Justice Brennan continued to argue that Texas was creating a lower class with its legislation and that the right to education was a vital state interest.[32] During oral argument, from the bench, he contended that the state was punishing innocent children with its policy.[33]

The Supreme Court eventually held that undocumented students could not be denied a public education. Judge William Wayne Justice, who presided over the *Plyler* district court case, later put it:

> Children raised without any education at all are likely to become burdens on the rest of society. They won't be able to make any real amount of money unless they get into crime, like dope traffic or something of that sort. If youngsters get an education, they can make a living.[34]

Without the decision in *Plyler*, these students who came to this country not on their own volition would not have a constitutional opportunity to obtain an education. In order to understand exactly how this opportunity came about, let us review the Supreme Court opinion in detail.

Plyler v. Doe[35] is the leading case regarding the education of Latino undocumented students in the United States. It stands among a pantheon of landmark educational cases, such as *Brown v. Board of Education*[36] and *Regents of the University of California v. Bakke*.[37] In addition to being a landmark opinion, *Plyler* is a vital opinion because of the nation's economic interest regarding the availability of the noncitizen work force.[38] The young undocumented students are a source of untapped talent for the United States.[39]

Plyler is a groundbreaking case in that, for the first time, the Supreme Court clearly stated that undocumented persons are protected under the Equal Protection Clause of the Fourteenth Amendment.[40] In earlier cases, the Court had established that noncitizens (aliens) are persons entitled to protection under the Due Process Clause of the Fourteenth Amendment,[41] but it had not interpreted the Equal Protection Clause to apply to persons not lawfully present in the United States.

The *Plyler* Court arrived at this conclusion by stating that "whatever his status under the immigration laws, an alien is surely a 'person' in any ordinary sense of that term."[42] The Court did so, building upon established precedent that aliens are "guaranteed due process of law by the Fifth and Fourteenth Amendments."[43] The Court had established in 1886, in *Yick Wo v. Hopkins*,[44] that the Fourteenth Amendment guarantee of equal protection of the laws was "universal in [its] application, to all persons within the territorial jurisdiction, without regard to any differences of race, of color, or of nationality."[45] In *Plyler*, the Court reaffirmed *Yick Wo* and extended the reach of the Fourteenth Amendment's Equal Protection Clause to the undocumented.[46] The Equal Protection Clause of the Fourteenth Amendment reads: "No State shall … deny to any person within its jurisdiction the equal protection of the laws."[47] The Court took this step because, under the Fourteenth Amendment, "persons" within the state's jurisdiction are to be protected under the Equal Protection Clause. Thus, the Court held that the amendment's Equal Protection Clause applies to those within a state's borders, even if they are unlawfully present.[48]

For the Court, the word "person" in the constitutional amendment meant exactly what it said—a person—without regard to immigration status. This had been the position urged by the plaintiffs undocumented children, who had sued the Tyler, Texas school superintendent for failing to provide them with a free public education under Texas law, thus treating them differently from lawfully admitted and U.S. citizen children. The state of Texas, in defending the lawsuit, argued against this textualist view, under the theory that the Equal Protection Clause could not apply to those not lawfully admitted in the United States.

In determining the applicability of the Equal Protection Clause to the undocumented, the Supreme Court reviewed the congressional debate surrounding the passage of the Fourteenth Amendment, including the following language:

> Is it not essential to the unity of the Government and the unity of the people that all persons, *whether citizens or strangers, within this land*, shall have equal protection in every State in this Union in the rights of life and liberty and property?[49]

Once the Court had determined that the Equal Protection Clause applied to the undocumented, its next task was to decide which level of scrutiny was in order. Not every state or government classification which treats persons differently violates equal protection. A reviewing court may choose among various standards of review. These standards examine the state interest behind the governmental classification at issue and the closeness between the classification and the interest. In such cases, the decision regarding which level of scrutiny to apply is nearly always outcome determinative. The three standards of review are as follows.

The lowest level is the rational basis standard of review. Under this standard, the governmental classification must be rationally related to the state's interest in enacting the legislation which contains the classification. This approach is typically used for ordinary economic legislation, not based on racial, alienage classifications, gender or illegitimacy classifications or ones impinging on fundamental rights. This standard of review is easily satisfied. Any rational reason for passing the legislation will suffice; in fact, sometimes, courts will find legislation constitutional if any conceivable set of facts could support it. One example of legislation which has passed constitutional muster is a state law which only allowed apprentices of riverboat pilots to serve as pilots, while not allowing any others to do so.[50]

The second standard of review is the intermediate scrutiny applied to illegitimacy and gender-based classifications. This midtier review requires that the law be substantially related to an important government interest. An example of the legislation upheld under this standard is the statutory distinctions which impose different requirements for a child's acquisition of U.S. citizenship depending upon whether the U.S. citizen parent is the mother or the father.[51]

Finally, the third and most exacting standard of review is strict scrutiny, under which a law must be narrowly tailored to promote a compelling governmental interest. Laws making distinctions are made based on race, alienage, national origin, or religion fall under this standard, as do laws impinging upon fundamental rights such as the right to vote, access to courts, and interstate travel.

The *Plyler* Court found that strict scrutiny was inappropriate for two reasons. First, undocumented noncitizens are not a suspect class because their unlawful presence in the country in violation of federal law is not, in the Court's words, a "constitutional irrelevancy."[52] Second, education is not a fundamental right that would require narrow tailoring and a compelling state interest.[53] Thus, the *Plyler* Court reaffirmed the holding in *San Antonio Independent School District v. Rodriguez*[54]—that education is not a fundamental right—despite Justice Marshall's plea to overrule it.[55]

Justice Brennan, who dissented in *Rodriguez*, yet wrote the majority opinion in *Plyler*, did not have the votes to overrule *Rodriguez* and find that education is a fundamental right.[56] In his *Rodriguez* dissent, Justice Brennan had disagreed with the majority's view that the only rights that may be deemed fundamental are those explicitly and implicitly guaranteed in the Constitution and instead stated that "'fundamentality' is ... a function of the right's importance in terms of the effectuation of those rights which are constitutionally guaranteed."[57]

Echoing the words of Justice Marshall, Justice Brennan wrote:

> As the nexus between the specific constitutional guarantee and the nonconstitutional interest draws closer, the nonconstitutional interest becomes more fundamental and the degree of judicial scrutiny applied when the interest is infringed on a discriminatory basis must be adjusted accordingly.[58]

Justice Brennan's majority opinion in *Plyler*, a little more than a decade later, reflected this same view.

In one respect, however, Justice Brennan's position departed from his statement in the *Rodriguez* dissent. There, the justice asserted that education is "inextricably linked to the right to participate in the electoral process and to the rights of free speech and association guaranteed by the First Amendment."[59] Based on the close nexus between the constitutional guarantees of the First Amendment and the non-fundamental right to an education, Justice Brennan wrote in *Rodriguez* that "any classification affecting education must be subjected to strict judicial scrutiny."[60] This turned out not to be the case in *Plyler*, however, where Justice Brennan did not find education to be a fundamental right and thus did not apply strict scrutiny to a state law denying education to undocumented children.

After the Court rejected strict scrutiny in *Plyler*, it applied a rational basis test to the Texas law that deprived undocumented children of a public education. Nevertheless, a close reading of the opinion reveals that the Court actually employed a more demanding standard,[61] a heightened, almost intermediate level of scrutiny. Some commentators have called this standard "rationality with a bite."

Application of a heightened rational basis test in *Plyler* began with the recognition that education is "perhaps the most important function of state and local governments."[62] Accordingly, the state's decision to deny an education to undocumented students could hardly be considered rational unless it furthered some substantial state goal.[63] The cost to the nation and to the innocent children involved should be taken into account.[64] As the Court put it: "it is doubtful that any child may reasonably be expected to succeed in life if he is denied the opportunity of an education."[65] Because the state took it upon itself to provide an education to children, it had to be made "available to all on equal terms."[66]

The unfairness of penalizing undocumented students for their parents' illicit act was another concern for the Court.[67] Such children "can affect neither their parents' conduct nor their own status."[68] Because the Texas law burdened children on the basis of a characteristic over which they had little control, penalizing them for their presence in the country was irrational.[69] Notably, this rationale echoes U.S. immigration law, in which, in the case a minor who is unlawfully present in the country while under age 18 no time accrues toward statutory bars to admission based on unlawful presence.[70]

Furthermore, the Court was concerned about the creation of a permanent caste of poorly educated undocumented resident aliens.[71] "[L]egislation imposing special disabilities upon groups disfavored by virtue of circumstances beyond their control suggests the kind of 'class or caste' treatment that the Fourteenth Amendment was designed to abolish."[72] It could also impose "a lifetime hardship on a discrete class of children not accountable for their disabling status."[73]

The Supreme Court expressed further concerns about the existence of this so-called shadow population—an undocumented underclass—allowed to remain in the United States by lax immigration enforcement and as a cheap labor source that need not receive any of the benefits afforded to citizens or legally admitted noncitizens.[74] In the Court's view, the existence of such an underclass "presents most difficult problems for a Nation that prides itself on adherence to principles of equality under the law."[75]

The Court next addressed the state's argument that the goal of reducing state expenditures by denying a free public education to the children of the undocumented was legitimate. The Court responded that the record lacked any "evidence ... suggesting that illegal entrants impose any significant burden on the State's economy."[76] In fact, the district court had noted in *Doe v. Plyler*[77] that "families of undocumented children contribute no less to the financing of local education than do citizens or legal residents of similar means."[78]

Additionally, the state's singling out of undocumented children for denial of a free public education because "their unlawful presence within the United States renders them less likely than other children to remain within the boundaries of the State, and to put their education to productive social or political use within the State," was similarly unpersuasive to the Court.[79] Even though an undocumented child might be deported, the Court found that many of them would remain in the country indefinitely, and some would even become lawful residents or United States citizens.[80]

Finally, "if the State is to deny a discrete group of innocent children the free public education that it offers to other children residing within its borders, that denial must be justified by a showing that it furthers some substantial state interest."[81] This formulation, of course, is a higher form of scrutiny than the traditional rational basis test, as discussed above. Ultimately, because the state made no showing of a substantial state interest, the Court invalidated the Texas law.

Thus, the *Plyler* Court contextualized the inequality inherent in the state's denial of an education to undocumented children. In this way, *Plyler*, an interest convergence case,[82] is also responsive to the hallmark Critical Race theme of antisubordination. It does so by leveling the playing field for undocumented children, who already have fewer rights than their U.S. citizen counterparts. The Court's equal protection analysis resulted in its use of a rational basis level of scrutiny in theory, but not in practice. Notwithstanding this contextualization and the Court's sweeping language regarding the existence of an undocumented underclass, undocumented students have not been afforded rights without struggle.

Three members of the Court wrote concurring opinions in *Plyler*. While they agreed with the result in the case, they wrote separately to state particular points of concern. Justice Marshall's concurrence reaffirmed his view that "an individual's interest in education is fundamental"[83] and rejected the rigid two-tier approach in equal protection jurisprudence. He called instead for varying levels of scrutiny "depending upon the 'constitutional and societal importance of the interest adversely affected and the recognized invidiousness of the basis upon which the particular classification is drawn.'"[84] Both assertions reiterated views that Justice Marshall had expressed in dissents in earlier cases.[85] But as discussed earlier, the *Plyler* majority tacitly endorsed his view when it employed a "sliding scale" approach to the standard of constitutional review.

Justice Blackmun's concurrence emphasized that "the nature of the interest at stake is crucial to the proper resolution" of the case and reaffirmed that, when analyzing whether a fundamental right exists for equal protection purposes, one must attend to the multitude of social and political interests regulated by the states.[86] In his view, "denial of an education is the analogue of denial of the right to vote: the former relegates the individual to second-class social status; the latter places him at a permanent political disadvantage."[87] The justice also enunciated his conviction that the classification of undocumented children was not a "monolithic" one and that many of the students would remain in this country permanently.[88]

Finally, Justice Powell wrote separately "to emphasize the unique character" of the case.[89] In his view, the undocumented children were being severely disadvantaged by the federal government's inability to control the border and the attractiveness of jobs in the United States, and he agreed that they were victims who should not be left on the streets uneducated.[90] However, excluding the undocumented children "from a state-provided education is a type of punitive discrimination based on status that is impermissible under the Equal Protection Clause."[91]

As seen earlier in this chapter, Justice Lewis F. Powell, Jr. played a key role in the evolution of the majority decision in *Plyler*. This fact should not be surprising, considering that he was a former member of the Board of Education in Richmond, Virginia. In addition to drafting his concurrence, Justice Powell engaged in several written exchanges with Justice Brennan and requested that Brennan share with him several versions of the draft opinion.[92] Thus, scholars have noted that the ultimate result in *Plyler* became "almost nothing more than a direct reflection of [Powell's] views of social policy."[93] In other words, some think that because the justice found the Texas statute problematic and misguided as a matter of social policy, he regarded it as unconstitutional.[94] In fact, another effect of Justice Powell's role in the evolution of the majority opinion is the dilution of the doctrinal arguments in the previous drafts, leaving it with "almost no generative or doctrinal significance because it invoked too many considerations."[95] This, of course, is one of the areas about which the dissent strongly criticized the majority opinion, as will be explored next.

The 5–4 decision in *Plyler* reveals a deeply divided court. Chief Justice Burger's dissent pointed out that the majority cobbled together a custom-made standard of review by "patching together bits and pieces of what might be termed a quasi-suspect class and quasi-fundamental rights analysis, [and] ... spin[ning] out a theory custom-tailored to the facts of these cases."[96] For Burger, if "ever a court was guilty of an unabashedly result-oriented approach, this case [would be] a prime example."[97] The choice to enact legislation was a political one, and not a function of the Court.[98] In Chief Justice Burger's view, it is up to Congress, not to the Court, to "assess the social costs borne by our Nation when select groups are denied the means to absorb the values and skills upon which our social order rests."[99] It is notable that this view would likely be shared by current Supreme Court Chief Justice John G. Roberts, Jr. At the time *Plyler* was decided, Roberts, as a special assistant to the Attorney General, argued that if the federal government "had taken a position in the case supporting the state of Texas and the values of judicial restraint," it could have "altered the outcome of the case."[100]

Justice Burger, in his dissent, did not dispute that denying children an education would create a permanent caste. In fact, the specter was a "disturbing one"; yet he contended that this was "one segment of a larger problem" for the "political branches to solve."[101] He further argued that the majority in *Plyler* "seeks to do Congress' job for it,"[102] and that it failed to allow the political process to run its course.[103]

As with any deeply divided opinion of the Supreme Court, it is likely that such a vigorous dissent may have contributed to *Plyler's* vulnerability to attack from both federal authorities and state entities. Also, in a sense, Chief Justice Burger's words are prophetic in that the only recourse for undocumented children who have received a K-12 education and want to further pursue the American dream still lies in the political process. Only by means of that process may the undocumented embark upon a path to legalization and become ability to work legally and attend postsecondary educational institutions free of the obstacles they face today.

Subsequent History of *Plyler*: Undocumented Today, Documented Tomorrow?

The named plaintiffs in *Plyler*, which was a class action lawsuit, were sixteen Mexican children who could not establish that they had been legally admitted into the United States.[104] The state argued that these children should be singled out because they were less likely to remain within Texas and put their education to "productive social or political use within the State."[105] As noted, the Court dismissed this argument, asserting that no state has such a guarantee.[106] The Court noted that "many of the undocumented children ... will remain in this country indefinitely, and that some will become lawful residents or citizens."[107] According to available data, this prediction proved true not only for the vast majority of the *Plyler* plaintiffs, but for noncitizens in general.[108]

Of the noncitizens that arrived in the United States before 1970, 82.7 percent had naturalized as U.S. citizens by 2004.[109] Furthermore, of those who entered the country between 1970 and 1979, 70.8 percent had obtained U.S. citizenship by 2002 and 49.7 percent who entered between 1980 and 1989 had obtained citizenship.[110] Finally, of those who entered in 1990 or later, 21.4 percent had obtained citizenship and of those who entered after 2000, 4.6 percent had become U.S. citizens.[111] This trend of smaller naturalization numbers in more recently arrived immigrants is a result of the legislation which requires a minimum amount of time of residence in the U.S before becoming a U.S. citizen. It may also be a consequence of more stringent application of naturalization requirements in recent post 9/11 years.

What about the *Plyler* plaintiffs? What has been their experience? More than a decade after the Supreme Court decision, journalists for a leading national newspaper interviewed thirteen of the sixteen children. The interviews disclosed that ten of them finished high school in Tyler, Texas.[112] All are now legal U.S. residents, and most of them have full-time employment.[113] Although many have taken college courses, none has graduated from a four-year institution.[114] They work as teacher's aides, automobile mechanics, assembly-line workers, managers, painters, and stock clerks.[115] Some work in the very school district that tried to bar them, and three are full-time housewives.[116] Of the four families from which these sixteen children came, only one has moved out of Tyler.[117] Indeed, they appear to have attained the American dream by moving from undocumented and illegal to legitimate members of United States society.

The experience of the *Plyler* plaintiffs reflects the view of Professors Alexander Aleinikoff and Rubén Rumbaut, who have cited studies showing that, despite the fears of a multicultural nation underlying this "immigration crisis," noncitizen acculturation within United States society is continuing its progress, as it has in the past.[118] Thus, the available evidence to date shows the falsity of the state's argument in *Plyler* that the undocumented children would not put their education to use to benefit the state of Texas. This evidence comports with economists' view of the social benefits of an education, which holds that education has a value to society beyond its value to the individual student.[119]

Among these social benefits are "a more-educated and better-informed electorate, lower rates of crime and violence, lower rates of poverty, better health and nutrition, and, generally a more smoothly functioning society."[120] These social benefits result regardless of immigration status because the undocumented person of today is very likely to become the permanent resident or citizen of tomorrow, as evidenced by the experiences of the *Plyler* plaintiffs.

Challenges to *Plyler v. Doe*

While *Plyler v. Doe* represents a high water mark in immigrants' rights jurisprudence, as legal precedent and as educational policy it has suffered criticism and challenges. Decided by a close 5–4 vote the *Plyler* opinion came in for criticism as result-oriented,[121] and because it "appear[ed] to be ad hoc and divorced from other related bodies of law created by the Court."[122] The challenges to the holding in *Plyler* have been found in the legislative realm.

Federal Challenges

At the federal level, U.S. Representative Elton Gallegly introduced a bill in Congress to amend the Illegal Immigration Reform and Immigrant Responsibility Act (IIRIRA).[123] The amendment would have authorized states to disqualify undocumented noncitizen students from public education.[124]

The amendment reflected the view that allowing undocumented students the opportunity to receive an education "promote[d] violations of the immigration laws" and imposed "significant burden[s] on States' economies and deplete[d] states' limited educational resources."[125] The amendment would have allowed states to regulate the conditions under which undocumented children could access public schools.[126] Thus, a state could even ban such children from its schools, and also could charge tuition fees to undocumented children. The Supreme Court in *Plyler* had found such a law to be a denial of equal protection under the Fourteenth Amendment of the U.S. Constitution.

The House of Representatives approved IIRIRA with the amendment attached.[127] It was dropped from the Act when President Clinton threatened a veto.[128] Texas senators Kay Bailey Hutchison and Phil Gramm opposed the amendment, and public interest groups began a publicity campaign against it. Both of these efforts contributed to the amendment's defeat.[129] Yet immigration to the United States has grown more rapidly in the last seven years than at any other time in U.S. history.[130] Furthermore, one commentator has argued that the federal government has a compelling interest in

> 1) upholding immigration law; 2) combating illegal immigration; 3) granting a free public education to those aliens whose residence is authorized by federal immigration law; and 4) relieving the states and public school systems from undue economic burdens caused by the federal government's own ineffectiveness.[131]

Thus, federal legislation such as this one could resurface at any time. It is therefore analytically useful to explore alternative grounds for undocumented students to have access to free public education in the United States. But before doing so, let us explore one more challenge to *Plyler*, this time at the state level.

State Proposals: California's Proposition 187 and Recent Look-Alikes in Other States

In California, following a highly contentious and divisive ballot initiative campaign in which its proponents chanted "Save our State," Proposition 187 passed by a close vote on November 8, 1994.[132] Proposition 187 read:

> [Californian citizens have suffered and are suffering economic hardship ... personal injury and damage caused by the criminal conduct of illegal aliens in this state. [Californians intend to] establish a system requiring notifications by and between such agencies to prevent illegal aliens in the United States from receiving benefits or public services in the State of California.[133]

Law enforcement officials would have been required determine the immigration status of every person "suspected of being in United States" without proper immigration authorization and to notify federal and state authorities.[134] One of its key provisions, section 7, contravened the mandate of *Plyler* in that it denied undocumented children in the state a free public school education.[135] A federal court in California invalidated this provision in 1997 in *League of United Latin American Citizens v. Wilson* ("*LULAC*").[136]

There are two opinions in the *LULAC* litigation. Both the 1995 and 1997 decisions explicitly reaffirmed *Plyler*. In 1995, a district court in the Central District of California held that federal law preempted section 7, which required the exclusion of undocumented students from public schools. The preemption arose from the Supremacy Clause, based on the Supreme Court's analysis in *Plyler*. In addition, in 1997, the court again followed *Plyler*, and noted also that section 1643 of the California law expressly deferred to *Plyler* in providing that "[n]othing in this chapter may be construed as addressing alien eligibility for a basic public education as determined by the Supreme Court of the United States under *Plyler v. Doe*."[137]

At the time of Proposition 187's passage, opinions as to whether the Court would overrule or affirm *Plyler* via the *LULAC* litigation varied, but most commentators believed that *LULAC* would reach the Supreme Court and result in an overruling of *Plyler*. *LULAC* was not brought before the Supreme Court, however, and the parties dropped their appeals following an agreement to enter into dispute resolution regarding the issues raised in the appeal.[138]

More recently, other states have tried similar initiatives. Indiana's HB 1383 would have barred undocumented children from public schools, prohibited hospitals from treating certain immigrants, and required law enforcement to report "suspected" undocumented persons to federal authorities.[139] The bill failed to pass the House of Representatives and did not make it out of committee.[140] The bill would have denied a variety of benefits, including food stamps and medical assistance.[141] Some legislators thought it was unfair that native Indiana students were losing their spots in university to children of the undocumented.[142] While there does not appear to be data supporting this view, it is representative of the misguided views on undocumented students which have emerged post *Plyler*.

In Arizona, two initiatives passed by referendum that attempted to limit services to immigrants. Although not a direct challenge to *Plyler*, they have caused uncertainty and fear of school attendance for undocumented children in the state. The first measure, Proposition 200, passed in 2004, requires that agencies verify the identity and immigration status of applicants for certain services and report any "discovered" immigration law violation to federal immigration officials.[143] The state Attorney General has determined that the law only applies to only a few programs which undocumented immigrants were already ineligible.[144] Supporters of Proposition 200 tried to expand its reach, by filing suit, but were unsuccessful.[145] Following on Proposition 200's heels, was Proposition 300, passed in 2006, which tried to restrict the access of adult literacy services, adult education, state-funded childcare, and in-state tuition for undocumented immigrants.[146] Proposition 300's reporting requirement was slightly different. It required a report on the number of persons denied access based on their status.[147] After Proposition 200 was approved, Arizona saw decreased clinic medical visits and participation other child health initiatives and increased confusion as to whether children should attend school, even though the proposition did not cover these services.[148]

Although the proposed federal legislation which would have overruled *Plyler* did not pass, and the state legislation so far has not excluded undocumented children from school—in fact, California's Proposition 187 was invalidated in a judicial reaffirmation of *Plyler*—these challenges serve as reminders of the tensions surrounding the education of Latino and other undocumented children. These attacks on *Plyler* reveal a deep-seated resentment towards undocumented immigrants, mostly due to the high cost that states bear when educating the children of the undocumented. This was an argument, however, that the Court rejected in *Plyler* as an insufficiently rational basis for denying educational opportunities to undocumented children.[149] It is an argument that has also seen further scrutiny and analysis in recent years as far as quantifying the financial contributions made by the undocumented children's families to their communities and to United States overall. If such an argument is reconsidered by the Supreme Court and, in light of new evidence, does not withstand rational basis scrutiny, then alternative legal bases for access to education for undocumented students must be found. The following section offers some alternative theories in this regard. First is the right to parent of an undocumented person under the U.S. Constitution, and second are state constitutional equal protection guarantees.

An undocumented Person's Right to Parent

The Supreme Court reasoned in *Plyler* that it would be unfair to punish children for the illegal acts of their parents.[150] This argument derived from earlier illegitimacy cases. Justice Powell made clear in his concurring opinion in *Plyler*:

> Although the analogy is not perfect, our holding today does find support in decisions of this Court with respect to the status of illegitimates. In *Weber* v. *Aetna Casualty & Surety Co.*, we said: "[Visiting] ... condemnation on the head of an infant" for the misdeeds of the parents is illogical, unjust, and "contrary to the basic concept of our system that legal burdens should bear some relationship to individual responsibility or wrongdoing."[151]

Plyler is fundamentally driven by the public policy consideration of society's interest in educating children. Because of its strong policy grounding and its perceived doctrinal weaknesses, it is worth exploring alternative grounds for the holding in *Plyler*.

The following alternative doctrinal grounds are available to support the continued access to education for undocumented children. Although children have no right to education in the U.S. Constitution, courts have found a "fundamental interest of parents, as contrasted with that of the [s]tate, to guide the religious future and education of their children."[152] Thus, parents have a right to direct the education of their children free from unreasonable state mandates. This right is focused on the parents' choice, rather than on the children's right to education.

Further, aliens or noncitizens[153] are "persons" within the meaning of the Fourteenth Amendment of the Constitution.[154] Thus, because the right to parent is largely derived from the Due Process Clause of the Fourteenth Amendment, it arguably applies to undocumented noncitizens.

Meyer v. Nebraska is the first case where the Supreme Court found a right to parent in the U.S. Constitution.[155] In *Meyer*, the Nebraska legislature had enacted a law prohibiting the teaching of foreign language to students in grades below the eighth grade.[156] This anti-German language law had been passed in the wake of post-World War I nativism. In fact, twenty-two other states had also passed such laws.[157] The purpose of the law, according to that state's Attorney General, was

> to create an enlightened American citizenship in sympathy with the principles and ideas of the country, and to prevent children reared in America from being trained and educated in foreign languages and foreign ideas before they had opportunity to learn the English language.[158]

The Court held that the Nebraska statute violated the Due Process Clause of the Fourteenth Amendment.[159] The Court stated that, "[c]orresponding to the right of control, it is the natural duty of the parent to give his children education suitable to their station in life; and nearly all States, including Nebraska, enforce this obligation by compulsory laws."[160] Thus, the right to parent in the U.S. includes the ability to direct the education of the child. Prohibiting foreign language instruction interferes with this duty.

The right to parent was reaffirmed in the case of *Pierce v. Society of Sisters.*[161] In this case, the Supreme Court enjoined the enforcement of Oregon's Compulsory Education Act of 1922.[162] The Act required every parent to send any child between the ages of 8 and 16 years old to public school.[163] The Society of Sisters operated many private primary and secondary schools.[164] Parents, as a result of the Act, withdrew their children from the private schools operated by the Society of Sisters.[165] The Society of Sisters brought suit seeking an injunction and claimed that the Act interfered with "the right of parents to choose schools where their children will receive appropriate mental and religious training."[166]

The Court relied on the *Meyer v. Nebraska* precedent, and stated the Act "unreasonably interferes with the liberty of parents to direct the upbringing of their children."[167] It further stated that, "[t]he child is not a mere creature of the state; those who nurture him and direct his destiny have the right coupled with the high duty to recognize and prepare him for additional obligations."[168]

The *Plyler* Court relied on *Meyer* as the original right to parent case, to explain that while there is no federal constitutional right to education, it is not an ordinary government benefit.

> Public education is not a "right" granted to individuals by the Constitution ... But neither is it merely some governmental "benefit" indistinguishable from other forms of social welfare legislation. Both the importance of education in maintaining our basic institutions, and the lasting impact of its deprivation on the life of the child, mark the distinction. The "American people have always regarded education and [the] acquisition of knowledge as matters of supreme importance." *Meyer* v. *Nebraska.* We have recognized "the public schools as a most vital civic institution for the preservation of a democratic system of government."[169]

Thus, while education is not a fundamental right, its central importance suggests that parents retain some degree of control and do not abdicate all responsibility to the state. By excluding undocumented children from primary education, parents would be deprived of the ability to give their children the benefits of America's "most vital civic institution." Not merely the prohibition against teaching a foreign language would be at stake but, most likely, the ability to study any language or any academic subject at all.

The Supreme Court has further elaborated on the "natural duty" a parent has to educate a child. In *Wisconsin v. Yoder*, it explained, "[t]he duty to prepare a child for 'additional obligations,' referred to by the Court, must be read to include the inculcation of moral standards, religious beliefs, and elements of good citizenship."[170] While the last obligation, to inculcate "good citizenship," would not apply at present to noncitizens, there is nothing in the Court's opinion to suggest that this is the only public policy justification for compulsory education. Further, such an obligation may be an avenue to better integrate noncitizens into the national community, and prepare them for our country's ultimate form of participation, citizenship.

However, this obligation and right of the parent is limited, when decisions of the parent will "jeopardize the health or safety of the child, or have a potential for significant social burdens."[171] In *Yoder*, the Court held that the state of Wisconsin breached the Free Exercise Clause of the First Amendment when it required Amish parents to comply with a compulsory attendance law.[172] Amish parents claimed that their religion expressly prohibited secondary education.[173] The Court ruled that the state's interest in compulsory education must be balanced with the interests of the free exercise of religion.[174] The significant social burden of illiteracy which undocumented students face absent their ability to attend U.S. public schools must be balanced with the state interests in denying public education to these children.

Finally, the Supreme Court has recently clarified the fundamental right to parent in *Troxel v. Granville*.[175] It stated, "we have recognized the right of parents to make decisions concerning the care, custody, and control of their children."[176] In *Troxel*, the Court struck down a Washington statute that allowed child visitation for "any person" at "any time."[177] A child's grandparents petitioned the Washington Superior Court for the right to visit their grandchildren.[178] Against the mother's wishes the trial court granted the order.[179] The Washington Supreme Court reversed the order because it was an unconstitutional infringement on the mother's care, custody, and control of her children.[180] The Supreme Court ruled that the Washington visitation statute violated the right to parent and was not in the best interest of the child.[181] This was based on the presumption that fit parents act in the best interest of their children and should be able to determine with whom the children associate.[182]

While the Court found a right in this circumstance, and it is not clear precisely where the limits of the rights of parents lie, undocumented parents arguably should be able to care for, have custody of and control their children by ensuring their attendance at public schools. Thus, while courts have been reluctant to give parents authority in curriculum decisions and, for example, courts have rejected parental rights to object to compulsory community service, academic testing, and mandatory sex education,[183] the mere decision to attend public schools may be one which the right to parent should support.

The Right to Parent as an Alternative Basis for *Plyler*

The right to parent, then, can be put forward as an alternative basis for holding that the children of undocumented persons should have access to primary education.[184] Supreme Court cases such as *Pierce* and *Meyer* concerned educational bans: one on sending children to private school, and another on the teaching of a foreign language in the public school, respectively. The Supreme Court found both to be unreasonable interferences with the ability of parents to direct their children's education. Further, if a state were to charge an undocumented parent unaffordable tuition, such as what happened in *Plyler*, this act could be considered an unreasonable interference as it would be akin to requiring the child be sent to private school or be home-schooled. In light of *Pierce*, a state law forcing a child to go to private school should similarly be unconstitutional because it would be directing his or her education against the parent's wishes.

And unlike *Yoder*, where Amish parents opted not to send their children to school in contravention of the state interest of compulsory education, the choice by undocumented parents to send their child to public school is consistent with such a state interest. In fact, Justice White's concurring opinion in *Yoder* quoted the same language from *Brown v. Board of Education* as did the *Plyler* court in acknowledging the significance of education. He stated, "Today, education is perhaps the most important function of state and local governments. Compulsory school attendance laws and the great expenditures for education both demonstrate our recognition of the importance of education to our democratic society ..."[185] Thus, because the state's interest furthers the parent's right to education of his or her child, the state interest and that of the parent should be one and the same. The interests may only diverge over specific issues such as the type of bilingual education and the like. A school district may want to pursue immersion education, or cut back on existing resources targeted to undocumented students. A parent of an undocumented child would usually want the opposite.

The right to parent is also beneficial in reinforcing the value of parents to be involved in their children's education. Studies show that parental engagement increases the chance of strong academic performance.[186] Students with involved parents are more likely to get higher grades, pass classes, develop better social skills, and go on to postsecondary education.[187]

Possible Negative Consequences of Using the Right to Parent as an Alternative Ground for *Plyler*

The use of the right to parent as a means to extend primary education to undocumented children has potential drawbacks. These drawbacks can be found doctrinally and conceptually under the law, as well as practically and politically.

Doctrinally, shifting the focus from the child to the parent poses the danger that the parent's action of being in the United States unlawfully would trump the educational access for the child. This is the case because the Court in *Plyler*, found that undocumented persons' unlawful entry was not a constitutional irrelevancy.[188] Also, in *Plyler*, the Court noted the children's innocence regarding their unlawful presence in the U.S., as they could not control the actions of their parents when they were brought to the country. However, under the right to parent, these parental actions could be taken into account and could result in a lowered standard of review for analysis under equal protection.

Another doctrinal concern regarding the right to parent lies in the distinction between positive and negative rights. While positive rights are traditionally conceived as rights to access certain protections, negative rights commonly imply freedom from governmental interference.[189] The prevailing view is that the right to parent is classically considered a negative right, so that parents can raise their children free from governmental interference. Yet raising children free from a denial of attending public school would appear to be a negative right that seemingly becomes positive. This is consistent with the view of scholars who note that the distinction between these two forms of rights is more theoretical than real.[190]

One drawback with this approach is that it could appear to enlarge parental control and for example, encourage parents to seek veto power over certain educational curriculum and programs. In the late 1990s, certain grassroots organizations lobbied state legislatures to pass so-called parental rights amendments.[191] These amendments sought to enhance the power of parents to be able to choose the curriculum and programs to which their children would be exposed. These laws were particularly favored by parents who object to teaching sexual education, evolution, and other controversial curriculum.[192] The New York City School District's plan to distribute condoms, and other attempts to teach students about sexual orientation with books such as Heather Has Two Mommies and Daddy's Roommate caused serious concern among such parents.[193] Most attempts at enacting such legislation have failed. Congressional attempts at passing similar legislation have also failed.[194] In 1996, a Colorado initiative was defeated 52 percent–48 percent.[195] Currently, Texas is the only state to codify a right to parent.[196] Yet it would appear that the right to parent as a form of educational access for undocumented children should not necessarily lead to the opening up of the entire school curriculum for parents to dissect.

Politically, parental rights amendments present many concerns. School districts may find themselves on the defensive in deciding school curriculum, and teachers may be forced to drop subjects they may have taught for years.[197]

Further, such a right may create more opportunities for litigation and its resulting legal fees, which would be an additional expense for school systems.[198] Finally, enhanced recognition of parental rights may weaken the state's power to protect children in child abuse cases.[199]

While as a policy matter there may be potential risks in the use of the right to parent, it is part of the legal landscape in the U.S. and could serve as an alternative ground for *Plyler*, as discussed above.

State Constitutional Provisions as Alternative Grounds for *Plyler*

Having seen alternative grounds for the *Plyler* holding in the right to parent under federal constitutional law, the following section analyzes what support state constitutions can offer for educational access for undocumented students. State constitutions have two important clauses that may be used to secure the right to access education for undocumented children. These are state education clauses, guaranteeing the right to an education, and state equal protection clauses, which are similar to the federal Equal Protection Clause of the U.S. Constitution. While there is much variation in the availability and in the scope of these two clauses in each of the fifty states, it is instructive to see how one state's constitution can be used to reach the result obtained in *Plyler*. The analysis conducted here is done through examination of the state constitution of Texas, the state where the *Plyler* litigation arose. While the possibility of inconsistent results exists because of the inevitable variations in the fifty state constitutions, using state constitutions is one way to protect the undocumented students' access to education. Specifically, using the Texas state constitutional cases concerning equal protection and education, the outcome in *Plyler* would be likely preserved. The case of *Richards v. League of United Latin American Citizens* illustrates this point.[200]

In *Richards*, Mexican American U.S. citizens who lived in the Mexican border area brought an equal protection challenge against the Texas system of higher education.[201] The Texas Supreme Court held that the state's appropriation of fewer resources to the border area did not violate the plaintiff's equal protection rights.[202] The trial court had ruled that the higher education appropriation was unconstitutional under the Texas Constitution.[203] The trial court found ample evidence of educational disparities, for example, that while 20 percent of Texans lived in the border area, only about 10 percent of the State funds spent for public universities are spent on public universities in that region.[204]

The state of Texas claimed such disparities in funding were a result of differences in hiring salary for certain faculty, different student–faculty ratios, and different equipment needs.[205]

In many ways, the Texas courts have analyzed their state's equal protection clause with a framework that is parallel to that of the federal system.[206] In this case, the trial court found that the state violated the Texas Constitution when it spent fewer resources on education in this portion of the state, thus denying Mexican Americans equal rights.[207] The Texas Supreme Court reversed the trial court's findings.[208] It did so for four reasons. First, approximately half of the Mexican American population in the state lived outside the border area.[209] Thus, it found that the class of people was really defined based on geography and not nationality.[210] For this reason, it found "territorial uniformity is not a constitutional prerequisite."[211] Second, because the difference was only a geographical disparity, the state only needed to show a legitimate basis for its funding scheme, and its efficient location of such monies was one such legitimate purpose.[212] Third, using a disparate impact analysis, the plaintiff failed to document an intent to discriminate against Mexican Americans.[213] The disproportionate impact was not enough to be "overwhelming and unequivocal" in order to show a discriminatory purpose.[214] Finally, higher education was not a fundamental right under the Texas Constitution.[215]

Unlike *Richards*, a *Plyler* type of situation, where undocumented students would be forced to pay out-of-district tuition, would have implications for Mexican Americans across the entire state, not just the border region. As a result, the class would be more likely to be an "easily identifiable group singled out for different treatment under the law and subject to prejudice in the community" and therefore less likely to be based on solely "territorial uniformity."[216] Further, the Texas Court noted "[the United States Supreme Court] has recognized Mexican Americans as a separate class in various equal protection contexts, and has treated discrimination against persons of Mexican ancestry as equivalent to racial discrimination."[217] However, under *Plyler* undocumented persons are not a suspect class.[218] Thus, it is unclear whether the Texas Supreme Court was referring to all persons of Mexican descent, or legal permanent residents and citizens of Mexican descent, when it used the words "Mexican Americans."[219] If the Texas Supreme Court found a distinction between the documented and undocumented Mexican Americans, it would likely not apply a heightened form of scrutiny to the undocumented and thus there would be no constitutional violation.

However, unlike *Richards*, a *Plyler* situation would involve primary education instead of higher education. The Texas courts have stated that primary education is a fundamental right.[220] Their finding is buttressed by the Texas Constitution's Education Clause that mandates the state to provide an "efficient system of public free schools."[221] Thus, because a fundamental right exists, "the state action is subjected to strict scrutiny" and would need to "serve a compelling government interest" in order to be constitutional.[222] Denying education to undocumented children would not be a compelling state interest because such children would be more likely to be impoverished, illiterate, uneducated, and more likely to engage in unhealthy decisions.[223] Further, such an action would create the very caste system that equal protection intends to abolish, as found by the *Plyler* majority.[224] For these reasons, the inability of undocumented children to receive an education would constitute a violation of the Equal Protection Clause of the Texas Constitution.

Finally, *Richards* is distinct from *Plyler* in that it sought to request a more equitable distribution of funds, whereas the plaintiffs in *Plyler* only sought the same right to access education as did the other children in the school district.[225] Thus, because the case does not involve a funding allocation decision of allocating funds, the Texas Supreme Court could be more inclined to rule in favor of the plaintiffs.

The state of Texas may also argue that denying education to undocumented children is a compelling interest because failure to do so would be very costly to the state. However, such an argument ignores the benefit the residents of the state receive in the form of cheap labor of the undocumented students' parents, as well other benefits that education provides for society.[226] It is also an argument rejected three times by three different courts in the *Plyler* litigation, among other reasons, as a consequence of the federal government subsidizing a portion of the undocumented students' educational costs.

Finally, if the Texas Supreme Court were to hold that undocumented students have a right to access primary education, it would overrule a Texas Court of Appeals decision, *Hernandez v. Houston Independent School District*.[227] In that 1977 case, the Texas Court of Appeals, Third District upheld the state and federal constitutionality of a statute that prohibited using public funds to educate undocumented children.[228] The Court of Appeals failed to find that education was a fundamental right or that undocumented aliens were a suspect class.[229] Thus, that statute was rationally related to the improvement of education and was constitutional.[230] *Plyler* would have overruled the federal constitutionality issue involved in this case.[231] However, the Court of Appeals' state equal protection conclusion has never been overruled.[232]

Complying with Plyler

Despite genuine attempts to comply with *Plyler*, many schools still face complications in providing for an undocumented student's right to access. In a recent case, a school official in Northern Chicago District 187 turned away a Latina mother trying to register her son for classes.[233] Originally, she had produced copies of utility bills and other documents verifying her residency in the district.[234] In addition, she produced a matrícula consular card, a photo identification issued by the Mexican Consulate. These cards are often used by persons who are in the U.S. without legal authorization as a form of identification, in the absence of U.S. identification. The Latina mother was advised that the matrícula card was no longer being accepted.[235] She then took her case to the district administrative office, where she administrative staff told her to produce state-issued identification.[236] While in the office, school officials gave her a document from the American Resistance, an anti-immigrant group, explaining why the matrícula was not a valid form of identification.[237] The school official then said she would contract "immigration" at the Department of Homeland Security to determine what identification was provided for individuals.[238] The school official then insisted on seeing work authorization, wanted to see proof of residency, and advised the parent that the children could be taught at home.[239] The matter was eventually resolved after two hours, and the child was enrolled.[240] Although this incident drew quite a bit of attention in the news, the school district did not initiate discipline against the school official.[241] This incident is surprising considering Illinois has been leading the nation in proactive policies to assist in the integration of immigrants. For example, then Governor Blagojevich signed the New Americans Executive Order, creating the Office of New Americans in November 2005.[242] The office is responsible for planning and coordinating policies to assist in welcoming Illinois's newest arrivals.[243] This includes information regarding childcare, preschool, and language services.

This incident in Illinois is also surprising, based on the case law precedent in the state, which allows a determination of residency and thus, school enrollment for noncitizen children who are in the U.S. with relatives who are not their parents.[244] If an aunt could enroll a noncitizen nephew from Mexico, how could a parent be denied in similar circumstances?

It is apparent that the best way to comply with *Plyler* is to ensure progress in effecting both the letter and the spirit of the opinion. Schools have in the past undertaken the practice of asking for Social Security numbers when parents enroll children. Most undocumented workers and their noncitizen children do not have Social Security numbers. Thus, this practice could be a clear violation of the right to access. Because the use of Social Security numbers by school officials in order to register children will cause parents to not enroll their children, states have become more cautious. For example, in 2003, the state of Virginia changed its Education Code to permit school officials to use another individual identifying number, and allowed authorities to waive the Social Security number requirement, if parents were concerned about disclosure.[245] The original law had mandated that parents provide schools with the student's Social Security number upon enrollment.

In contrast, California and Illinois have a policy of requiring only voluntary disclosure of Social Security numbers.[246] States such as Indiana and Tennessee have prohibited school districts from requiring Social Security numbers as a condition of enrollment to comply with the decision by *Plyler*

Court.[247] Other states prepare materials to inform parents and to train school officials.[248]

Despite these efforts, some school districts encounter difficulties in complying with *Plyler*. The lack of Social Security number also creates obstacles even beyond enrollment, such as verifying the identity of parents and other adults who will be picking up children at school. Further, the inability to obtain a driver's license and the unavailability of foreign documents also make these transactions difficult, because these documents are used an alternative to presenting a Social Security number.[249]

Because of these and other compliance problems in trying to ensure the education of undocumented students under *Plyler*, education policy analysts have suggested that schools *may not*:

- deny admission to a student on the basis of undocumented status;
- when determining residency, treat a student fundamentally differently from others;
- engage in practices to "chill" school access (see below);
- require students or parents to disclose or document immigration status;
- make inquiries of students or parents that may expose their undocumented status;
- require Social Security numbers from all students.[250]

Further, these analysts have highlighted and described specific areas of concern, for schools, which are set forth as follows:

- *Chilling.* Chilling refers to actions that create fear among undocumented students or their families. Many families are understandably fearful of completing forms such as vaccination records. They know their residency in this country is precarious and are generally unclear about how U.S. institutions function. For example, the free-lunch application requests Social Security numbers, but does not require them. Indeed, the need to complete enrollment forms can dissuade many parents from enrolling their children in school in the first place.[251]
- *Exposure.* Educators are not to "expose" children and families to the Immigration and Naturalization Service ("INS" now Department of Homeland Security). Fear of exposure, however, leads parents to keep their children from school, and causes children to worry about being arrested, separated from their parents, or kicked out of school.[252]
- *Disparity.* Disparity refers to the imposition of different rules according to individual or group characteristics. An example would be a clerk who demands original documents of "suspicious" students but accepts

copies from all others. Such procedures, whether gratuitous or a matter of written policy, can jeopardize the already fragile security of undocumented children. They increase the probability of exposure or chilling and can easily violate the requirements of Plyler.[253]

The recommendations above would assist in trying to ensure that undocumented children of undocumented parents are fully integrated. On the other hand, clear violations of the right of access may result in liability for a school district. Thus, there is a need for further analysis of specific aspects of compliance with *Plyler* and is undertaken in this next section.

Asking Questions Regarding Immigration Status

In order to comply with *Plyler v. Doe*, many states and school districts have adopted policies in which the school administration is advised not to even inquire as to a student's immigration status as a condition of enrollment. Further, schools may not require students or parents to disclose or document their immigration status.[254] The school district in Tyler, Texas, the party to *Plyler v. Doe*, has such a policy. The state of Indiana also does have a "do not ask" policy.[255]

The state of Michigan follows an education policy analogous to that of Indiana. The policy divides students into categories: nonimmigrant students, immigrant students, migrant students, and all other foreign students. "All foreign students residing in the district are considered residents and are entitled to enroll in the district *(Plyler v. Doe)*."[256] For the categories of "Immigrant students, Migrant Students, and All Other Foreign Students," it provides that "tuition may not be charged, a resident may not be counted in membership for state aid purposes, a student with a high school diploma, or its equivalent may NOT be counted in membership for state aid purposes."[257] Finally, the policy clarifies that the residency requirements for each of these groups must be the same as all other students.[258]

Other states and school districts follow the opposite approach and ask for the disclosure of citizenship status and visa status from parents wishing to enroll their children.[259] As stated before, these states cite the need to comply with federal immigration law and verify status such as that of F-1 and J-1 student visa holders, as the reason for their inquiry.[260] However, the official legal interpretation of section 274B of the Immigration and Nationality Act states that it "neither expressly prohibits nor authorizes any school district to require an alien to produce his or her visa or passport. ..."[261] Further, under this official interpretation, the Act:

[n]either prohibits nor allows any school district to require an alien to produce a visa, passport, or I-20 identification form in order to establish

residency within a school district. However, a school district is free to apply to alien students the established criteria for determining residence as it applies that criteria to any other student who seeks admission.[262]

Despite the differences between schools in their application of these rules, an educational law treatise advises:

> School authorities should recognize that the Congress has not overruled Plyler and, accordingly, where a student already present in the United States does not affirmatively indicate a desire to attend school as an F-1 student and the circumstances of that case are relevant, it is probably unwise to introduce immigration status into the dynamic.[263]

Ultimately, the law concerning whether a school should ask immigration status appears to be settled. Proposed requirements to verify that status of children within the school have been found unconstitutional as having intent of denying children the protection of *Plyler*.[264] Furthermore, it is true that then having such a "don't ask policy" could also be seen as overly cautious, since schools could request for such information for motives such as calculating the number of undocumented students so that they can obtain funds from the federal government.[265] Yet the difficulties in obtaining data from the undocumented population and the possibility of estimates yielding the information used by the state would support the use of caution in this instance.

Some schools also maintain a "do not ask" requirement for the added purpose of complying with Family Education Rights and Privacy Act ("FERPA").[266] However, it is not at all certain that FERPA would be violated in the absence of a "do not ask" policy, as FERPA is liberally interpreted to include immigration status information on students. FERPA prohibits the release of personally identifiable information about a student without the written consent of their parents.[267] Under FERPA, "personally identifiable information" is defined as:

> ... (a) the student's name, (b) the name of the student's parent, or other family member; (c) the address of the student, or the student's family; (d) a personal identifier, such as the student's social security number or student number; (e) a list of personal characteristics which make the student's identity easily traceable: or (f) other information which would make the student's identity easily traceable.[268]

It is apparent that immigration status may be considered "personally identifiable information." Thus, the disclosure of information relating to the immigration status of undocumented students or their parents would make the students' identity traceable, and it is prohibited by FERPA. If a school official voluntarily reveals the immigration status of an undocumented child to the Immigration and Customs Enforcement ("ICE"), this act would likely constitute a FERPA violation because it is personally identifiable to that child. In the above case, where the Northern Chicago school official threatened to call the Department of Homeland Security (DHS), the school would have committed a FERPA violation if it had contacted DHS to inquire into the immigration status of the student. Conversely, if the school were to just generally mention in an interview with newspaper reporters that "about 50 undocumented children go to school here," such information alone may not be FERPA violation because that information is not personally identifiable to the specific students.

FERPA's prohibition of the release of personally indentifiable information is subject to certain exceptions. FERPA only allows for the release of personally identifiable information when there is parental consent or under court order or subpoena.[269]

Schools would be well advised not to communicate with immigration officials barring a subpoena. In fact, it is a longstanding practice that principals are advised to deny requests for information by the immigration officials without a valid subpoena or warrant.[270] In practice, principals are further advised that if given a subpoena, they should consult an attorney before complying with the request.[271]

However, new post-9/11 requirements require schools to check student F, M, or J visas via the SEVIS (Student Exchange and Visitor Information System).[272] It is important to note nothing in FERPA directly references noncitizens. The only change in law is that there is a specific exemption from FERPA for those with a F, M, or J visa, so that their personal information may be shared with the immigration authorities via SEVIS. This change has caused confusion among school districts to the extent that it has led, for example, the Indiana state attendance officer to assert in a formal opinion that:

> No child should be denied enrollment in public schools (K-12) in Indiana due to immigration status. Any reports of the student's immigration status to any federal government office is [sic] the responsibility of the local school corporation in accordance with federal law. The child in question should be enrolled and enrollment should continue during the appeal process. In review of the federal law I find nothing preventing the enforcement of this state law.[273]

Furthermore, certain state and local privacy laws may be applicable to protect the privacy of the students. One example is Executive Order 41 signed by New York City Mayor Michael Bloomberg that protects the privacy of all residents seeking assistance from city agencies. The order protects those seeking assistance from schools, hospitals, and law enforcement from questions regarding sexual orientation, status as a victim of violence, income tax records, or immigration status.[274]

Assessing and Addressing the Cost of Compliance with *Plyler*

The cost of compliance with *Plyler* is not easy to quantify. Predictably, those who oppose immigration calculate their numbers expansively. For example, educating the children of undocumented workers costs states $7.4 billion dollars, according to a study by the Federation for American Immigration Reform ("FAIR"), an anti-immigrant group.[275] The number is further broken down to show that California spends an estimated $2.2 billion annually to educate undocumented immigrant children while Texas and New York rank second and third.[276] The FAIR report used the Urban Institute's estimate of 1.1 million undocumented alien schoolchildren in United States, and then disaggregated that number using Census Bureau statistics.[277] The calculation also uses per-pupil averages and does not account for costs associated with teaching English as a second language.[278]

On the other side of the spectrum, the National Council of La Raza, a Hispanic American advocacy group, asserts that if such a number is correct, the amount of funds expended is only a small portion of the national expenditure on education, estimated at roughly $700 billion by the Department of Education.[279] To date, no authoritative estimate exists of the cost of educating undocumented children nationwide. The General Accounting Office attempted to calculate a number of undocumented students in public schools and the resulting cost for doing so, and was unable to reach a reliable result because of difficulties in data collection.[280] Thus, the federal government has no official estimate of the cost of education for undocumented children.[281]

Proponents of education maintain that it is an investment that will reap benefits in the future. Additionally, they dispute some of the existing attempts to quantify the cost. Schools are funded by state and federal aid funding that is usually based on enrollment. Thus, funding usually keeps pace with enrollment increases. Thus, local taxpayers are not likely to suffer an increased tax burden from serving undocumented children. Some studies have found that undocumented persons use public services at a lower rate than other U.S. residents.[282] This is explained by an undocumented person's fear that accessing public services would lead to exposure. However, the cost of educating the undocumented is seen as a burden, since educating all children regardless of immigration status deprives U.S. citizen and lawfully admitted noncitizen children of greater enjoyment of the limited resources available.

The frustration of the states at the federal government's lax enforcement of immigration law and with the states' own inability to control what happens has led some localities to attempt to legally compel federal government to enforce immigration law.[283] Others have gone so far as to attempt a lawsuit against Mexico for the cost of educating school children. A resolution sponsored by Anaheim Union High School District Board member Harald Martin in 1999 sought $10 million a year from Mexico to cover the continuing costs of educating undocumented schoolchildren.[284] In relation to his resolution, Board member Martin stated: "We're providing a service just like anybody else, and why should the American taxpayer have to pay for this?"[285] The debate of this resolution took a racially charged twist. Some during the debate of the proposal charged Martin as a racist. A Latino member of the community addressed Mr. Martin by saying: "I'm saddened to feel the hostility in this room, but you folks chose us to have as neighbors. We didn't choose you."[286] Another person said during the meeting in reference to the Ku Klux Klan, "where are all your sheets?"[287] Yet Mr. Martin, himself a German immigrant, considers himself assimilated and criticizes those who are not. "To have an America of different groups, of different enclaves, is divisive and dangerous ... I am not a German American. I am an American of German heritage. There is a big problem in the world today with all this hyphenation."[288]

Mr. Martin expressed his frustration at a time of turmoil in California, after Proposition 187 was passed, but before the court had ruled on its provisions, Gov. Gray Davis had said that he would not order the removal of undocumented children from California schools.[289] Others at the Board meeting thought it was unfair to single out Mexico. "This resolution singles out one country, and we do not want to appear to be racist, so we should send a bill to every country that has illegal aliens in the schools," was the statement of Mr. Chad Morgan, the Orange County chair of Young Americans for Freedom, an extreme right-wing organization.[290] However, many in the school system argued that the district did not spend any extra money on illegal immigrants. Schools receive funding according to a state formula based on average daily attendance, regardless of the number of undocumented students.[291]

Similarly, the Anaheim Union High School Board of Trustees voted to have its attorney draw up a resolution billing Mexico for the education of its students enrolled in the district whose presence in the U.S. was unlawful.[292] Meliton Lopez, former superintendent of the Anaheim City School District and a member of Los Amigos of Orange County, a Latino advocacy group, opposed this action, stating that "They should be focusing on creating an environment that is risk free and where children do not feel afraid or diminished."[293]

Two Anaheim school trustees eventually abandoned the idea.[294] Instead, the Board decided to present a new resolution holding the federal government accountable "for failing to protect our borders." Additionally, part of

Board member Harald Martin's proposal that the INS be asked to count the number of undocumented students in the district still had broad support. However, critics were not pleased with this turn by the Board. As one community leader indicated: "[w]e don't need the INS in our schools. We need more schools and more teachers who are role models to our students who are flunking."[295] Eventually, the Board revised its plan. The revised plan demanded that the Immigration and Naturalization Service and Attorney General Janet Reno count the number of undocumented students in the Anaheim school district.[296] The Board passed a resolution to ask the federal government to reimburse the district for the costs of educating illegal immigrants, and to negotiate with foreign countries "to recover the costs of educating their citizens." The Justice Department declined Anaheim's demand to bill foreign countries for the cost of educating illegal immigrant children.[297] The Justice Department claimed it had no legal standing to do this. In 2002, Mr. Harald Martin was defeated in his bid for reelection to the school board.[298] He continued his initiatives, having lobbied the city council unsuccessfully to ask the federal government for power to arrest suspected illegal immigrants.[299] Should the city council have agreed, Anaheim would have been the first city in the nation to do so.[300] Many Latinos feared racial profiling.

Mr. Martin's saga as a Board member has continued in recent years. In 2007, he was appointed by the Anaheim Union High School District Board to a vacant seat of the board but later resigned, once community members obtained over five thousand signatures to force the board to hold a special election for his seat. For now, the chapter seems to be closed on any actions in Anaheim regarding undocumented children in their schools. Having seen the costs of compliance with Plyler, consider now the possibility of applying Plyler to early childhood education.

Applying *Plyler* to Pre-Primary Education

One aspect of the education of undocumented children in the United States which has not been analyzed of yet is pre-primary education, and whether the Plyler v. Doe's holding could apply to pre-K public programs. Currently, one quarter of three-and four-year olds attend publicly funded preschool and another quarter attend private preschool in the United States.[301] The threshold question the Supreme Court would address in this situation is whether the right to access pre-primary education warrants the same heightened constitutional scrutiny that the Court applied in Plyler. Because the Court has made clear there is no fundamental right to education in the U.S. Constitution, state constitutions may be the best vehicle to implement such a policy.

A counselor at Douglas Elementary School in Tyler, Texas, the district where the Plyler v. Doe dispute originated, has witnessed many undocumented mothers being hesitant to enroll their children in a federal program, even though immigration status was not a factor in the program.[302] Indeed, while federal law prohibits undocumented workers from receiving "federal means-tested public benefit for five-years," Congress exempted school lunch programs, Head Start, and means-tested programs under the Elementary and Secondary Education Act of 1965.[303]

It is sound policy to extend pre-primary education to children of undocumented workers. Assistant Secretary of Education Susan Neuman, of the most recent Bush Administration, has expressed the view that, "from the beginning, the playing field is ... not equal."[304] She has also stated that early education provides "the rich language interactions that are necessary to allow children to explain, describe, inquire, hypothesize, and analyze."[305] She has concluded that "our failure has been to adequately compensate for the gap when it can be best overcome in the earliest years."[306]

Advances in neuroscience have made it clear that the first few years of life are crucial for cognitive development and that early experiences can influence the emerging architecture of the brain.[307] Some preschool programs have reduced grade retention and placement in special education, increased graduation rates, and decreased crime and delinquency.[308] Research shows that taxpayers would save twice the amount of money part on children preschools by the time those individuals reach the age of 27.[309] Further, the Federal Reserve Bank in Minneapolis has found that investment in preschool carries with it an unusually high rate of return at 12 percent.[310] Other studies have estimated the rate of return between 4 and 9 percent.[311] Finally, the Brookings Institution calculated a $2 trillion gain to the U.S. Gross Domestic Product by 2080 from the adoption of a universal preschool initiative.[312]

Many states are beginning to introduce universal pre-K programs, and proposals have been made at the national level for similar initiatives. Illinois is creating a universal Pre-school for All program, and is making an effort to specifically include the undocumented.[313]

The best vehicle for asserting that undocumented children have a right to pre-primary education would be the state constitution's education clause.[314] Every state, except Mississippi, has an education clause.[315] As applied to kindergarten, the Supreme Court of Indiana struck down on state constitutional and statutory grounds a district's $20 student services fee, imposed upon parents of all students without regard to financial need.[316] Further, the Supreme Court of New Jersey recognized the right of poor, urban students right to access preschool.[317] In contrast, courts in Massachusetts, North Carolina, and Arkansas have not found such right.[318] However, in Massachusetts in the case of *Hancock v. Driscoll*, the trial court in school finance litigation ordered publicly funded preschool as part of an "adequacy" remedy.[319] The judge did so underscoring that in addition to its short term benefits, "[h]igh quality early child education has longer-term advantages as well, including increased high school graduation rates, increased college attendance rates, better employment, and less involvement with any criminal or juvenile justice system."[320]

Any attempt to restrict access to pre-primary education by undocumented students would likely be unconstitutional using a *Plyler v. Doe* analysis. The *Plyler* Court noted the government has exclusive power to classify aliens, and states have authority to act only when "such action mirrors federal objectives and furthers a legitimate state goal."[321] Conserving state educational resources did not mirror congressional objectives, and thus the state could not enforce the law.[322] "In the area of special constitutional sensitivity by these cases, and in the absence of any contrary indication fairly discernible in the present legislative record, we perceive no national policy that supports the State in denying these children an elementary education."[323] Similarly, attempts to make undocumented children pay tuition or denying them access altogether would likely be impermissible under the same reasoning. The Court in *Plyler* held "if the State is to deny a discrete group of innocent children the free public education if offers other children residing within its borders, the denial must justified by a showing that it furthers some substantial interest."[324] Because the benefits associated with pre-primary education are well documented, it is unlikely that there would be a substantial state interest that could show that pre-primary education should not be available to undocumented children. The Texas law at issue in *Plyler* "promoted the creation and perpetuation of a subclass of illiterates within our boundaries, surely adding to the problems and costs of unemployment, welfare, and crime."[325] Similarly, because preschool lowers the costs of unemployment, and crime, there would be no rational basis under *Plyler* for denying undocumented students a pre-primary education.

A complicating factor in making the case for undocumented children attending pre-primary education is that kindergarten still is not universal in the United States. Only fourteen states provide full-day kindergarten, and 55 percent of kindergartners attend full-day classes.[326] Thus, because pre-primary education is currently not universal or mandated, it may be more difficult to argue for its access. Opponents will likely argue that *Plyler* only applied to primary education, and that pre-primary education would be closer to higher education than it would be to primary education. Of course, unlike higher education, children still are innocent parties who should not be punished for the sins of their parents. Thus, while a noncitizen that has matured into adulthood might consider the option of higher education, the pre-primary education child has no choice.[327]

The availability of Head Start to the undocumented is clearly a national policy. Further, as a general principle, Congress's regulation in the area of noncitizens benefits and education makes clear that the states cannot limit benefits to aliens without violating the Supremacy Clause. While the 1996 welfare reform, in the form of the Personal Responsibility and Work Opportunity Reconciliation Act of 1996 ("PRWORA"), limited many assistance programs to the poor, it did not do so for Head Start and pre-primary education.[328] Further, Congress expressly addressed other areas of noncitizen education such the rule regarding noncitizen higher education in IIRIRA section 505. If Congress wanted to restrict another type of education, pre-primary education, it would have done so. Any attempt to regulate education or prohibit educational advancement by the undocumented would thus then be inconsistent with immigration policy and barred by the Supremacy Clause.

Finally, the Court in *Plyler* was driven by the importance of education as a value in society and the strong public policy associated with allowing easy access to it.[329] Thus, because the benefits associated with pre-primary education are so high in comparison with the costs, extending the holding in *Plyler* to pre-primary education would advance this same principle.

The twenty-first century demands a greater commitment to education. Primary education will not be enough to truly realize the economic, health, and societal benefits of education. Thus, it is a benefit for all to allow undocumented children access to pre-primary education.

This chapter concludes with an examination and assessment of the manner in which other countries have handled their undocumented students' educational needs.

Towards What is Possible: Lessons From Europe

Let us now compare the United States' treatment of undocumented students with that of the nations of the European Union ("EU"). Since its inception, the EU has experienced expansive growth in its undocumented population, with migrants coming from Africa and non EU countries, to find work in "Fortress Europe." Unlike the United States, the EU has developed a comprehensive, multi-faceted approach towards integrating noncitizen children into its public schools. This approach utilizes several techniques such as conducting lessons in the language and culture of their country of origin in mainstream school curricula, promoting inter-cultural education for all children, access to support services and financial aid, the use of orientation measures, and special human resource development for educational faculty.[330]

In contrast to the United States, where the Supreme Court has stated that education is not a fundamental right, not even for U.S. citizens, most countries grant the right to education to all children of compulsory school age, regardless of immigration status.[331] This right has been affirmed by a variety of international human rights instruments, including the United Nations Universal Declaration of Human Rights, and the United Nations Convention on the Rights of the Child.[332] Other applicable conventions include the International Covenant on Economic and Social Rights.[333] At the European regional level, the Charter of Fundamental Rights states that "(1) Everyone has the right to education and to have to vocational and continuing training. (2) This right includes the possibility to receive free compulsory education."[334] Finally, human rights instruments ban discrimination based on race or ethnic origin in education.[335]

The European Court of Human Rights interpreted Article 2 of the Protocol to the European Convention on Human Rights in one of its earliest education cases. This case was *Case Relating to Certain Aspects of the Laws of Languages in Education in Belgium*.[336] The case was filed by French-speaking parents residing in areas of Belgium in which their children were required to attend schools in which Dutch was the language of instruction.[337] The Court held that the schooling in French-language and Dutch-language in certain areas constituted discrimination on the basis of language, and thus violated Article 2 of the Protocol and Article 14 of the European Convention.[338]

Since the Court's testing of this right, the right to education has become more widespread by the use of policies implementing its universal nature. Under European law, minors from third countries who have the status of long-term residents are entitled to the same treatment in education as that of citizens of the EU member state.[339] Minors who are children of asylum seekers or are themselves asylum seekers have been able to access the education system under conditions similar to those applicable to citizens of the host member state.[340] In the case of children who are "irregularly present" on EU territory, no education entitlement is articulated by EU legislation. Thus, the law of individual nations is applicable in this case.

Nations vary in how they provide the right to education to undocumented students. Certain countries such as Belgium, Czech Republic, Greece, France, Ireland, Italy, Luxembourg, the Netherlands, Austria and Portugal explicitly permit school enrollment for undocumented children.[341] The right to education is implicit in certain European countries where there is no obstacle to the enrollment of children who have no legal status in the country. Countries where this is the case include Germany, Estonia, Spain, Cyprus, Latvia, Hungary, Malta, Slovenia, Finland, the United Kingdom, Bulgaria and Romania. These countries either do not link student enrollment to residency status, or do not distinguish categories of children who have a right and duty to attend school.[342] Only in a few European countries do schools have no obligation to enroll children who are not in the country legally. These countries include Denmark, Lithuania, Poland, Sweden, and Iceland.[343]

Most countries also provide a variety of support services to low-income and noncitizen children. Students obtain these services on an as-needed basis. France and Luxembourg allow low-income children to apply for special grants, and exempt them from some financial contributions for school services.[344] Other countries subsidize travel to and from school, meals, uniforms, and books for the children. Usually the provisions for noncitizen children are no more generous than are those for natives. However, Cyprus is one country where noncitizen children enjoy slightly more special treatment. Children who do not speak Greek as a first language are encouraged to stay at school in the afternoon for remedial classes and homework assistance. The children get a free lunch if they do so.[345]

Additionally, what makes European countries truly unique are the special orientation services that are provided to noncitizen parents. These include written information about the school system, special allowances for inter-preters, special resource persons, additional meetings specifically for noncit-izen families, and information about pre-primary education.[346] Several countries employ the first measure, written information about the school system in different languages. Ireland publishes information in the nine main languages of asylum seekers, unaccompanied minors, and parents of non-national children.[347] A few countries use interpreters. In Sweden, schools must provide interpretation at special introductory meetings for newly arriv-ing families, explaining rights to pre-schools and schools, and the national curriculum.[348] This interpretation right also extends also extends to the twice yearly "personal development dialogue" held with all parents. Further, coun-tries such as the Netherlands, Finland, and the United Kingdom have spe-cially trained "intercultural mediators."[349] Such persons deal mostly with language concerns, but their role is flexible, with a focus on linking the home, school, and community. Luxembourg has set up "consultative councils of foreigners" for a municipality where more than 20 percent of the population is foreign.[350] These councils address the unique issues specific to foreign pupils in the municipality. Other countries such as Spain, Finland, and Swe-den provide informational meetings to orient noncitizen parents.[351]

European schools use a combination of bilingual and immersion tech-niques to integrate noncitizen children. These are used either in an integrated approach where children get special instruction during schools hours or by extracurricular tuition where special instruction is given after school.[352] Greece uses an approach where noncitizen pupils form special learning groups for two years. Noncitizen pupils are taught separately, but can join the native schoolchildren for lessons in music, sports, artistic subjects, and for-eign languages, where the language barrier does not impair understanding as much as in other lesson areas.[353] A few countries such as Estonia, Latvia, and Cyprus offer bilingual education in which the teacher uses both the native language and their school language of instruction.[354] In Germany, Greece, Slovakia, and Slovenia, teachers are specially trained at the outset to face the linguistic and educational challenges posed by immigrant students.[355] In Cyprus, teachers with noncitizen pupils in their class are entitled to a reduc-tion in their work time as an incentive to teach these students.[356] In addition, the government offers afternoon and evening classes in Greek for all foreign parents of pupils.[357]

A novel approach undertaken by a few countries is noncitizen access to pre-primary education. The Czech Republic, Finland, and Sweden operate special groups for noncitizen children at pre-primary level so they will be ready for formal primary education.[358] In the United Kingdom, pre-school staff are advised to give particular attention to children whose second language is English.[359]

Finally, a few countries have recognized that noncitizen children are at high risk of dropping out of school because of their socioeconomic circumstances. Belgium, Spain, and the Netherlands have special programs targeted to these children.[360]

Another special feature of the European system is the accommodation made for noncitizens to continue the practices of their native culture. In Germany, compulsory "physical education and swimming" is taught in a co-educational environment. However, schools must offer to teach girls and boys separately, if the parents request it.[361] The Muslim community uses this accommodation frequently. School lunch menus in Spain are also culturally sensitive for similar reasons.[362] Additionally, all countries, with the exception of Iceland and Bulgaria, have a form of multicultural education that teaches tolerance and discusses racism and xenophobia.[363] At present, the United States does not seem to be on par with Europe on these fronts.

The concept of education as a right is not new, nor is it unique to Europe though. Education is categorized as an economic right. It pre-dates the Universal Declaration of Human Rights and other international covenants. In 1941, President Franklin Delano Roosevelt outlined his "Four Freedoms." These include freedom of speech, freedom of religion, freedom from want, and freedom from fear.[364] Surely, freedom from want should encompass freedom from want of schooling, and want from the ill effects of lack of schooling. Further, as seen earlier in this chapter, every state constitution except Mississippi has an education clause within its constitution that forces the state to create a public school system.[365] A great many of these education clauses compel the state legislatures to provide for "a thorough and efficient system" of public schools.[366] Unfortunately though, the Supreme Court of the United States has not recognized a right to education in the U.S. Constitution,[367] although at least one commentator has suggested that a federal right to education remains possible today.[368]

Furthermore, some suggest the level of education that is guaranteed should be more of a political question, and not one for the courts. Economic rights are based on state tax revenue and the right to education, unlike a political right like freedom of speech, brings associated costs.[369] Thus, an economic right will never be fully enforced so long as public resources are scarce.[370] This argument fails to take into account that education, unlike other economic rights, is more seen as an investment, that with proper levels of funding it can contribute more to economic productivity, less crime and poverty, and thus be in the state's interest to be provided for adequately. Undocumented students would be more fully integrated and productive members of society if the United States followed more a human rights approach associated with education. This would prevent the current quagmire of being embroiled in equal protection analysis and ensure *Plyler*'s vitality.

2

Documented Dreams, the Underground Railroad and Underground Undergraduates

Higher Education for the Undocumented and the Use of Student Movements to Achieve this Goal

Introduction

The Supreme Court in *Plyler* recognized that undocumented children are a vulnerable subclass in the United States. While under *Plyler* undocumented children receive a free elementary and secondary education, the promise of an education ends once they complete secondary education. Their irregular immigration status poses unique challenges when seeking higher education, very often leading to prohibitively high tuition rates—even for those students who have lived in a state for many years—or worse yet, a complete prohibition against enrolling in postsecondary institutions.

These obstacles, when added to the routine financial, societal and emotional pressures most college students face, make higher education an impossible dream for nearly all undocumented students. Thus, this chapter begins with actual stories of successful undocumented students, showing how they navigate the roadblocks they encounter in their pursuit of further education, having completed their K–12 studies. The chapter then explores the phenomenon of undocumented student movements in pursuit of higher education, and shows that the imagery used in these movements is vivid, using names evocative of either the students' quest for achievement or current status as being hidden, in the shadow of mainstream United States society. For example, a recent volume compiling the narratives of undocumented high school students is entitled DOCUMENTED DREAMS,[1] in a manifest reference to the DREAM Act, but also to the students' aspirations of reaching their full educational potential and lawful immigration status. In contrast, the imagery of being concealed, underground, because of their undocumented status is also present. Some of its leaders refer to the network of student activists and their allies in this movement as the Underground Railroad, in a clear reference to the antislavery movement.[2] A number of these students, once they overcome many obstacles and reach college, have identified themselves as Underground Undergrads.[3]

These undocumented student movements appear to be a subset of the current immigrant rights movement, which has been growing steadily in recent years but emerged in full force as part of the nationwide immigration reform marches in the spring of 2006. This immigrant rights movement has identified as been, potential new civil rights movement.[4] During the marches of 2006 and afterwards, the undocumented student participation in public political expression was curtailed by those arguing that their undocumented status precluded them from exercising any First Amendment rights. The examination and analysis of these student movements will assist in the understanding of whether undocumented students possess First Amendment rights to free speech and can in fact protest and express their political views while at school.

A Bittersweet Victory

Four undocumented high school students from Hayden High School in West Phoenix, Arizona won a national robotics competition in early 2005.[5] Their robot, named Stinky, was built from cheap plastic pipes and the foul-smelling glue that gave it its name. The team of undocumented students won the prestigious Marine Advanced Technology Remotely Operated Vehicle Competition, an underwater robotics contest sponsored by NASA and the Office of Naval Research. Observers at the competition were surprised that the robot could compete with one from Massachusetts Institute of Technology ("MIT"), a better-looking robot decorated with an ExxonMobil sticker. The company donated $5,000 to the twelve engineering students from MIT to build it.[6]

The Hayden High team came together after two teachers offered to coach a team and put up fliers at school advertising the competition. The team members were Cristian Arcega, the school's science wiz, who lived in a wooden shack attached to his parents' trailer; Lorenzo Santillan, a former gang member who enjoyed fixing cars; Oscar Vazquez, an ROTC student; and Luis Aranda, a burly student who carried the heavy robot.[7] They raised $800 from local businesses to build the robot. In the end, the team won awards for best design and technical writing, since Stinky could perform a task that the MIT robot could not. It sucked fluid out of a tiny container 12 feet underwater.[8]

However, their victory did not last. Vazquez and Aranda graduated from Hayden High School, but could not attend college immediately. Their unlawful immigration status made them ineligible for in-state tuition and low-interest student loans.

This inspiring account of an underdog team triumphing against incredible odds made for a prominent story in *Wired* magazine.[9] Support for the students came in from all around the world. Over $3,000 poured into a "La Visa

Robot Scholarship Fund," an account opened after hundreds of people e-mailed both *Wired* magazine and the high school offering financial assistance. The story was picked up on English and Spanish nationwide broadcasts, including National Public Radio and ABC's Niteline, and Warner Brothers purchased the rights for the movie.[10] Arcega received a full tuition, four-year scholarship to the California Institute of Technology, and wanted to become an engineer. Vazquez was able to attend classes part time at Phoenix College.[11] Both of them eventually enrolled at Arizona State University, where Vazquez is an engineering senior, while Arcega had to withdraw after one year "when all the immigration issues were coming up."[12] Because he is unable to work in the U.S., Vazquez plans to go to Canada after graduation.[13] Santillan and Aranda have both studied culinary arts, and Santillan plans to open his own catering business, so as not "to worry about showing identification to a potential employer."[14]

In the past, undocumented students in Arizona were eligible to receive in-state tuition rates at state colleges. However, Arizona Proposition 300 now bars such in-state treatment.[15] Instead, these undocumented students, even though they have resided in Arizona nearly all their lives, must pay out-of-state tuition, just like international students. Such students thus are delaying or altogether terminating their education because of this situation. Unfortunately, many students in this situation, even the most talented and hard-working, are effectively denied the opportunity for higher education. Not every student is fortunate enough to receive press attention and scholarships. In fact, another undocumented student has also entered a robotics competition with his school team and has encountered obstacles to participating.[16] Because of his lack of proper identification owing to his undocumented status, Amadou Ly, a Senegalese high school student resident of New York, was unable to travel on an airplane to the competition with the rest of the team. Instead, he had to take a long train ride to Atlanta.[17] His plight became widespread news throughout the media, leading to his obtaining a temporary student visa.[18]

Getting Deported from Princeton

Dan-el Padilla Peralta, a full-scholarship senior and class salutatorian at Princeton University, was an undocumented student who received a two-year scholarship to study at Oxford University's Worcester College after graduation.[19] Recognizing that he might be barred from reentering the United States for ten years under current immigration law, Mr. Padilla took his chance and left for Oxford in fall 2006.[20]

Mr. Padilla's parents brought him to the United States from the Dominican Republic when he was four years old.[21] The family had originally entered the U.S. seeking medical care for his mother, who had diabetes complications associated with pregnancy.[22] His parents applied unsuccessfully for legal immigration status in the United States.[23] His mother decided to stay in the United States after their initial visitor visas expired.[24] Like his younger U.S-born brother and other U.S. citizen children, Mr. Padilla then was raised in the United States and educated all the way through his elementary and secondary school here.[25]

Mr. Padilla overcame a childhood living in homeless shelters and slums to become a star classics student at Princeton. His mentor, Jeff Cowen, first discovered him as a nine-year-old living in a shelter curled up reading a biography of Napoleon. Mr. Cowen became involved in his life and assisted him in his education, especially with his admission to Collegiate School, an elite New York City private institution.

Mr. Padilla requested adjustment of status to obtain legal immigration status in the U.S. because of the extraordinary circumstances in his life, such as moving thirteen times and being abandoned by his father. Mr. Padilla's story received much media attention, and U.S. Senators and Congresspersons intervened on his behalf. However, the U.S. Customs and Immigration Service ("USCIS") refused to change his status because of concerns that he would set a precedent for the treatment of other undocumented immigrants. Padilla also applied for a discretionary waiver that would allow him to come back to the U.S. He would have liked to teach social studies, history, and literature to disadvantaged middle-school children. At his Princeton graduation ceremony, Padilla met former President Bill Clinton, who wrote a letter to immigration authorities on his behalf.

Senator Hillary Clinton from New York and several members from the Congress pleaded with the USCIS on behalf of Mr. Padilla once they learned Mr. Padilla's story. In summer 2007, Mr. Padilla was able to obtain a temporary waiver and returned to Princeton on an H-1B visa to conduct research for his former mentor.[26] In most circumstances, the H-1B is a temporary visa of six years' duration. After this six-year visa expires, Mr. Padilla Peralta may again face removal from the United States, unless he finds another lawful path to immigrate or there is a change in the law.

Dan-el Padilla Peralta in his own words

Mr. Padilla has shared with us the following thoughts reflecting on his experience and offering a message of hope to other undocumented students:

> My opinion on the situation of undocumented students in the U.S: Their predicament is a cruel travesty that violates some of our country's basic moral and legal principles. We don't sanction punishing children for their parents' decisions—except in the case of undocumented students. We prize hard work and high achievement among our nation's

students and encourage them to pursue their dreams of higher education—except in the case of undocumented students, who have to run through a depressingly effective gauntlet of restrictions and obstacles. And we believe that our children above all else should be protected from hate, from embarrassment, from shame—except in the case of undocumented students, who have to contend, at every turn, with the invidious sneers and slanders of those who would have them believe that the only thing they deserve is a fast-track deportation.

I would say to all the undocumented students out there to keep on striving to perform at the very highest level, and to shut out all that slander and hate as best you can. I know how frustrating and draining it is to be made to feel that you don't deserve even the scraps of educational access that are tossed your way, to live in constant fear that someone near and dear to you will be arrested and deported in the middle of the night, to endure poverty. But who'll be able to marginalize you when you continue racking up As and earn admission to the best universities in this country? Face the challenges with pride and purpose.[27]

Mr. Padilla's words, while abundantly evidencing the plight of the undocumented student, also show a sense of hope in the power of higher education. His words echo what the teachers of undocumented students have said in order to keep their undocumented students motivated: "Look, you can get deported tomorrow. Do you want to get deported as a garbage collector? Or deported as a doctor?" and "There will be people all over the world who will have you, the U.S. is too stupid to keep you."[28]

Mr. Smith Goes to Washington for Undocumented Students

On July 25, 2007, Immigration Customs Enforcement ("ICE") arrested Juan and Alex Gomez in Miami. They were just two of the many youths who have been apprehended nationwide by immigration authorities.[29] Juan and Alex were toddlers when their parents brought them to the U.S. from Colombia, fleeing persecution.[30] Both children excelled in school. Juan did especially well on fifteen advanced placement exams and nearly scored perfectly on the SAT exam.[31] However, because of the law which prevented the boys from receiving in-state tuition benefits, and the family had limited financial resources, they were only planning to attend community college.[32] Their friends and supporters used the Internet to spread the message to support them, and to enlist the help of non-profits such as the Florida Immigration Advocacy Center. They have been successful in attracting national media attention. As a result, U.S. Representative Lincoln Diaz-Balart agreed to sponsor a private bill to give them relief. Private federal bills to grant lawful immigration status are the only narrow remedy for these students under current law.

Furthermore, USCIS agreed to suspend their deportation and release them from detention for at least forty-five days.[33] Finally, Senator Christopher Dodd managed to have a private bill passed, so that then the young men could stay in the U.S. until 2009.[34] TIME magazine described the lobbying effort "like something out of *Mr. Smith Goes to Washington*."[35] The lobbying may only pay off for the students, since both their parents and grandmother have been removed from the U.S. and deported back to Colombia.[36] Juan has been accepted at Georgetown University and continues his education there, while Alex is a graduate of the Miami Dade Community College.[37]

Although it is rarely done, from time to time Congresspersons have introduced and secured passage of private bills in the past for undocumented students. Congressman Paul Gilmor (R-Tiffin) introduced a bill to grant legal permanent relief status to an undocumented youth from Gilboa, Ohio.[38] The eighteen-year-old, Manuel Bartsch, was jailed over Christmas of 2006 and was expected to be deported for overstaying a ninety-day visa used when he arrived from Germany with his stepgrandfather when he was ten years old. ICE granted a stay as a matter of courtesy until spring 2009. USCIS also granted employment authorization to Mr. Bartsch.

Similar success stories are told repeatedly in immigrant communities around the United States.[39] Yet, only very few undocumented students are so fortunate as to have the spotlight shining on them like the Hadley High students, Dan-el Padilla, the Gomez brothers, and some of the others whose lives we have shown.[40]

Let us now examine the data regarding how many undocumented students nationwide would be likely beneficiaries of the higher education they seek and what benefits higher education provides.

Data regarding Undocumented Students Eligible to Pursue Higher Education and Obstacles they Face

The Pew Hispanic Center estimates that 1.5 million undocumented children currently reside in the United States.[41] Of these, approximately 765,000 youths arrived in the United States before they reached their sixteenth birthday.[42] Furthermore, the Migration Policy Institute estimated that there were 360,000 undocumented high school graduates aged between eighteen and twenty-four in the United States in 2006.[43] However, it is estimated that each year only 5 to 10 percent of undocumented high-school graduates—about 65,000 nationwide—are eligible to attend college.[44] In 2005, only an estimated 50,000 undocumented students enrolled in the United States colleges and universities.[45] Among them, approximately 18,000 were enrolled in California community colleges in the academic year 2005–2006.[46] Only an estimated 271 to 433 undocumented students enrolled in the University of California during the academic year 2006–2007.[47]

The Importance of Higher Education

Receiving basic education is essential to those children and to the society as a whole.[48] Today, more than twenty-five years after *Plyler v. Doe*, obtaining a college degree is even more important than before. Without college training, a person will likely have difficulties negotiating potential employment in the twenty-first-century job market.[49] Moreover, technology dominates today's society and influences individuals' lives in almost every dimension. Most people cannot escape poverty without higher education which will provide the tools and opportunity to use technology. Additionally, college courses help form individuals' critical thinking ability, a key foundation of a democratic society. Finally, a college education tends to inspire individuals to pursue their areas of interests. Those individuals will be able to apply themselves and contribute to the society in a constructive way.

Private and Social Benefits of Higher Education

College education significantly increases income, as compared with the income of persons with a high school diploma. For example, a typical worker with a high school diploma earned 62 percent less than a typical full-time worker with a four-year college degree in the United States.[50] Additionally, an individual with a four-year college degree is less likely to be unemployed. In August 2005, the unemployment rate for those over twenty-five without a high school diploma was 7 percent, 4.5 percent for high school graduates, and 3.5 percent for those with some college, and 2.4 percent for those with a bachelor's degree.[51] The available data suggest that this is the case even during harsh economic times, such as the ones currently facing the U.S.[52] By extending these private gains to the undocumented student, the United States can provide greater social mobility to these individuals and help the economy at large as well.

However, the social returns are more important, especially in light of anti-immigrant accusations that undocumented workers cost taxpayers money. Education can provide the groundwork for more win–win thinking, as opposed to a zero sum game where undocumented workers are perceived as taking something away from the United States. This thinking is exemplified in the words of a spokesperson for Federation for American Immigration Reform ("FAIR"), who, in commenting about undocumented students being admitted to U.S. colleges, has said that: "there is another kid who wasn't admitted to school because we admitted the illegal alien."[53] The assumption, of course, is that the other "kid" is a U.S. citizen left out of higher education.

Such nativist fear of competition embodies several misconceptions. First, the U.S. citizen college applicant has many other opportunities, not having any restrictions based on citizenship, whereas the undocumented student only fits narrowly into the admissions profiles of certain institutions of higher education. Second, there are benefits to the whole of U.S. society when more individuals overall achieve higher education. Research has found that for every percentage point increase in the supply of college graduates, there is a raise in the wages of high school drop-outs by 1.9 percent, the wages of high school graduates by 1.6 percent, and the wages of college graduates by 0.04 percent.[54] Further research has also shown other benefits relating to health, voting, and reduced crime. Thus, even those persons not going to college enjoy the benefit of more people graduating from college.

There are further benefits to higher education society in terms of higher democratic participation. For example, in the 2004 presidential election, of every age group, adults with higher levels of education were more likely to vote than those with less education. Between 1980 and 2004, the voting rate for high school graduates declined more than the voting rate for those with higher levels of education.[55] Voting may also be a particular benefit to undocumented persons, to the extent that undocumented status or possibly race currently excludes such persons from participation the political process. Voting is a function of citizenship and if undocumented persons are more educated it may become more likely for them to find a pathway to citizenship. With more education, such persons are more likely to find opportunities for lawful immigration status and hence maybe also more likely to become citizens. Thus, they will have an ability to better participate in the U.S. sociopolitical community.

Greater education also leads to healthy behaviors. Those with more education are also more likely to have higher rates of physical activity and are more likely to control diabetes.[56] Such persons are less likely to smoke during pregnancy, become obese, and have two or more risk factors for heart disease.[57] Encouraging healthy behaviors is important because such behaviors will prevent chronic diseases that contribute to increased health costs for the population as a whole.

Finally, allowing access to college education, by requiring completion of high school or a GED would reduce high school drop-out rates. In 2000, only 59.8 per cent of noncitizens in the United States had completed high school.[58] Immigration status and barriers to higher education contribute towards a higher drop-out rate. Having a clear opportunity for higher education following graduation would provide an incentive to finish high school. The social benefits of higher education of undocumented persons are evident. For example, the RAND Corporation found that the average thirty-year-old Mexican immigrant woman who has graduated from college will pay $5,300 more in taxes and cost $3,900 less in criminal justice and welfare expenses than if she had dropped out of high school.[59] Thus, the economic benefit associated with providing pathways to college for undocumented students can be substantial.

Neither education nor public benefits attract noncitizens to the U.S. Even the Supreme Court has observed that "few if any illegal immigrants come to this country ... in order to avail themselves of a free education."[60] Thus, there is no merit to the argument that undocumented persons will come to the U.S. solely in search of a college education. Further, when comparing the possible benefits to society, the costs associated with this unsubstantiated fear would be clearly outweighed. One Massachusetts study showed that if undocumented aliens were allowed to gain residency, the state would gain millions of dollars.[61] The money was identified as "net new revenues to the state, since public colleges would incur little or no added costs in accommodating these small numbers of additional students, a tiny fraction of the 160,000 public college students in Massachusetts." Finally, when more people obtain higher education, this of course, leads to higher-paying employment, and thus more tax revues in the long term.[62]

Obstacles Undocumented Students Face in their Pursuit of Higher Education

At present, their immigration status determines those undocumented students' future, regardless of their talents. If undocumented high school graduates, as beneficiaries of *Plyler v. Doe*, are able to obtain regular immigration status, they may be able to pursue higher education and likely realize their full potential. Because undocumented students often come from lower socioeconomic backgrounds, they do not have financial support to attend colleges. This is particularly true when these undocumented students are required to pay out-of-state tuition rates.[63] In fact, undocumented students are ineligible for federal financial aid such as student loans, scholarships, or work-study programs because of the prohibition of a 1996 federal law.[64]

Many undocumented students fear that if they apply for college, they and their family members might risk being deported as a result of the information they disclose in the applications.[65] Furthermore, undocumented students, through their application process, find that they are not allowed to attend public universities or colleges after they finished their K-12 education because of their immigration status. An example of this is the ban on undocumented students entering North Carolina community colleges enacted in May 2008.[66] Even when some undocumented students are admitted to colleges, they usually discover that they have to pay non-resident out-of-state tuition, usually three times or more compared to resident students.[67] For example, in the 2007–2008 year, tuition at the University of California, Los Angeles for undergraduates was $7,713.23 for residents, while it was $27,333.23 for nonresidents.[68]

Federal and State Legal Obstacles to Higher Education for Undocumented Children: the Debate

The granting of in-state tuition to undocumented students is at the center of political and legal debates and, as seen above, one of the main obstacles for these students in obtaining higher education. Although the determination of residency for state tuition purposes is a state law matter, and in fact, the Supreme Court has recognized that "illegal entry into the country would not, under traditional criteria, bar a person from obtaining domicile within a State,"[69] it is through federal legislation that this debate has ensued. Two federal laws, which will be discussed in detail below, appear to restrict the states' ability to grant in-state tuition to undocumented students. This is what has caused the heated debate.

Proponents of granting in-state tuition rates to undocumented students argue that it is within a state's prerogative and not that of the federal government to grant or deny undocumented students in-state tuition. Immigration status should not be the primary factor determining whether undocumented students can pursue higher education and realize their dreams. Echoing the argument that persuaded the Supreme Court in *Plyler*, proponents argue that undocumented children came to the United States through no fault of their own. While those youngsters are raised alongside their native-born peers, they should be rewarded for their hardwork, not punished for the actions of their parents.

Opponents of granting in-state tuition rates to undocumented students believe that these students should not receive preferential treatment for competing with legal permanent residents and citizens of the United States to enroll in postsecondary educational institutions. Opponents further argue that allowing one undocumented student to attend college means the denial of the same opportunity to a U.S. citizen student. Opponents also argue that states should not waste tax dollars to educate undocumented students. Without valid immigration status, those undocumented students could not even obtain lawful employment in the United States after they have their college diplomas. Moreover, opponents argue that the *Plyler* decision recognized undocumented children did not have free will when they were brought to the United States. When those undocumented students complete their free elementary and secondary education, however, those undocumented students become individuals.[70] Thus, in their view those undocumented individuals are responsible for their own decisions. When they choose to continue staying in the United States, those undocumented students knowingly and purposefully break the U.S. laws. They are personally responsible for their own actions.[71] Thus, opponents argue that undocumented students should either voluntarily leave or be deported from the United States. This view is unrealistic since many of the students have virtually no ties to the countries they left as infants or young children and often do not even speak the language of the country. Additionally, the resources of the federal government are limited so that deporting all the undocumented students in the county is impossible at the present time.

Opponents also argue that allowing undocumented students to pay in-state tuition rates when they attend colleges clearly violates the federal mandates. Specifically, the Personal Responsibility and Work Opportunity Reconciliation Act of 1996 codified at 8 U.S.C. § 1621 ("PRWORA") and the Illegal Immigration Reform and Immigrant Responsibility Act of 1996 codified at 8 U.S.C. § 1623 ("IIRIRA") prohibit undocumented persons from receiving government benefits.

Heated debates over interpretations concerning PRWORA and IIRIRA have raged throughout the postsecondary education institutions around the nation. The following subsections focus on different interpretations of the 1996 laws and how they are obstacles in the achievement of higher education for undocumented students.

Federal Law Obstacles: PRWORA, IIRIRA and in-state tuition bans

PRWORA is a comprehensive welfare reform that also creates a scheme for determining aliens' eligibility for federal, state, and local public benefits and services. It does not prohibit college admission to undocumented students. It categorizes aliens as either "qualified" or "not qualified" and then denies state or local public benefits based on that characterization in 8 U.S.C. § 1621. Federal law defines the term state or local benefit as any postsecondary education benefit for payments or assistance provided to an individual by an agency of the State or local government.[72] This legislation denies state and local benefits to any alien who is not a qualified alien, a nonimmigrant under the Immigration and Naturalization Act, or an alien paroled into the United States. Undocumented persons would fall outside of the definition of noncitizens who can receive benefits under this law.

Another federal law, IIRIRA, expressly limits the eligibility of aliens "not lawfully present" in the United States for higher education benefits. Under § 1623 of 8 U.S.C., which is part of IIRIRA, an alien who is not lawfully present in the United States shall not be eligible on the basis of residence within a state (or political subdivision) for any postsecondary education benefit unless a citizen or national of the United States is eligible for such benefit without regard to whether the citizen or national is such a resident.[73]

Those who oppose granting in-state tuition rates to undocumented students argue that these two 1996 laws intended to prohibit states from offering in-state tuition rates to undocumented students, as they are within the definition of the term "benefit" of both laws.[74] Thus, in their view, except certain emergencies, these two federal laws bar undocumented persons from receiving public benefits, including in-state tuition for postsecondary education.[75]

Those who support granting in-state tuition rates to undocumented students, however, argue that the 1996 laws made undocumented persons ineligible for postsecondary education benefits based on state residence unless equal benefits were made available to all U.S. citizens, regardless of state of residence. Professor Michael Olivas, an expert in this field, has found this view to be "clear, by plain reading of the provision as a whole."[76] In the wording of § 1623, "unless" means that "Congress enacted a condition precedent for states enacting rules" concerning postsecondary education.[77] Additionally, the word "benefit" in § 1621 clearly indicated that Congress intended it to be a "monetary benefit." Applicants applying for in-state tuition rates request schools to consider them as residents for in-state tuition purposes. The determination of residency is a "status benefit," not "monetary benefit." Applicants do not receive any funds from states or federal government. Thus, the term "benefit" in § 1623 should mean dollars (amount, duration, and scope), such as scholarships, fellowships or similar monetary benefits. However, the benefit of granting in-state tuition rates for college education is a benefit to be considered for in-state resident status, not a benefit defined under § 1623. Reading these provisions together, Professor Olivas concludes that §§ 1621 and 1623 allow states to consider residency status regarding the undocumented students in their public postsecondary institutions. That is, states have authority to determine whether students are eligible for in-state tuition rate under states' laws.[78]

As a result of these provisions, states like Colorado verify the lawful presence of students before extending in-state tuition.[79] These provisions do not affect U.S. citizen students, even if their parents are present in the U.S. without legal authorization.[80] Neither of these statutes can be interpreted as a mandate to deny admission to undocumented aliens.[81] The word "unless" in § 1623 suggests that states have the power to determine residency of the undocumented students.[82] Finally, PRWORA does not completely oust states power to regulate the matter. States can also pass in-state tuition for undocumented aliens so long the laws apply equally to residents and nonresidents.

Recently, the North Carolina Attorney General has called upon ICE to clarify what constitutes a benefit. In response, the Department of homeland security (DHS) stated in a July 9, 2008 letter that the benefits under 8 U.S.C. § 1621 mean "monetary assistance for post-secondary education."[83] At least one state's court of appeals has agreed with this view. The California Court of Appeals concluded that paying in-state tuition rates is a monetary benefit within the scope of Sections §§ 1621 and 1623.[84] The court was persuaded by the fact that undocumented students would be eligible to pay in-state tuition rates, which would be at least three times less tuition than that for non-residents, and that this amount was quantifiable. The Supreme Court of California has recently granted review of the case, so the value of this California Court of Appeals decision is in question at this writing.

The DHS has further addressed the issue whether a public community college can enroll undocumented persons.[85] The agency has stated that a school has discretion to decide whether to admit out-of-status or undocumented students.[86] However, the DHS notes that by enrolling in college, undocumented students are taking the risk of being apprehended and possibly removed from the United States. Furthermore, if they choose to leave the United States in the future, they could be barred from reentry.[87] Additionally, if they apply for a change of status for a student visa, the DHS has indicated that it will deny their request.[88]

The DHS has also clarified that no college or university is required to determine a student's immigration status, except for students present in the U.S. lawfully on student visas. That is, other than for students already on visas, an institution of higher learning is not obligated to determine whether or not a student is legally present in the U.S. and allowed to study. The DHS does not require school officials to obtain immigration status information before they admit students or "to report to the government if they know a student is out of status."[89]

The DHS has also reiterated that it is up to the states to decide if they will admit undocumented students into their public postsecondary institutions. States may do this either as a matter of policy or through legislation.[90] However, if they choose to address this issue, states must apply federal immigration status standards to identify which applicants are undocumented students. Such a view is consistent with the fact that all immigration law is federal law. Accordingly, the DHS has concluded that, absent any state policy or legislation addressing this issue, it is up to the individual institutions of higher learning to enroll undocumented students.[91]

The two federal law provisions regarding in-state tuition and benefits, 8 U.S.C § 1621 and 8 U.S.C § 1623, have generated confusion among admissions administrators in state colleges and universities. As a result, public university administrators have turned to the Attorney Generals in their states for legal advice on this issue. For example, the Attorney General of Virginia has concluded that (1) illegal or undocumented aliens should not be enrolled in Virginia public instructions of higher education, and (2) illegal or undocumented aliens are ineligible for in-state tuition status in Virginia.[92] In contrast, the North Carolina Attorney General's Office has advised the North Carolina Community College System that schools are free to develop their own admission guidelines because admission is not considered as "benefit" under federal law.[93] Yet, the community college's board has continued to deny admission to undocumented students to avoid potential litigation in the future. In summary, the DHS has clarified that states can admit undocumented students to public postsecondary educational institutions under the federal law. But, it there is still continuing debate regarding whether states are free to grant in-state tuition rates or financial aid to undocumented students.

State Obstacles: Litigation Regarding Higher Education for Undocumented Students

As opposition to higher education for undocumented students has mounted, legal challenges to state actions have taken place in Virginia, Kansas, and California.[94] Undocumented students seeking a higher education have been dealt severe blows in nearly all of the recent litigation in several of these states. In the earliest case, undocumented students sued the leading Virginia higher education institutions for failure to admit them under state policy. In *Equal Access Education v. Merten*,[95] the plaintiffs, several undocumented students and one association, alleged that federal immigration law preempted the denial of admission to Virginia institutions of higher education, and that such denial violated the Commerce and Due Process Clauses of the Constitution.[96] Thus, the federal District Court for Eastern Virginia had to decide whether states could deny undocumented students admission to institutions of higher education.[97] The court found that states had the right to limit the admission of undocumented students to university.[98] However, schools had to adopt policies consistent with immigration laws.[99]

The case arose when the Virginia Attorney General issued a memorandum discouraging institutions of higher education from admitting undocumented students.[100] It stated "the Attorney General is strongly of the view that illegal and undocumented aliens should not be admitted into our public colleges and universities at all. ..."[101] In fact, the Attorney General strongly encouraged school officials and all public employees in higher education to report facts and circumstances regarding the presence of undocumented students on campus to the immigration authorities.[102]

The undocumented plaintiffs in this Virginia case found themselves on the losing side of all of the rulings in the case. For instance, unlike *Plyler*, where the plaintiffs proceeded anonymously, the five undocumented students in *Merten* were not allowed to proceed without revealing their identities.[103] As a result, three of the individual plaintiffs were unable to continue in that role for fear of being deported.[104] The next setback was a pretrial dismissal of a large part of the plaintiffs' case.[105] Finally, the undocumented students lost the case altogether when the remaining aspects of the case were dismissed after the court found that the universities were using the appropriate federal standards to identify the undocumented students.[106] The undocumented student plaintiffs argued that by categorically denying them higher education, the defendant higher education institutions prevented them from obtaining future higher earnings associated with a college education.[107] The court rejected this argument for several reasons, including the fact that if the students graduated without obtaining legal immigration status, they would be unable to work lawfully in the U.S. and the fact that the students failed to show how their earnings would affect foreign commerce.[108] In any event, the court pointed out that there were other institutions of higher learning in Virginia where the undocumented students could attend without regard to their immigration status.

The litigation in Kansas yielded a different result, in which the court reaffirmed the ability of undocumented students to receive higher education, via the use of in-state tuition, even if in a procedural manner. This is how it happened. Once the Kansas legislature enacted House Bill 2145, two dozen U.S. citizen students and their parents, who paid non-resident tuition at Kansas universities, filed a lawsuit seeking injunctive relief. They also sought a declaration from the court that in violation of federal law, H.B. 2145 offered in-state tuition rates to undocumented students who have graduated from and attended high school in Kansas for at least three years or have obtained their GED in Kansas. In the case, styled *Day v. Sebelius*,[109] the plaintiffs challenged that H.B. 2145 violates 8 U.S.C. § 1623, which prohibits undocumented persons from receiving a benefit for which a United States citizen is ineligible.[110] In the same complaint, the plaintiffs also alleged that H.B. 2145 contravened federal law because H.B. 2145, only operating in Kansas, created distinct immigration classifications which are not based on federal standards. The plaintiffs also argued that implementation of H.B. 2145 would encourage and induce the "transport of aliens into and across the United States" in violation of federal immigration law. The plaintiffs further alleged that a law drawing a distinction on the basis of alienage needed to meet the requirements of the Equal Protection Clause under a heightened standard of review. Finally, the plaintiffs alleged that, because undocumented students will not be able to work once they are educated, any arguments regarding their contribution to the U.S. workforce are unpersuasive.

The court dismissed this lawsuit because the plaintiffs had no standing.[111] The court concluded that even if H.B. 2145 violated the federal laws and U.S. Constitution, the plaintiffs did not suffer any injury. The plaintiffs would still be considered non-residents and be required to pay out-of-state tuition rates. The plaintiffs appealed the case to the Tenth Circuit Court of Appeals, which affirmed the findings of the trial court.[112] The United States Supreme Court declined to review the case.[113]

In a similar lawsuit filed in California, nonresident U.S. citizen students and their parents brought a lawsuit in state court challenging the legality of the California Education Code § 68130.5, also known as A.B. 540. A.B. 540 grants undocumented students exemption from paying out-of-state tuition for postsecondary education if the applicants satisfy three-year high school attendance or obtain GED in California. Like the plaintiffs in *Day v. Sebelius*, the plaintiffs in *Martinez v. Regents of the University of California* sought injunctive relief and declaratory relief, alleging that A.B. 540 violated federal law, the Fourteenth Amendment to the U.S. Constitution and the California state constitution. The plaintiffs also claimed that the Supremacy Clause preempted A.B. 540 because implementation of A.B. 540 conflicted with the federal immigration laws, 8 U.S.C §1621 and 8 U.S.C. §1623. Since undocumented students could apply to be considered state residents if they attended California high school for at least three years or obtained GED in California while the plaintiffs were unable to do so, they argued that the requirement of California high school attendance was a *de facto* residence requirement.[114] Furthermore, A.B. 540 exempted certain undocumented students from paying nonresident out-of-state tuition, but U.S. citizen students from states other than California were not, and were required to pay out-of-state tuition. Therefore, they argued that A.B. 540 conferred a benefit as defined under federal law to undocumented students based on "residence."

Although the trial court found that plaintiffs had standing in this case, the court ruled in favor of the defendants, state colleges and universities and dismissed the plaintiffs' complaint because evidence was insufficient to support the plaintiffs' complaint.[115] Subsequently, the plaintiffs appealed and the California Court of Appeal reversed the trial court's ruling, concluding that A.B. 540 violated federal law because the high school attendance requirement of A.B. 540 is a substitute for residence requirement regarding in-state tuition rates.[116] By paying less than out-of-state tuition rates, those A.B. 540 students received a benefit within the definition of 8 U.S.C. §§ 1621 and 1623, without conferring the same benefit to U.S. citizens.[117] Thus, A.B. 540 conflicts with the federal laws and is preempted under the Supremacy Clause of the U.S. Constitution. The court did not enjoin A.B. 540 and the law is still enforced. However, the case is now on appeal to the California Supreme Court, which granted review on December 23, 2008.[118]

Thus, the record on the litigation of higher education of undocumented students yields mixed results, and the trend shows what would appear to be the beginning of an erosion of *Plyler*'s promise of educational equality.[119] The next sections will examine actions taken in pursuit of legal avenues for higher education for undocumented students in the United States.

Federal and State Efforts Regarding Undocumented Students and Higher Education

Plyler v. Doe provides a constitutional guarantee to undocumented students of a free public elementary and secondary education, but not postsecondary education. Thus, federal legislation is essential to afford undocumented students access to higher education. For undocumented students, the obstacles to access to higher education range from the denial of admission, to an inability to obtain student loans, to being charged nonresident tuition—all because of lack of legal immigration status. The following two sections will detail the efforts being undertaken at the state and federal levels to ensure access to postsecondary education for undocumented students in the United States.

Federal Efforts to Assist Undocumented Students: The DREAM Act and Student Adjustment Act

Chief Justice Burger, in his dissenting opinion of *Plyler v. Doe*, took a dim view of the Supreme Court's actively making societal policy in the case.[120] Furthermore, it is clear that Congress has plenary power to regulate and legislate in the area of immigration. Thus, to tackle the ongoing debate regarding higher education of undocumented students, Congress must confront the concerns raised head on. First, Congresspersons must clarify to their constituents that undocumented students are distinct from those adult migrants who enter this country purposefully. Second, the *Plyler* Court guaranteed free elementary and secondary education over twenty-five years ago. This guarantee creates dilemmas where undocumented students currently continue to achieve. While those undocumented students are entitled to a basic education, only Congress can and must exercise its power to resolve this collision of education and immigration policy. Successful undocumented students work hard to obtain advanced degrees, but despite all the obstacles detailed above they cannot practice, work or teach—all because of their immigration status. Their choices are limited by their immigration status, through no fault of their own.

If the undocumented students have received their *Plyler* guaranteed education and excelled, it is truly a waste of talent to deport them. Recognizing this as a waste of talent, Congress is legally and morally responsible to resolve these dilemmas by providing a path to legalization undocumented students.[121] Thus, those undocumented students can apply their talents to U.S. society. Let us see how the U.S. Congress has addressed this moral imperative in recent times.

Proposed Legislation in the 107th Congress

Initially, in 2001, Congress considered several bills, including H.R. 1563 (Preserving Educational Opportunities for Immigrant Children Act, introduced in the 107th Congress and reintroduced as H.R. 84 in the 108th Congress by Representative Sheila Jackson-Lee), H.R. 1582 (Immigrant Children's Educational Advancement and Dropout Prevention Act, introduced in the 107th Congress by Representative Luis Gutierrez), H.R. 1918

(Student Adjustment Act, introduced in the 107th Congress and reintroduced as H.R. 1684 in the 108th Congress by Representative Chris Cannon) and S. 1291 (Development, Relief, and Education for Alien Minors Act, DREAM Act, introduced in the 107th Congress and reintroduced, after some modification, as S. 1545 in the 108th Congress by Senator Orrin Hatch). These legislative proposals would all enable certain undocumented students in the United States to obtain Lawful Permanent Resident ("LPR") status.[122] After receiving bipartisan support, S. 1291 was revised and introduced by Senator Richard Durbin as S. 1265 (Children's Adjustment, Relief, and Education Act), "CARE" Act.[123] To be eligible for LPR status under this bill, an undocumented student must have been: (1) at least age twelve on the date of enactment, and (2) have a high school diploma or equivalent credential, among other requirements.[124] However, none of these bills made any further progress.

Proposed Legislation in the 108th Congress

The following year, Senator Orrin Hatch (R-Utah) proposed and the Senate Judiciary Committee reported on a bill, S. 1545, also known as the Development, Relief, and Education for Alien Minors Act, or the "DREAM" Act. The DREAM Act, like the previous proposed bills, would enable certain undocumented students to become LPRs and eventually eligible to apply for U.S. citizenship.[125] The DREAM Act would implement a two-stage process.[126] In the first stage, those undocumented students would be eligible for conditional LPR status if they (1) were under age sixteen at the time of initial entry into the United States, (2) resided continuously in the United States for at least five years preceding enactment of the DREAM Act, and (3) had a high school diploma (or equivalent credential) or had gained admission to an institution of higher education.[127] In the second stage, if those undocumented students were (1) successful academically in the first two years of higher education, or (2) enlisted to serve in the military, then they could petition to remove the condition of their LPR status.

Additionally, several proposals in some guest worker bills and other immigration bills in the Senate would have also provided certain undocumented students the opportunity to become LPRs.[128] Meanwhile, members of Congress introduced similar bills, including the Student Adjustment Act of 2003, H.R. 1684, in the House, all without success.[129] The Student Adjustment Act of 2003, if passed, would have made undocumented students eligible for federal postsecondary education benefits, while their immigration applications were pending.[130] This Act would have also permitted states to determine residency requirements for higher education purposes. The House version also contained provisions for the adjustment of an undocumented student's illegal status. These bills were unable to attract more support out of concerns over homeland security and negative views of a so-called amnesty for undocumented persons. They all failed.

Proposed Legislation in the 109th Congress

In the 109th Congress, Senator Durbin again introduced the DREAM Act of 2005 (S. 2075) in the Senate.[131] Meanwhile, Representative Diaz-Balart introduced the American Dream Act (H.R. 5131) in the House.[132] Similar to previous legislative proposals, both the DREAM Act and the American Dream Act, if passed, would have repealed 8 U.S.C. § 1623 and enabled eligible undocumented students to adjust to LPR status. Among the requirements for adjustment to LPR status, both bills would have required the undocumented student to demonstrate that (1) he or she had been physically present in the United States for a continuous period of not less than five years immediately preceding the date of enactment of the bill, and (2) had not yet reached age sixteen at the time of initial entry.[133] Both bills also would have required an applicant to demonstrate that he or she had been admitted to an institution of higher education in the United States, or had earned a high school diploma or the equivalent in the United States. Both bills failed, as they were unable to garner enough support.[134]

Proposed Legislation in the 110th Congress

In 2006, with the support of Bush administration, bipartisan congressional efforts produced the Comprehensive Immigration Reform Act, S. 2611. S. 2611 would have codified the DREAM Act.[135] Again, S. 2611 would have repealed 8 U.S.C. § 1623, the provision which limits eligibility for higher education benefits for aliens unless such benefits are available to all U.S. citizens and permanent residents regardless of their residence.[136] S. 2611 would have required that eligible undocumented student applicants be admitted to college at the time of their applications, and have earned a high school diploma or GED.[137] Under S. 2611, a person subject to a removal or deportation order would be ineligible to obtain benefits under the bill, unless the order was issued before he or she reached the age of sixteen. S. 2611 also gave the Department of Homeland Security discretion to cancel removal of and adjust the status of a person present in the U.S. unlawfully, provided that (1) the person has been in the U.S. for a continuous period of at least five years preceding the date of enactment of the law and (2) the person was under the age sixteen at the time of initial entry. Moreover, S. 2611 specifically required that the applicant, an undocumented individual, must be a person of good moral character since the time of application.[138] Applicants would be denied if they had criminal violations and were thus inadmissible under the INA. S. 2611 also made it clear that a person would be ineligible if he or she had committed fraud after age sixteen.[139] Applicants under the DREAM Act, if determined eligible, would be granted conditional permanent residence for a period of six years.

Opponents argued this comprehensive immigration reform bill was a form of amnesty. In their view, it would have encouraged more lawbreakers if the bill became law. Therefore, Congress yielded to political pressures and it was not enacted into law.

In 2007, Senator Richard Durbin introduced the DREAM Act of 2007 (S. 774) in the Senate. He later placed the DREAM Act as an amendment to the 2008 Department of Defense Authorization Bill (S. 2919).[140] After some modifications, Senator Durbin and co-sponsors Senator Charles Hagel and Senator Richard Lugar, introduced the DREAM Act as S. 2205.[141] S. 2205 gained more support from some Republican senators, such as Senator Kay Bailey Hutchison, who had previously opposed the DREAM Act. Despite this support, the DREAM Act fell short of the votes needed.[142]

Proposed Legislation in the 111th Congress

The efforts to pass federal legislation that provides a path to legalization for undocumented students have continued in this most recent Congress. Senator Richard Durbin and seven other Senators have introduced the DREAM Act of 2009 (S. 729) and Representative Howard Berman (D-CA) introduced H.R. 1751, the American Dream Act. These bills are essentially identical to the ones introduced in previous Congresses; they are both currently being considered in committee.[143] The support of the Obama administration for this bill is evidenced by the testimony of the Secretary of the Department of Homeland Security Janet Napolitano. She has stated that it is a "good piece of legislation and a good idea."[144]

DREAM Act Arguments: Pro and Con

"It's unfair to make these young people pay for the sins of their parents," Senator Durbin (D-IL), a frequent sponsor of the DREAM Act has said.[145] Department of Defense officials had spoken favorably of the DREAM Act, and specifically the bill's promise of legal status to members of the military as a means of boosting recruitment.[146] The Army has struggled to recruit soldiers as a result of the Iraq war. Senators, though, remain committed to bringing the DREAM Act up separately or attaching it to other pieces of legislation. Interestingly, there have been many grassroots campaigns to assist undocumented students seeking higher education. Some students such as Marie Nazareth Gonzalez, Martine Mwanj Kalaw, and Tam Tran have even testified before Congress on the need for the DREAM Act.[147] In addition, a few stories have become very high-profile.

Critics of the bill call it the "Nightmare Act," or a sleeper amnesty. Representative Brian Billbray, a leader of the Immigration Reform Caucus in the House, stated. "We're giving status to immigrants based on the fact that they are here illegally. It sends a mixed signal to both legal and illegal immigrants."[148] Furthermore, he noted that undocumented persons resident in the United States: "owe obedience to the laws of the country in which [they are] domiciled."[149] Thus, critics claim that the DREAM Act diminishes the responsibility of the undocumented to correct their residency status, and if unable to do so, then to depart from the United States. The DREAM Act is seen as rewarding the undocumented for remaining unauthorized. What this argument ignores is the lack of choice the undocumented students have to change their immigration status.

Opponents are further concerned that the DREAM Act gives preferential treatment to undocumented students, resulting in inconsistent treatment to other noncitizens who "have waited in line for their turn." However, this argument ignores the fact that under most formulations of the DREAM Act, an applicant who overstays a student visa is not eligible for residency. Furthermore, the last version of the DREAM Act was in the process of being amended to change the immigration benefits the applicant would receive from the grant of conditional residency to temporary visas instead.[150] Thus, under such a scenario, a person who came through a lawful immigration channel will in fact receive better treatment than those who have remained in the U.S. undocumented.

Additionally, opponents claim that *Plyler's* principle was to allow education of children who had no say in the decision to come to the U.S., and that now that they are adults, they should be responsible for their immigration status. However, this argument ignores the fact most young people apply to college when they are still in high school, and in order to make a smooth transition to college, such students need to be able to apply at that time. It would be much more difficult and disruptive to their studies for noncitizens students to return to their parents' countries of origin and apply for visas. In any case, such visas are unlikely to be granted under current immigration law. Often students do not even know their immigration status until they apply to college. Further, if caught, noncitizens who are adults would face a ten-year bar to reentry. Thus, this would be quite unfair to many young students who have made their home in the U.S. and would be forced out of the U.S. or into using a procedure ill-suited for undocumented aliens in the U.S.

Others criticize the DREAM Act because, in its last version, it did not offer community service as an alternative to military service.[151] There is concern that undocumented students could be exploited by the military as its human resource needs during wartime grow. However, adding a community service option would mean the bill would be less attractive to the military constituency that in the past helped to secure its passage. Such critics should allow the bill to become law first and then introduce legislation to allow more civilian service options later.

Another concern is the direct rise in spending predicted as a result of the DREAM Act. The Congressional Budget Office ("CBO") estimates that passage of the DREAM Act would result in increased spending in student loans, and Food Stamp, and Medicaid programs by 90 million dollars over ten years.[152] However, the report made clear that undocumented students would be less likely than other students to participate in federal loan schemes for fear of exposing their family.[153] The CBO also estimated that 13,000 students would enroll in higher education because of the DREAM Act, as well as 46,000 college students who would be eligible for adjustment of status to conditional permanent residency over a ten-year period.[154] While federal outlays may be increased slightly, as mentioned previously, the federal government will gain social benefits as well as increased tax revenue in the long run.

The rationale of *Plyler v. Doe* and public policy considerations support the view that undocumented students should not be penalized for their parents' decisions years ago when they were young. Had they had the opportunity to receive additional education, including financial aid, the students would be able obtain better paying employment after college. This of course, provided they are able to work legally in the United States. By equipping them with higher education, undocumented students would earn higher compensation and will be able to spend or invest in the U.S. economy, not to mention paying more in taxes.[155] "[E]ducation prepares individuals to be self-reliant and self-sufficient participants in society."[156] Denying undocumented students access to higher education excludes them from becoming full participants in a society which has invested in them with a K–12 education. The DREAM Act is essential to help overcome this current dilemma for undocumented students in the United States.

Having seen the efforts Congress has made to resolve the legal obstacles towards higher education for undocumented students, consider now the state efforts as well.

State Efforts to Eliminate Higher Education Obstacles for Undocumented Students: Early Litigation in California

In 1990, the Court of Appeals of California decided a case which challenged the constitutionality of legislation providing that a noncitizen could be a resident for tuition purposes, unless precluded by the Immigration and Nationality Act.[157] The court held that that the law was constitutional, noting that "... the privilege withheld here—subsidized public university education—is considerably less significant [than the right to vote, work, get public assistance, medical care.]"[158] In fact, the other rights mentioned by the court are routinely withheld from undocumented persons under the U.S. legal system.

Furthermore, the court noted an absence of a "fundamental right" needed for a successful equal protection claim.[159] The court also noted that the state had a number of legitimate interests such as "not subsidizing violations of law, in preferring to educate its own lawful residents, in avoiding enhancing the employment prospects of those to whom employment is forbidden by law, in conserving fiscal resources for the benefit of lawful residents …"[160]

The court distinguished *Plyler v. Doe* by reviewing the Supreme Court's language about the stigma of illiteracy and the possibility that the undocumented student cannot contribute "even in the smallest way to the progress of our Nation" to find that "[t]here is, of course, a significant difference between an elementary education and a university education."[161]

If this same case were litigated today, the court might rule differently. Following the Critical Race Theory tenet of legal indeterminacy—the idea that not every case has one correct outcome[162]—we will find that because many of the premises the court used are different, the result could be the opposite. More students in the U.S. now attend college than in 1990 and higher education is increasingly essential in the skills-based information economy that was emerging in 1990. Also, the Court appears not to have been sympathetic at that time to the undocumented because Congress had just passed an amnesty for undocumented persons to become legalized in 1986.[163] In contrast, at present, no significant immigration benefits legislation has been approved since 2001.

In 1997, the U.S. District Court for the Central District of California invalidated Proposition 187, which enacted a law denying higher education to noncitizens unlawfully present in the United States.[164] The court held that states have no power to effectuate a scheme parallel to that specified in federal law, even if the parallel scheme does not conflict with federal law because Congress has expressly occupied the field of regulation of public postsecondary education benefits.[165] It also held that because federal law regulates the ability of immigrants to obtain postsecondary education benefits, it was Congress's intent to occupy the field and oust state power in this area.[166] Thus, the early record of litigation in California also yielded mixed results for undocumented students seeking higher education in that state. We will see later how California's undocumented fared in more recent times.

States Leading the Way, Despite Challenges

State legislatures nationwide have considered different types of proposals allowing undocumented students access to higher education. A recent examination of the laws of the fifty states on this topic discloses the following results. Since 2001, ten states, namely Texas, California, Illinois, Kansas, New York, Oklahoma, Texas, Utah, and Washington, and Nebraska, have enacted legislation offering in-state tuition rates to undocumented students at public institutions of higher education.[167] Currently, the state of New Jersey is considering a similar bill, recommended by a blue ribbon commission, while in Colorado and Arkansas such bills have been defeated in recent times.[168] Reports show that those states experienced neither a large influx of noncitizen students nor added financial burdens on their educational systems.[169] Instead, the states have experienced school revenues increase by bringing in tuition from students who otherwise would not be in college.[170]

Texas was the first state to allow undocumented students to apply for in-state tuition. Since June of 2001, undocumented students are eligible for in-state tuition rates if they meet certain criteria as follows.[171] First, applicants must have graduated from a Texas high school or received the equivalent of a high school diploma from the state of Texas. Second, applicants must be enrolled in a state institution of higher education. Third, applicants must have resided in Texas for at least three years. And, fourth, applicants must sign an affidavit in which they promise to file a petition to become a lawful permanent resident of the United States at their earliest opportunity.[172] Despite the narrow criteria contained in the law, some commentators believe that these requirements are too generous and treat undocumented students better than nonimmigrants.[173] In 2005, Texas further enacted laws to make state financial aid available to undocumented students.[174]

Texas Governor Rick Perry has vetoed an attempt to overturn the current law allowing students to qualify for in-state status.[175] Texas state legislator Representative Debbie Riddle was the sponsor of House Bill 104, a proposal that would limit in-state tuition to only legal residents.[176] She stated:

> ... people of my district are demanding that we do something regarding illegal immigration ... they're demanding that both federal and state governments do something about securing the borders ... and they are incensed that illegal immigrants are getting in-state tuition.[177]

Another legislator, Representative Rick Noriega disagreed with that contention, stating that "... [w]hen you have students that we know have a higher degree of education, they're able to contribute back to the economy ... [i]t just makes sense for us to protect out economic investment."[178] He pointed out that Texas already spends $100,000 per student per year on primary and secondary education.[179] Since it was enacted, 11,130 students have used the law to qualify for in-state tuition.[180]

California, following Texas, beginning in November 2001, also implemented similar but slightly different legislation, also known as A.B. 540, allowing undocumented students to apply for in-state tuition.[181] By avoiding use of the term "residence," A.B. 540 established exemptions for undocumented students from paying non-resident tuition.[182] Students are eligible to apply for a California nonresident tuition exemption if they (1) have attended a California high school for three years or more, (2) have graduated from a California high school or attained the equivalent to a high school degree, (3) register as a student after fall of the 2001-02 school year, and (4) file an affidavit promising to apply for permanent residency at their earliest opportunity.[183] Notably, the filing of affidavit is aspirational. Applicants only need to state that they intend to apply and promise to do so as soon as possible if they are eligible. This is the legislation discussed earlier in this chapter[184] which has been found to be preempted by federal law and is currently on review by the California Supreme Court. The California law differs slightly from the Texas law. Instead of categorizing a qualified individual as a resident for tuition purposes, it exempts a student from paying nonresident tuition.[185] Yet, just as with the Texas law, this legislation does not appear to run afoul of federal law, as it does not base in-state tuition on residency.

California has also considered, but not enacted, other legislation to assist undocumented students in their quest for higher education. In 2005, the California Assembly proposed and passed S.B. 160, also known as the California Dream Act.[186] This act would have allowed those undocumented students eligible for in-state tuition under A.B. 540 to apply for state financial aid or grant programs.[187] Despite its evident potential benefits to extend educational opportunity to undocumented students, Governor Arnold Schwarzenegger vetoed S.B. 160. In 2007, the California Assembly passed another version of California Dream Act, S.B. 1, similarly allowing undocumented college students to apply state financial aid and grant programs.[188] Claiming that California faced serious budget deficit issues, Schwarzenegger vetoed this bill as well, on fiscal grounds.[189]

In 2002, Utah adopted a law similar to those of Texas and California. It allows students to be eligible for in-state tuition if they (1) attended a Utah high school for three or more years, (2) graduated from a Utah high school or received the equivalent of a high school diploma in Utah, (3) registered at an institution of high education after the fall of the 2002–03 academic year, and (4) filed an affidavit promising to apply to become a LPR as soon as possible.[190] Joining Texas, California and Utah, seven other states have implemented similar policies offering in-state tuition rates to students who meet certain requirements, regardless of their immigration status.[191] Table 2.1 details those states which grant in-state tuition rates to undocumented students.

These states grant students in-state status for tuition purposes based on graduation from a high school in that state, not on residency. Three additional states have considered legislation allowing undocumented students to pay in-state tuition rates.[192] Most of these bills, however, never even made it to a vote or were postponed indefinitely in committees.

Meanwhile, some states have introduced legislation regarding undocumented students, with the aim of denying them higher educational

Table 2.1 States Granting In-State Tuition Rates by Statute to Undocumented Students (Alphabetical Order)

States	Policy	Date of Enactment	Statute
California	A.B. 540, 2001–2002 Leg., Reg. Sess. (Cal. 2001)	1/1/2002	CAL. EDUC. CODE § 68130.5
Illinois	H.B. 60, 93rd Gen. Assemb., Reg. Sess. (Ill. 2003)	5/20/2003	110 ILL. COMP. STAT. ANN.
Kansas	H.B. 2145, 2003–2004 Leg., Reg. Sess. (Kan. 2004)	7/1/2004	KAN. STAT. ANN. § 76–731A
Nebraska	L.B. 239, 99th Leg., 1st Sess. (Neb. 2006)	4/13/2006	NEB. REV. STAT. ANN. § 85–502
New Mexico	S.B. 582, 47th Leg., Reg. Sess. (N.M. 2005)	4/8/2005	N.M. STAT. ANN. § 21–1–4.6
New York	S.B. 7784, 225th Leg., 2001 Sess. (N.Y. 2002)	8/1/2003	N.Y. EDUC. LAW § 355(2)(H)(8)
Oklahoma	S.B. 596, 49th Leg., 1st Reg. Sess. (Okla. 2003)	5/12/2003 (repealed on 11/1/2007)	OKLA. STAT. ANN. TIT. 70, § 3242
Texas	H.B. 1403, 77th Leg., Reg. Sess. (Tex. 2001)	6/16/2001	TEX. EDUC. CODE ANN. § 54.051, 54.052, 54.0551, 54.057, 54.060]
	S.B. 1528, 79th Leg., Reg. Sess. (Tex. 2005)	9/1/2005	
Utah	H.B. 144, 54th Leg., Gen. Sess. (Utah 2002)	7/1/2002	UTAH CODE ANN. § 53B-8–106
Washington	H.B. 1079, 58th Leg., 2003 Reg. Sess. (Wash. 2003)	7/1/2003	WASH. REV. CODE ANN. § 28B.15.012

opportunities. Georgia[193] and Colorado[194] have passed legislation denying in-state tuition rates to undocumented students.[195]

In early 2007, the Oklahoma legislature passed H.B. 1804, the Oklahoma Taxpayer and Citizen Protection Act. It repealed earlier legislation which offered undocumented students in-state tuition rates if they satisfied certain requirements. Undocumented students enrolled in college prior to the 2007–08 academic year and who received such benefits were grandfathered and could continue paying in-state tuition. Additionally, those undocumented students graduating from Oklahoma high schools will also be exempt if they attended two or more years prior to graduation. On May 7, 2007, Governor Brad Henry signed H.B. 1804 into law.

The National Coalition of Latino Clergy and others filed a lawsuit to prevent the enforcement of the law, but the trial court dismissed the lawsuit without addressing the merits of the case. It did so based on the plaintiffs' lack of standing.[196] In finding that the plaintiffs did not have the legal capacity to bring the case, the most notable aspect of the court's opinion is the court's refusal to acknowledge the reality of the undocumented student plaintiffs' lives. These students live in the shadows of an immigration law system which is broken, and which does not afford them any opportunity to obtain legal immigration status. What the court did, in fact, was to use their irregular immigration status against them as a prudential limitation to deny them standing to sue in court to prevent enforcement of this law.[197]

In the court's view, the only way the undocumented students could file a lawsuit to challenge the Oklahoma law would be to obtain regular immigration status. Its own words are instructive: "For these Plaintiffs, the remedy for their alleged injuries is simple, *act in accordance with federal law.*"[198] The court does not appear to understand that if these students were able to obtain lawful immigration status under current federal immigration law, they would do so. The court also distinguishes *Plyler* by noting that the plaintiffs are not children, and that as adults they have choices. Of course, undocumented young adults seeking higher education are actually choiceless in the sense that most of them do not have the option because of family circumstances, language ability, etc. to go back to the countries they left as young children.

Table 2.2 details the current status of legislative state actions regarding postsecondary access to education of undocumented students.

As of June 30, 2008, an estimated 1,267 bills concerning immigration have been considered in forty-five states in the year.[199] Among them, since January seventy-four bills related to education were introduced in twenty-two state

Table 2.2 State Legislative Actions Regarding Undocumented Students and Higher Education

Grant in-state tuition to undocumented students	Texas, California, New York, Utah, Illinois, Washington, New Mexico, Kansas, Nebraska
Legislation passed would grant in-state tuition to undocumented students, but waiting for Governor's signature	Florida, Hawaii, Maryland
Pending legislation would grant in-state tuition to undocumented students	Massachusetts, Minnesota, New Hampshire, New Jersey, North Carolina, Oregon, South Carolina, Tennessee
Legislation passed would grant in-state tuition to undocumented students, but vetoed	Connecticut, Wisconsin
Deny in-state tuition to undocumented students	Georgia, Colorado, Arizona, Alabama (after repeal in 2007), Oklahoma (after repeal in 2007)

legislatures, including Arizona, California, Connecticut, Florida, Georgia, Hawaii, Idaho, Indiana, Maryland, Minnesota, Mississippi, Missouri, New Jersey, New Mexico, Oklahoma, Rhode Island, Tennessee, Utah, Virginia, Washington, West Virginia, and Wyoming.[200] Most proposals are related to tuition benefits, grants, or scholarships, while some of these bills deny unauthorized students access for higher education.[201] Of these, twelve laws were enacted in eight states, including Arizona, Georgia, Hawaii, Maryland, Minnesota, Oklahoma, Utah, and Washington.[202] Primarily, these laws address in-state tuition eligibility, student loans, English language acquisition, and access, as well as ESL programs.

Other states like Washington offer other alternatives to higher education for undocumented students. One program in Big Bend seeks to assist noncitizen populations of Washington by helping them learn English, as well as a trade.[203] The intensive ten to eleven week program serves "a population that otherwise would not walk through our doors," according to Big Ben's director, Sandy Cheek.[204] Many workers are able to get much better jobs. One was able to get a job for a construction company, and learned to drive trucks. His salary was $2,300 a month, more than twice as much as he earned working in the fields.

The majority of bills proposed to limit higher for undocumented students failed.[205] In one example, a Virginia bill that would have banned in-state tuition for undocumented students was changed to specifically allow in-state tuition for these students after the sponsor of the legislation was personally touched by stories of those the change in law would affect. Three states have restricted tuition benefits, as well as other public benefits to undocumented students. Alaska has adopted legislation that requires a student to be a U.S. citizen or legal resident to qualify as a state resident for tuition purposes.[206]

The state law that has been the most successful in denying state higher education access to undocumented students is Arizona Proposition 300, passed in 2006. This is the law mentioned earlier in this chapter which affected the Hayden High School students who won the robotics competition with Stinky the robot. Estimates show that Proposition 300 has blocked at least 5,000 students from in-state college tuition, financial aid, and adult education classes.[207] The law limits participation in adult education and child care programs to citizens, legal residents, or other persons lawfully present in the U.S.[208] It also prohibits those who are not lawfully present from being classified as in-state or in-county for tuition purposes, and prohibits such persons from receiving any state aid.[209] State agencies must also report the total number of persons qualifying for these programs and the number of them who are ineligible based on immigration status.[210]

The effects of this law are clear. In 2007, the community colleges in Arizona reported 124,000 students classified as paying in-state tuition, in contrast to the 1,470 students who were not entitled to be classified as in-state because of a lack of lawful immigration status.[211] Additionally, during the same time period, 40,900 students applied for financial aid, of which only 320 were not entitled to aid because they were not a citizen or legal resident. In addition, both Arizona State University and the University of Arizona reported 77,300 students registered for the fall 2007 semester.[212] The university could verify the legal immigration status of 59,300 students. Roughly, 16,500 did not require verification because they did not request or did not receive in-state tuition. 1,500 were unverifiable due to lack of information.[213]

Further actions affecting undocumented students took place when the Arizona treasurer's office began an investigation to determine whether Arizona State University violated Proposition 300 by providing private aid to some of its students who may have been unlawfully present in the U.S.[214] Dean Martin, the state treasurer, was the lead sponsor of Proposition 300. It is unlikely there will be any wrongdoing, because the university paid the private scholarship money out of its non-profit organization, which is a private entity.[215]

This exclusion from higher education is not unique to undocumented students. Even U.S. citizen children of undocumented parents "pay the price" for their parents' unlawful status. As seen earlier in the introduction to this book, the state of Indiana sought to deny higher education assistance, called the Indiana Twenty-first Century Scholars program, to U.S. citizens and legal permanent residents whose parents were undocumented.[216] A young Hoosier Latina born in the U.S. to undocumented parents filed suit, seeking injunctive and declarative relief that the discrimination against students such as herself violated the Equal Protection Clause. The Indiana scholarship program is important, as it has helped over 25,000 students since it was established in 1990, and the state spends $19 million a year to assist students.[217] The case eventually settled, and the exclusion of U.S. citizen children of the undocumented was discontinued. Had the young woman lost in court, the children of over 75,000 people believed to be undocumented would have been excluded.

In fact, such a phenomenon is not new. The national chain Toys"R"Us offered a $25,000 savings bond to the first baby born in the U.S. at midnight on New Year's day of 2007.[218] The first baby born was Yuki Lin. However, she lost the prize upon the company finding out that her mother was an undocumented person; the prize was then awarded to another baby in Gainesville, Georgia. Under mounting pressure, Toys "R" Us ultimately gave the prize to both babies.[219] This shows that many U.S. citizens are treated differently because of their parents' unlawful immigration status. So despite the fact that Yuki Lin was legally a U.S. citizen, the Gainesville baby's mother told reporters that, "If [the mother is] an illegal alien, that makes the baby illegal."

The First Amendment Rights of Undocumented Students

With names such as Underground Undergrads and Mexican-Americans Students' Alliance ("MASA"), undocumented student organizations show their commitment to activism toward attaining higher education. For example, when the City University of New York denied in-state tuition to undocumented students starting in late 2001, "MASA decided to fight to preserve the right of undocumented students to get a higher education and to improve themselves."[220] The MASA students conducted a series of protests, and held a three-day hunger strike at the headquarters of the CUNY's trustees.[221]

The denial of in-state tuition was part of the crackdown against noncitizens following the September 11, 2001 attacks, "where allowing undocumented students to go to CUNY was [seen as] a national security issue and an insult to every citizen and legal immigrant seeking a higher education."[222] What these students did was to reaffirm the right to express themselves, even if they were not lawfully present in the U.S. However, in our experience, state and local authorities have threatened undocumented persons with negative repercussions, saying that because they are present in the United States without legal authorization, they have no First Amendment rights. This allegation, in view of the undocumented student organizing aimed at reaching higher education and lawful status in the United States—which has taken the form of marches, protests, and the like—makes imperative an inquiry into the First Amendment rights of undocumented students.

Applicability of the First Amendment to Undocumented Persons

At the outset, let us review the First Amendment in its entirety:

> Congress shall make no law respecting an establishment of religion, or prohibiting the free exercise thereof; or abridging the freedom of speech, or of the press, or the right of the people peaceably to assemble, and to petition the Government for a redress of grievances.[223]

A review of the text discloses that the people have the right to assemble peaceably, to excercise free speech, and to petition the government for redress of grievances. The key question to ascertain the applicability of the First Amendment to those present in the United States without lawful immigration status is: Who are the people whose rights are protected? This precise question has not been answered by the United States Supreme Court. There is case law in other contexts which may prove instructive to ascertain the free speech and right to petition of undocumented students.

In the context of noncitizens being deported from the United States based on their political beliefs and associations, the Supreme Court has held that "an alien unlawfully in this country has no constitutional right to assert selective enforcement as a defense against his deportation."[224] Based on this language from *Reno v. Arab-American Anti Discrimination Committee*,[225] some have suggested that the Court completely excluded undocumented noncitizens from the protections of the First Amendment.[226] Others suggest limitations only apply when the First Amendment claim is raised in deportation or removal proceedings.[227] Yet a leading free speech scholar, R. George Wright, has found that the purposes of the Free Speech Clause would not be served if U.S. citizens cannot be engaged in free speech exchanges with undocumented persons. Thus, he suggests an uncontroversial approach to freedom of speech for undocumented speakers.[228]

Immigration scholar Michael Wishnie has studied the history of the First Amendment and found that noncitizens have the right to petition for grievances.[229] The existence of such a right is also good policy because it encourages reporting crimes to the police. Furthermore, it is consistent with historical precedent, where aliens were able to petition as early as the time of the founding of the Massachusetts Bay Colony.[230] Thus, if undocumented students were to argue that their deportations should be blocked because they were apprehended while they tried to petition to the principal, superintendent, or member of the school board, they might arguably find protection, in this scholar's view. A similar right to petition case may arise when a student skips class to attend an immigration march.

Similarly, Wishnie points out that while the courts have dealt with issues generally surrounding the First Amendment and noncitizens, no court has addressed a noncitizen's right to petition,[231] or more generally, the rights of an undocumented person while residing in the U.S. and not subject to deportation proceedings. Thus, by analogy, case law interpreting other constitutional provisions with analogous language might assist in ascertaining the scope of this right.

Can Fourth Amendment Jurisprudence Help Interpret First Amendment Rights?

The Fourth Amendment to the United States Constitution also protects the rights of the people, again, a term left undefined in its text. The only interpretation of the term comes from the United States Supreme Court in the case of *United States v. Verdugo-Urquidez*.[232] In that case, the Court ruled that the people are "a class of persons who are part of a national community or who have otherwise developed sufficient connection with the country to be considered part of that community."[233] The Court added that, "[a]liens receive constitutional protections when they have come within the territory of the United States and developed substantial connections with the country."[234] Arguably, then, undocumented students who have come to the United States through no fault of their own, brought by their parents as infants, and who are raised in this country for years, could have developed substantial connections to the U.S. Thus, they should be considered part of the people for First and Fourth Amendment purposes. The Supreme Court has also recognized that undocumented persons are entitled to the protections of the Equal Protection Clause, even if they are present in the United States without authorization.[235]

Student First Amendment Free Speech Rights

The First Amendment rights of students at school are also an area of murky jurisprudence. While all students at school do not "shed their constitutional rights to freedom of speech or expression at the schoolhouse gate,"[236] the Supreme Court has weakened their First Amendment rights at school in recent cases. The original student freedom of speech case, *Tinker v. Des Moines* stated that "student expression may not be suppressed unless school officials reasonably conclude that it will materially and substantially disrupt the work and discipline of the school."[237]

In *Tinker*, students protested against the war in Vietnam by wearing armbands, and the school disciplined them for doing so. The Court held that the armbands did not disrupt the work of the school.[238] Since *Tinker*, the Court has found exceptions for school speech that implicated drug use and explicit sexual metaphors.[239] Another case which is an exception to the right of a student's speech would make it possible that a school could discipline a student for attending a civil rights march.[240] The case is *Dunn v. Tyler Independent School District.* In this case, hundreds of African American youth walked out of school and sued to enjoin their school officials from disciplining them, yet the students lost. The court in *Dunn* found that a regulation subjecting to automatic suspension any student who participated in a boycott was not overbroad.[241] The court distinguished *Tinker* by establishing that in *Dunn*, it was a mass refusal of pupils to take part in the classroom process.[242] In *Tinker*, there was no disruption. This holding is consistent with educational policy and practice, which aims to have the students present in class and learning. It is also a view which appears to be favored by Latino leaders and politicians. Los Angeles Mayor Antonio Villaraigosa told immigrant marchers on April 15, 2006, "I want our kids in school."[243] However, it is still an open question if undocumented students should be subject to discipline when there is no disruption while they engage in marches for immigration reform.

In 2007, the Supreme Court held in *Morse v. Frederick*[244] that schools can abridge the free speech of students in order to enjoin the promotion of illegal drug use. Though this case, colloquially known as "BONG HiTS 4 JESUS," the Court delineated student free speech rights when advocating illegality. One question that the Court failed to answer is: What is the mission of public schools? While the National School Boards Association believes that the educational mission of schools goes beyond the classroom curriculum, Justice Roberts stated that schools have "special characteristics which circumscribe students' free speech rights" and that "Congress has declared that part of a school's job is educating students about the dangers of illegal drug use."[245] So the question still remains whether the freedom of speech co-exists with the basic educational mission of schools. Two principles framed the Justices' analysis in *Morse*. First, students do not lose their constitutional rights to freedom of speech or expression at the schoolhouse gate.[246] However, Justice Thomas contended that the "Constitution does not afford students a right to free speech in public schools. The second principle is that there is a limitation of students' rights in schools and that they are not exactly the same as adults in the rest of society.[247] Thus, the schools may be in a bind, and will need to decide if it is part of the educational mission to discuss illegal immigration.

What do *Morse*, *Dunn*, and *Tinker* suggest about the future of undocumented student speech in schools? It appears that if the advocacy is for the rights of the undocumented, some might argue that it is promotion of illegal immigration. However, the marches and other protests seen in spring of 2006 and then periodically around the U.S. advocate immigration reform, not illegal immigration. Thus, such actions are most consistent with *Tinker*, as long as the school disruption is low. Otherwise, the precedent of *Dunn* might apply and the students' rights will be curtailed.

The Effects of Restricting Free Speech in Schools

K–12 students want to speak out against the problems that they see in the world, their community, and the school they attend—and many of these are very important. Along with concerns about drugs, violence, and racial discrimination, another issue of concern is immigration reform. If student speech regarding immigration reform is restricted by the school using the standards set forth in *Tinker*, *Dunn*, and *Morse*, then who will stand up for these students' rights? One student who attempted to stand up for his rights paid the ultimate price.

On March 25, 2006, eighth-grader Anthony Soltero organized a march in his hometown of Ontario, California to protest a proposed immigration law.[248] He worked to organize this walkout to coincide with a larger Los Angeles-area demonstration against a law which would cause undocumented workers to be categorized as felons.[249] On March 28, Soltero walked out of school to follow along with the statewide protests. On March 30, Soltero was taken to a school administrator's office where he was allegedly threatened with being excluded from graduation, and fines, and up to three years in prison.[250] After this meeting, Soltero went home and committed suicide.

While school officials claim that Soltero had nothing to do the protests and he was simply skipping class, others paint a more positive picture of Soltero's plight. His mother, Louise Corales lamented, "He was just fighting for his rights. He would be proud that we are here now to honor him because he is a hero."[251] One of Soltero's peers added: "He was 14 years old, and he was thinking he's going to jail. That was a big pressure on him."[252] On internet blogs about the walkouts, many anonymous posters regard Soltero as a martyr for the cause.[253]

Nativo López, President of the Mexican American Political Association, who organized many of the March 28 protests, spoke with Soltero's family following the tragic event. López commented:

> Anthony was born here, and his mother was born here. This is an example of a native-born citizen who identifies with this movement and takes a leadership role in a middle school to organize a walkout of his peers. He did this, and the school authorities threatened him with incarceration if he did it again. … It's fine if they read passages from the Constitution, the history of the country, biographies of George Washington and Thomas Jefferson—who the English, back in the era of the American Revolution, accused of terrorism. But then these children who are willing to practice these same precepts and theories can be reprimanded for actually living the Constitution.[254]

While Anthony Soltero's story is one of the sadder ones, it is far from the only story of a student's loss of free speech rights. These instances range from the absurd, to poignant and, as much in the case of Soltero, tragic; nevertheless, they are all indicative of an unfair and seemingly arbitrary denial of First Amendment rights.

The First Amendment operates as a check on the actions of the government. It imposes constraints on government actors and their activities in their governmental capacity. The Supreme Court's free speech doctrine facilitates the ability for government actors to regulate free speech activities in the United States—in places such as schools, government buildings, and even newspapers. Notre Dame Law professor Richard Garnett states: "In the school-speech cases, the doctrine does not reflect the speaker's age, but rather her situation and status as a student-in-school. It is the school enterprise—the public school's 'mission'—that drives the decisions."[255] Thus, in a school that views its mission as that of educating its students about current legal and sociopolitical issues, undocumented students might have the ability to start movements to advocate for the passage of the DREAM Act and comprehensive immigration reform. But this ability is by no means guaranteed.

Although the First Amendment states that free speech shall not be abridged, the Supreme Court has stated in the last century that it may be abridged in certain contexts—one of those being schools. What does this say about how this society views students and young adults? Some school officials contend that speech may not disrupt the educational mission, thus making it appropriate to lower the amount of free speech rights students have. However, this is not taking into account student speech which is integral to the guarantee of fundamental rights. Holding up a sign that reads "BONG HiTS 4 JESUS" does not further any educational goals, but is it arguable that it is worth abridging a student's right to free speech?

The problem with *Morse* and the *Tinker* standard is that they limit free speech concerning critical societal issues. One of these issues is rights for immigrants. In the case of Anthony Soltero, the school alleges that he was leaving the school and thus breaking the rules. However, others closer to him claim he was threatened for protesting about his beliefs. A walkout during the school day may be a disruption to the school, but a one-day disruption is not important enough to leave a young student feeling threatened in his own school. Anthony Soltero's story brings light to the need for the courts to re-evaluate the level of free speech protection that there is in schools.

Concluding Thoughts: Using Critical Race Theory to Understand the Quest for Higher Education for Undocumented Students and their First Amendment Rights to Express their Views

Critical Race Theory shows how the seemingly race-neutral decisionmaking in the education and immigration systems in fact subordinate the interests of the students. Undocumented students cannot obtain lawful immigration status until the passage of the DREAM Act. Without lawful immigration status, even though they reside in particular states and should be considered state residents, they are unable to pay in-state tuition except in ten states of the Union. Without lawful immigration status, undocumented students will be no more than highly educated farmworkers.[256] If we take the fact that most undocumented students are from racial minorities, we can see how the educational system ignores the interests of the students in pursuit of political agendas which ignore the realities of the benefits that these students can contribute to the United States. In the face of the permanence of racism in the U.S., it will be only when the interests of the nation and those of the students converge in the form of immigration reform that these students shall reach the equality contemplated in *Plyler*.

3
Speak No Evil
Language Education Policy from *Lau* to the Unz Initiatives and Beyond

In October of 2003, a teacher at the East Valley Institute of Technology[1] in Mesa, Arizona prohibited several cosmetology students from speaking Spanish in her classroom. When students and parents protested the teacher's actions at a community meeting, school administrators defended their employee, arguing that the school's official policy was consistent with the state's "English immersion" mandate approved by Arizona voters. The administrators further claimed that the teacher was merely using effective classroom management skills, and therefore, acted in a manner consistent with "best practices" in teaching.[2] In effect, the school maintained the professional integrity of the teacher, while casting doubt on the student's conversations in Spanish which they automatically assumed not to be related to the lesson being taught. The school administrators further supported the teacher in stating that such conversations could have disrupted daily classroom functioning, and potentially caused the teacher to "lose control of the classroom."[3]

Because the teacher's actions were defended as an acceptable form of classroom management, school officials implicitly argued the teacher needed to "be fair" to *all* students in her class—since effective classroom management calls for treating every student equally and curtailing potential activity that could serve as a basis for chaos in the classroom. Because the English-speaking students were not privy to the student conversations in Spanish, school officials implied that allowing students to speak in Spanish was not "fair" to the English-speaking students in class.[4] This argument not only placed English-dominant students at the center of the classroom discourse, but relegated Spanish to a type of commodity or good that either all students needed to have, or no one could. This was particularly useful, of course, for those students who were perceived to be at a disadvantage for not knowing the Spanish language.[5]

By defending the teacher's actions, the school and district not only justified the teacher's behavior, but created a precedent of acceptable teaching practices surrounding language regulation in the classroom. Since their defense also hinted that the teacher was merely responding to the broader English immersion mandate, school officials were simultaneously crafting a type of "street-level" policy justification—where local adaptations to the larger state mandate can be negotiated or interpreted at the classroom level.[6]

A side effect of this type of retroactive policy formation is that it is summative and justificatory in nature, as opposed to being formative, holistic, and instructive. Consequently, it set off a maelstrom of protests within the Latina/o community, prompting the League of United Latin American Citizens to submit a formal complaint to the U.S. Department of Education's Office of Civil Rights.[7] Eight months after this incident, the school found itself under federal investigation to determine if its policy overstepped the controversial Arizona mandate.[8] Unfortunately, this type of incident is not an isolated one. For example, these authors have encountered anecdotal evidence showing that students are banned from speaking Spanish in buses on their way to school.

In this chapter, we argue that the teacher's actions (and the district's defense of her actions) are problematic, yet quite understandable, given the current backlash against language rights in the classroom and the rise of "English only" initiatives that are gaining increased national support. We will make the argument that this backlash is, at least in part, informed by those very same acts, court decisions, policies, and referenda that aim to *promote* the language rights of language minority students. Our position is that language rights policies, while enormously important, nevertheless promote a deficit perception of English language learner students. By tracing these important legal and policy initiatives, we hope to highlight how they largely aim to fix or rectify the "language deficiencies" of children, as opposed to fixing deficient school structures, curricula, instructional practices, and policies that enable non-English language speakers to flourish in an English-dominant school setting.

Our hope is to highlight the various ways in which language policy targets particular under-represented groups including, but not limited to, Latino students, immigrant students, English language learners of all racial/ethnic backgrounds, as well as undocumented students. Although undocumented students may be represented in one (or all) of the aforementioned categories, we believe they also occupy a precarious space in the language education discourse by virtue of their position: they are a tangible symbol of the very reason this country implements policies of this nature, and a daily reminder of our need for comprehensive immigration reform.

The Backlash Against Language Rights

In several states across the nation, English immersion initiatives have gained increased popularity, putting language maintenance and other bilingual education programs on alert. In fact, Arizona's Proposition 203, the legislation at issue in the case detailed in this chapter, was one of four such initiatives where voters decided the preferred method and delivery of English language instruction.[9] This new approach to educational change via direct democracy is a recent phenomenon, entirely consistent with the devastating impact of the initiative process on Latina/o immigrant communities.[10] It is a voter-driven language reform policy which has found considerable economic and ideological support from Mr. Ron Unz. Mr. Unz is a California software developer and multi-millionaire who has personally financed and/or spearheaded the statewide language initiatives in California, Arizona, Massachusetts, and Colorado. All four of these initiatives were structurally similar in that they were voter initiatives that mandated a uniform method of instruction, and that they did not aim to eliminate bilingual education but replace it with structured English immersion.[11]

Under classic or traditional bilingual education, students are encouraged to maintain high levels of proficiency in two languages—most often the student's native language and the English language. Under two-way bilingual education, both English dominant and Limited English Proficient ("LEP") students are encouraged to become proficient in two languages, in order to remove the uni-directionality of traditional bilingual education approaches. In contrast, English immersion programs place *only* the LEP student in a "sheltered" learning environment for a specified amount of time, upon which the student is transitioned into classrooms where English is the predominant language of instruction. Although both teachers and students in the English immersion are allowed to use the native language to clarify understanding of content knowledge, the new teaching environment is unequivocally "English only."[12]

Arizona's Proposition 203, an example of the English immersion model, applied to all *language* learners—including those who speak sign language or any of the numerous Native/tribal languages in the state.[13] Other limitations under Proposition 203 include (1) a ban on all teaching materials that were not exclusively in English, (2) the repeal of all previous Arizona statues regulating English-language learning, (3) the denial of parent "opt out" petitions without explanation or the possibility of legal repercussion, (4) the inability to repeal or change the proposition by legislative action alone, and (5) a stipulation that any changes to the proposition can only be made through direct democracy or statewide ballot.[14]

When viewed holistically, the voter initiatives aimed to dismantle the spirit of bilingual education at its core and place English-language learners in a "sink or swim" environment.[15] Despite the fact that research overwhelmingly supports the efficacy of bilingual education as a sound curricular and pedagogical approach,[16] and despite sound evidence that finds the majority of LEP students in bilingual education programs transfer in three years and are successful in mainstream academic settings,[17] bilingual education, nevertheless became the target of ideological and political opposition.

Such a backlash is not particularly surprising, given the recent rise in immigration-related hate crimes coupled with the rampant xenophobia and racial politics that dominate state and federal political agendas.[18] Bilingual education is often criticized because it fragments the country's national identity and is a divisive force that threatens national unity.[19] It is also widely believed that holding on to one's "mother tongue" places an English-learning child at academic disadvantage.[20] Other criticisms aimed at bilingual education reinforce a popular, though largely unfounded, belief in the efficacy of "sink or swim" strategies as the *only* way to learn a new language. Although research consistently challenges each of these stock stories, they nevertheless persist because they are so firmly rooted in this country's collective ideology.[21] Not only are such beliefs grossly exaggerated and unfounded, but emerge from a deep-seeded paternalism that views non-English speakers as deficient and in need of shedding their ability to speak another language in order to blend into a English-dominant social order. Such nativist linguistic sentiment has a long tradition in U.S. history. For example, at the time of World War I, Nebraska enacted legislation banning teachers from instructing their pupils in German and the Supreme Court invalidated the law.[22] Thus, in the wake of the current "immigration crisis," it is not surprising to find bans on Spanish in the classroom, such as the one which took place in Arizona.

Deficit thinking in the "language rights" discourse?

This type of deficit thinking is not only found in conservative or right-wing circles, but also functions—albeit at more subtle levels—in more progressive arenas, including those sympathetic to bilingual education. In effect, the nature of deficit thinking about second-language acquisition in the U.S. is so pervasive that even progressive educational scholars have fallen prey to its views. They have internalized its poisonous logic by unconsciously subscribing to a language rights discourse that regards non-English speakers as having specific deficiencies or shortcomings.

From the terminology used to describe second-language learners (e.g., *Limited* English Proficient, Language *Minority* Students, etc.), to the methods implemented in bilingual classroom settings (e.g. *Sheltered* English Instruction, *Structured* Immersion, etc.), there is an implicit belief that non-English-speaking children are somehow broken, inferior, or lacking and that the only way they can get better is by shedding their language-based limitations. In other words, the importance of "learning English" remains firmly at the center of the language learning discourse. Not only does this ontological move position English as the dominant language, but it implicitly suggests that academic, career, and economic opportunities are *dependent* on learning and mastery the English language.

We are not suggesting that a strong command of the English language is unimportant, but rather we argue that we need to separate the learning of the language from the concomitant "benefits" that one gains from simply having learned the language. In other words, there is a slippage between language learning and social benefits that needs to be interrogated and problematized. For such an argument not only presupposes that English-language learning is the key to success, but also it entirely disregards the social, economic, political, structural, and racial context which keeps undocumented students, indeed, all underrepresented students (second-language learners *and* English-dominant learners alike) in a subordinate position in society.

To be certain, many marginalized communities (e.g., Chicanos) have been speaking English for decades, yet their command of the English language has not largely translated into academic, economic, political, or social gain. In this regard, students who are second-language learners have the potential of exposing the falsity of American idealism and disrupt the stock stories that circulate in the larger social order about English language acquisition. They also have the potential to challenge taken-for-granted assumptions about what constitutes language deficiency, and help us open a theoretical space to interrogate how the term is deployed in academic and policy circles.

Interestingly, the notion that English language learners have a "language deficiency" formally entered the policy discourse in 1970, when the Office of Civil Rights ("OCR") issued a memorandum detailing the Title VI requirements of the Civil Rights Act for school districts. The memorandum read, in part:

> Where the inability to speak and understand the English language excludes national origin-minority group children from effective participation in the educational program offered by a school district, the district must take affirmative steps to rectify the **language deficiency** in order to open its instructional program to these students.[23]

By positioning the student's inability to speak English as a "deficiency" in need of remediation, the OCR inadvertently began a string of signifying practices that would eventually make their way into the language rights discourse.

In that memorandum, the OCR was merely trying to provide guidance to school districts that were ignoring a student's linguistic needs. However, because the memorandum positioned students as having a language deficiency, it reproduced a particular form of linguistic paternalism: where schools are "charged" to take affirmative steps to rectify or cure students of their linguistic ailments. By focusing on the linguistic deficiencies of the student, the OCR ignored, or downplayed the deficiency of the district to meet the student's language needs.

This rhetoric of language deficiency was once again seen in the *Lau v. Nichols* decision, in which the United States Supreme Court found that the San Francisco Unified School District violated the Civil Rights Act of 1964 by failing to provide a meaningful educational experience to Chinese-origin LEP students. The majority opinion, written by Justice Douglas, opened with the following statement:

> The San Francisco, California, school system was integrated in 1971 as a result of a federal court decree. ... The District Court found that there are 2,856 students of Chinese ancestry in the school system who do not speak English. Of those who have that **language deficiency**, about 1,000 are given supplemental courses in the English language. About 1,800, however, do not receive that instruction.[24]

In this opinion, the logic of deficiency is explicitly stated and assumed from the onset. In contrast to the OCR memorandum which identifies how "language deficiencies" can prevent certain students from participating in school, the majority opinion in *Lau* is very specific and direct: it is the Chinese students *themselves* that have a language deficiency. In other words, while the language of deficiency is unquestionably present in both the OCR memorandum and the Supreme Court decision, the OCR memorandum tempers its approach by focusing more on the accommodations needed to rectify the language deficiency, while the Supreme Court focuses on the student as the source of the deficiency.

The concurring opinion of Justice Stewart in *Lau* was quite reminiscent of the language used in the original OCR memorandum and differed somewhat from the principal opinion. For example, he utilized the term "language deficiency" but deployed it in a way that was more diplomatic and change-oriented:

> It is uncontested that more than 2,800 schoolchildren of Chinese ancestry attend school in the San Francisco Unified School District system even though they do not speak, understand, read, or write the English language, and that as to some 1,800 of these pupils the respondent school authorities have taken no significant steps to deal with this **language deficiency**.[25]

Clearly, both the majority and concurring opinion in this landmark case not only viewed the inability to speak English as a deficiency, but viewed it as an aberration that needed to be fixed or remedied by the school. Unfortunately because schools were positioned as the solution to this language problem, the focus of the deficiency was not on the school but on the individual student.

In 1974, the Equal Education Opportunities Act ("EEOA") required school districts to have special programs for second-language learners, regardless of federal or state funding. Similar to previous policy and judicial mandates, section 1703(f) of the EEOA utilized similar language to frame its argument, but shifted the signifier surrounding deficiency. Instead of focusing on language deficiencies, the EEOA focused instead on the presence of language barriers:

> No State shall deny equal education opportunity to an individual on account of race, color, sex, or national origin, by ... the failure by an educational agency to take appropriate action to overcome **language barriers** that impede equal participation by its students in its instructional programs.[26]

On the one hand, the EEOA made a significant shift in focus to hold schools accountable for rectifying any barriers that might exist that prevent LEP students from equal participation in school. However, and in the same breath, it positioned the barrier as student problem, and the school as the agent responsible for rectifying the problem. As such, the EEOA still reproduced and reified a deficit-driven logic that seemed to blame children for their linguistic shortcomings.

This paternalistic belief reappeared in 1981 under *Castaneda v. Pickard*, a court case in which the plaintiffs argued that a language remediation program offered by the Raymondville Independent School District in Texas violated the EEOA. In *Castaneda*, the Fifth Circuit Court of Appeals overturned the decision of the lower court, concluding that second-language learners were at a particular disadvantage because they did not know the language of instruction. The court further found that in having to learn the language of instruction, they fell behind their peers in other academic areas. According to the Fifth Circuit:

> Limited English speaking students entering school face a task not encountered by students who are already proficient in English. Since the number of hours in any school day is limited, some of the time which limited English speaking children will spend learning English may be devoted to other subjects by students who entered school already proficient in English. In order to be able ultimately to participate equally with the students who entered school with an English language background, the limited English speaking students will have to acquire both English language proficiency comparable to that of the average native speakers and to recoup any deficits which they may incur in other areas of the

curriculum as a result of this extra expenditure of time on English language development. ... If no remedial action is taken to overcome the academic deficits that limited English speaking students may incur during a period of intensive language training, then the **language barrier**, although itself remedied, might, nevertheless, pose a lingering and indirect impediment to these students' equal participation in the regular instructional program.[27]

While the ruling correctly recognized the double burden placed on second-language learners, the court never fully clarified whether the "language barrier" emerged from the student or the school district. Clearly, and in concert with the spirit of the original OCR memorandum, the court recognized the duty of the school to acknowledge and rectify this barrier. However, in leaving the genesis of the language barrier undefined, the Fifth Circuit Court of Appeals never moved away from suggesting that the barrier was, at least in part, student-imposed. As such, we believe that this void serves only to reinforce a deficit discourse that views second-language learners as having "language deficiencies" because it positions schools as the primary agents responsible for inculcating and assimilating students into the linguistic and cultural norms of this society.

Word Play: Structuring Inequities through Language Policy

While *Lau v. Nichols* was perhaps the most significant court case since *Brown v. Board of Education* in addressing and remedying disparities in the classroom, it was also quite different than *Brown* in that it addressed the unintentional ways in which schools and districts also harm students.[28] In other words, *Brown* was a case about intentionality—and how separate schools are not necessarily equal schools. *Lau*, on the other hand, was more about unintentionality—and how equal schools may not be very equal in how they treat their students.

However, by looking at language as a problem in need of a remedy, *Lau* highlighted the language deficiencies of students while ignoring the deficiencies of the schools to address their linguistic needs. Moreover, it simultaneously ignored the fact that LEP students might also have assets and strengths—as opposed to just needs, shortcomings, and deficits. In other words, by framing language as a problem as opposed to an asset, *Lau* reinforced popular negative perceptions of languages other than English, while curtailing more holistic policy solutions that build on a student's prior knowledge in his/her native language.[29]

Richard Ruiz has identified three basic orientations in language policy: (1) language-as-problem, (2) language-as-resource, and (3) language-as-right.[30] It appears that every major decision, policy recommendation, and reform initiative to date—from the initial OCR guidelines, to the *Lau* decision, to the more recent Unz initiatives—all seemed to emerge from the "language-as-problem" framework. This lens not only positions English language students as deficient, but severely curtails the possibility of putting forth alternative policy options that build on a student's linguistic strengths.

In effect, the language policies and proposed solutions and interventions not only emerge from a deficit perspective but ensure that LEP students are viewed as second-class-citizens merely because of the language they speak.[31] As Patricia Gandara and Russell Rumberger surmise, the vast majority of LEP programs reinforce a deficit perception about language minority children:

> … by framing the needs of immigrant and EL pupils as a "language problem," the appropriate policy was easily understood as transitioning these students as quickly and efficiently as possible *from* their native language *into* English. However, if … programs for EL immigrants had been conceptualized as responding to language as a *resource*, educational policies might have evolved quite differently. We might have seen more political support for programs that built on students' native language as an avenue to enhanced academic competence, and there might have been a greater emphasis on academic achievement rather than merely on acquiring English. Education policy often seems to overlook the fact that immigrant students also bring assets, not just needs. All have linguistic and cultural resources that can be built on, and many have hopefulness and the desire to take advantage of opportunities in their new setting.[32]

In short, the language and metaphors used in language education policies not only reflect societal perceptions of languages other than English, but also the perceptions of the individuals who speak these languages. Policy is a powerful tool, not only because it reflects reality, but because it shapes and structures how we view the world. If the inability to speak English is solely viewed as a deficiency to be overcome, then the policy solutions we embrace will only continue to perpetuate deficit understandings of LEP students.

Speak No Evil: Language Ideology and Popular Democracy

As states like California, Arizona, and Massachusetts have increasingly moved toward ballot initiatives to regulate student language learning and capacity, we have a responsibility—as educators and as human beings—to critically examine the ideological and political underpinnings that drive such initiatives. In this discussion, we have argued that the logic of deficiency and assimilation is what largely drives these and other similar initiatives. However, rather than suggesting that these sentiments exclusively emerge from those who are unsympathetic to bilingual education, we have also argued that it is a discursive problem that plagues our very thinking about English language learning.

The incident at Arizona's East Valley Institute of Technology is not an aberration or an unusual event, but is part of a larger hegemonic discourse in which English language learning is privileged and normified. The need to regulate Spanish, or any other "minority" language, has become a form of social control: where schools and/or their agents are responsible for "fixing" the language deficiencies of language minority students. It is an epistemological and ideological form of language control, as well as a deeply paternalistic ideology that language minority students need to be "saved" from their own (unacknowledged) language deficiencies.

Perhaps it is time we critically examine the ideological cloth from which both English Only and Bilingual Education movements and ideals are cut. It is likely that we will find that they both reproduce and reify a paternalistic discourse which privileges the universality of English and the role of ideological state apparatuses in regulating, monitoring, and controlling language differences.

Undocumented students are at the center of this discourse since, by virtue of their origin, they enter the classroom cloaked in a different language. It is important that these vulnerable students not be further disadvantaged by the educational system and policies that are charged with providing them an education and instead allow persistent inequalities to continue and render them second-class citizens in this society.

4

Accountability under No Child Left Behind

Implications for Undocumented Students

The No Child Left Behind Act of 2001 ("NCLB")—perhaps the largest and most significant educational legislation since the Elementary and Secondary Education Act ("ESEA") of 1965—was signed into law on January 8, 2002 by former President George W. Bush. With bipartisan backing, NCLB reauthorized ESEA and aimed to usher in a renewed focus on quality education for all children throughout the United States. In fact, NCLB's promise to improve schools for our most marginalized children was perhaps the most appealing element of the legislation, for it was a healthy reminder that educational *access* was not coterminous with educational *outcomes*. Indeed, in following the spirit of the original ESEA bill, which provided targeted monies to schools with the greatest educational need, NCLB also sought to "improve the academic achievement of the disadvantaged" by providing funds to improve basic programs at the local level.[1]

NCLB's mission is straightforward: To ensure that all children—regardless of race, class, gender, creed, or ability—have an equal opportunity at a high quality education. That is, no child enrolled in public education will be left behind with regard to his or her learning and academic success. Its framers believed that such an outcome would be achieved through (1) development and implementation of high quality educational standards, (2) alignment of assessments, curricula, and accountability systems to meet those standards, (3) meeting the educational needs of all children through the strategic use of resources, (4) holding schools accountable for educational outcomes, and (5) empowering parents and communities with real-time data about their school's performance.[2] NCLB, in its statement of purpose, specifically outlines how it aims to accomplish these goals.[3]

In order to receive federal grant money under the NCLB, each state must develop and submit a comprehensive reform plan to the Secretary of the U.S. Department of Education.[4] The state's plan must show proof of high academic standards,[5] proposed academic assessments to meet those standards,[6] and the accountability measures used to gauge success.[7] The U.S. Department of Education needs to approve this plan prior to its implementation.[8] With respect to formulating academic content standards, NCLB has very specific guidelines: States must specify what children are expected to know and be able to do in specific content areas, demonstrate that the proposed course content is both coherent and rigorous, and demonstrate that they are promoting the teaching of advanced skills.[9] Moreover, states must specifically implement high academic content area standards in mathematics, reading/language arts, and science and they must specify the knowledge, skills, and levels of achievement expected of children in these content areas.[10]

NCLB also requires states to show that they meet challenging academic achievement standards typically measured via a standardized test in every school in the state. NCLB encourages states to gauge academic proficiency every year while providing information to parents about the individual progress of children, the schools they attend, and the overall performance of their respective school districts as they move toward mastery of the state standards.[11]

Perhaps the most contentious element of NCLB is its emphasis on accountability. Under NCLB, a state must show that it has developed and implemented "a single, statewide state accountability system that will be effective in ensuring that all local educational agencies, public elementary schools, and public secondary schools make adequate yearly progress ("AYP")"[12] towards the state standards. NCLB allows each state to define how it will determine what constitutes its AYP so long as said measure meets the following criteria:

- It applies the same high standards of academic achievement to all public elementary school and secondary school students in the state,
- It is statistically valid and reliable,
- It results in continuous and substantial academic improvement for all students,
- It measures the academic success and progress of students enrolled at public elementary schools, secondary schools, local educational agencies as well as the state, and
- It includes separate measurable annual objectives for continuous and substantial improvement for all public elementary school and secondary school students in the state, and allows for disaggregation of data to observe the progress of specified subgroups—including those who are economically disadvantaged, from major racial and ethnic groups, students with disabilities, and students with limited English proficiency.

Additionally, a state must use data to establish benchmarks for measuring the percentage of students meeting or exceeding the state's proficient level of academic achievement on the state assessment or test.[13] Under NCLB, states are required to measure student progress at three critical periods in the K–12 trajectory: once during grades 3–5, once during grades 6–9, and once during grades 10–12.[14] By the 2014 school year, NCLB specifies that all children will be at the "proficient" level on all areas of a state test.[15]

To help meet this goal, NCLB raises the requirements for all teachers and paraprofessionals in the schools, requiring schools and school districts to employ highly qualified teachers for all subject areas, and raising the required training for paraprofessionals in each school. While states are free to define the parameters of teacher quality, most "highly qualified" teachers must be fully certified (which is usually shown by the completion of a bachelor's degree) and have demonstrated competency in the core academic subject(s) they teach.[16]

NCLB's Double-edged Sword

While some individuals welcome many of the measures adopted by NCLB, others question its effectiveness and are deeply troubled by the over-emphasis on standardized testing and high-stakes examinations. National consensus, however, is that the current educational system is broken and something must be done to help children be successful in school. Where there is substantive disagreement is in the method or strategy for accomplishing that goal.

Proponents of NCLB embrace the idea of accountability. They argue that well-planned accountability systems emphasizing assessment and incentives for improvement and community involvement can improve public education as a whole. They contend that such an accountability plan ultimately leads to measurable gains in student performance. These proponents found much support in the administration of President George W. Bush,[17] which consistently touted the benefits of accountability and achievements gained under NCLB.[18] It pointed to "turn-around" schools and districts—such as Garden Grove School District in California, where 75 per cent of the student spoke English as a second language and 60 per cent were low-income, and still managed to meet the AYP—as "proof" that NCLB was working. According to the superintendent of Garden Grove, the district used data from NCLB and set targets in order to close the achievement gap to get all students on target towards success.[19] Proponents argued that such examples and anecdotes provided evidence of the effectiveness of high standards coupled with strong accountability systems.

Proponents further posit that NCLB is designed to maximize a students' learning, by arguing that the results of tests can be used as "benchmarks" to gauge a students' progress. Sandra Feldman, president of the American Federation of Teachers, has used the analogy of a thermometer when discussing the role of the standardized tests in a system of accountability:

Tests are vital tools for measuring student progress and for identifying where students' and schools' achievement can be improved. But a test is a thermometer, not a treatment. More and more testing is not a "cure" for poor student achievement. That can only be solved through a comprehensive program of lower class size, highly qualified teachers, appropriate instructional materials and adequate school facilities. Good tests, used properly, will help us understand how children are doing, help direct resources to those in need, and reassure parents that their children are getting a broad and rigorous education.[20]

Proponents believe that when tests are used to gauge student performance in this fashion, then schools can target their resources accordingly to improve in content areas where students are lacking.

In sum, proponents believe that NCLB is designed to help every child in public school be academically successful. With highly qualified teachers and paraprofessionals in place to monitor student progress, rigorous performance measures implemented to gauge that progress, and communities empowered with real options to "vote with their feet," many believe that NCLB can move the country in a positive direction.

Not Everyone Agrees

Although proponents applaud the potential benefits of NCLB, opponents of the legislation are firm in their belief that it is fundamentally flawed both pedagogically and theoretically. Opponents contend that NCLB equates "testing" with "learning" and places schools on a testing regimen that is high on rhetoric and low on evidence. They insist that no scientific study has conclusively found a direct relationship between test scores and success later in life, and believe that the over-reliance on a single performance measure not only sends out the wrong message about the role and function of the test, but can ultimately serve to *lower* the overall quality of schools.[21]

Critics maintain that testing—particularly in a "high-stakes" situation—creates more problems than it solves. They believe that it leads to a narrowing of the curriculum (both with and across content areas), an over-reliance on teaching practices that are strictly focused on the test, and the virtual elimination of subject areas that are not tested (e.g., social studies, art, music, humanities, etc.).[22] In other words, they argue that great teaching is not only stifled but actually sacrificed in the name of Adequate Yearly Progress.[23]

Moreover, critics believe that NCLB has a negative effect on the environment and climate of a school. They contend that the intense and exclusive focus on testing in schools sends the wrong message to children about "what's important" in the classroom, and squelches a teacher's passion for teaching and learning. They argue that with such an intense emphasis on test scores, teachers rarely get an opportunity to engage children in learning activities beyond what's being tested. As a result, teacher and student creativity in the classroom is stifled and students fail to see the beauty of learning beyond rote memorization.[24] Indeed, research suggests that as the school curriculum becomes increasingly focus on the test, teachers, students, parents, and the broader community becomes less satisfied with schools[25] Critics contend that the only thing "left behind" in such a test-centric environment is the energy, excitement, and passion for learning that emerges in the creative exchange between a teacher and her/his students. Nowhere is this more evident than in inner city schools—where the pressure to meet AYP is so intense that the environment, culture, and climate of the school often borders on the toxic.[26]

In fact, Jonathan Kozol has repeatedly argued that the school system in the U.S. is severely broken and provides very little to students of color except broken dreams and limited opportunities. His recent book, THE SHAME OF THE NATION, carefully illustrates how black and Latino children attend schools that are more racially isolated, severely overcrowded, structurally inadequate, and academically poor than the schools that white students attend.[27] As a result, Kozol maintains that the majority of inner city children of color are the default objects of NCLB: they are expected to perform well on the state test despite the vestiges of racism, concentrated poverty, and inadequate school funding to support success.[28]

In fact, Kozol argues that NCLB places enhanced demands *specifically* on urban schools to lift themselves out of their pervasive "academic funk" and demonstrates how these schools now focus obsessively over meeting state AYP mandates. Far too often, Kozol argues, they resort to pre-packaged curricular offerings, mechanistic teaching methods, and reform-oriented "miracle cures" that are high on promises but low on results. The unfortunate victims of this obsession—i.e., the black and brown students caught in the middle—quickly learn that testing is the only thing that is valued at these schools. Not surprisingly, it is often the state test that presents the biggest hurdle for children of color to overcome.

Although NCLB was designed to close the gap between affluent white students and their minority counterparts, research often finds that the achievement gap has actually increased[29] or remained stagnant[30] since the implementation of NCLB. This is generally true for student performance on the state test as well as national tests of student academic progress.[31] Although data show that test scores increased for children of color from 2004 to 2008, they also indicate that test scores increased for white students during this same time period—effectively leaving the achievement gap untouched.[32] In other words, while proponents of NCLB correctly claim that a focus on accountability has raised test scores for children of color, critics maintain that the available data does not demonstrate much progress in closing the achievement gap between white and non-white students.[33]

NCLB is thus a double-edged sword: on the one hand, it calls for increased accountability for *all* students—including those who are low-income, limited English proficient, Latino, African American, and those with a special education designation. The Act calls for 100 per cent proficiency in Mathematics, Reading, and Science by the year 2014 and holds schools accountable for meeting AYP in state-level exams by requiring that teachers and paraprofessionals be "highly qualified" in their content area. On the other hand, NCLB is having a disproportionate impact on teaching and learning, especially in schools that serve linguistically and culturally diverse students.

Given the high-stakes nature of these tests, many schools find themselves forced to take extreme measures to avoid the sanctions under the AYP requirement. For example, many schools are increasingly pushing remedial programs for students who fail to pass the state test, while others are frenziedly revising classes to "teach to the test."[34] Others are increasingly counseling failing students into alternative education or high school equivalency programs in order to avoid having these failing students as liabilities on their school rosters.[35] In this race to meet AYP, the linguistically and culturally diverse student is the one who often gets left behind.[36]

The Linguistically and Culturally Diverse Student and NCLB

Public concern over the growing number of LEP, immigrant, and other student from culturally diverse backgrounds has intensified in recent years.[37] In fact, since the early 1980s, social policy analysts have alerted educators of the growing population of people of color—many of whom come from immigrant backgrounds and speak languages other than English.[38] These assertions have already been confirmed by recent census figures which point to the fact that cities and states across the nation have witnessed a dramatic change in their racial and ethnic compositions.[39] Moreover, census figures indicate that this transition is largely fueled by a significant growth in the Latino population which is the fastest growing "minority" group in the United States.[40] Needless to say, this demographic shift—commonly referred to as the "Browning of America"[41]—places enhanced demands on educational institutions and other social service providers to meet the needs of an increasingly diverse student population.[42]

One of the challenges schools face is the sharp increase in the number of students from immigrant families where at least one of the parents was born outside the United States. To be certain, research by Randy Capps and his colleagues at the Urban Institute suggests that children of immigrants currently comprise one-fifth of all school age children and will represent up to 25 per cent of the K–12 student population by the year 2010.[43] Not surprisingly, the vast majority of these children are identified as Limited English Proficient (LEP). Capps finds that the vast majority of these students are Latinos, come from families that are primarily monolingual Spanish speakers, and live in racially isolated communities. Moreover, a sizeable number of these students also attend linguistically segregated schools—many of which lack basic knowledge of how to academically accommodate English Language Learners.[44] As Cosentino de Cohen attests:

> Only 10 per cent of U.S. elementary schools educate 70 per cent of LEP students. And nearly half of elementary schools serve no LEP students. In addition to serving high proportions of English Language Learners, High-LEP schools are more likely than other school types to be located in urban areas, and therefore have many characteristics associated with urban schools: larger enrollments, larger class sizes, greater racial and ethnic diversity, higher incidence of student poverty and health problems, etc. Important differences are also found in terms of resources. Teachers and principals at High-LEP schools have, on average, less experience and qualifications than those at schools with few or no LEP children.[45]

In fact, this emerging student population has caused considerable stress and frustration for teachers and administrators, as they adjust their teaching practices to accommodate this diverse student body. Adding to this stress are the increased demands placed on schools by NCLB and state-level accountability policies that are unforgiving in their push to demonstrate Adequate Yearly Progress.

Indeed, the demographic shift has presented public schools with the challenge of quickly needing to adapt in order to effectively serve the needs of this particular population. However, since many schools and districts in these new diaspora[46] states have little knowledge of and/or firsthand experience with LEP students, many of the adjustments and/or educational accommodations have occurred at the surface level: e.g., hiring bilingual paraprofessionals, translating documents between the home and the school, and professional development and/or training in cultural competency. While these accommodations are tremendously important, they are but a first step in truly understanding students and families, their cultural and linguistic backgrounds, and how to best accommodate them in the school and larger community.

Moreover, because many of these students often fall into multiple categories within NCLB's identified breakout groups, it often proves to be quite a challenge for schools and districts to navigate AYP for each particular subgroup.[47] Under NCLB, schools are required to demonstrate student performance and progress by disaggregated subgroup and demonstrate that they are meeting performance targets for each particular group every year.

Since undocumented and LEP students fall under multiple categorical designations (e.g., Latino, LEP, and Low Income), schools that serve these students are more likely to miss particular performance targets for some of the respective categories. Consequently, there is a built-in incentive for schools not to have culturally and linguistically diverse students identified and/or tested because the student's disaggregated test scores might end up harming the school's overall ability to meet AYP. As Randy Capps and his colleagues at the Urban Institute suggest:

> For a school to make AYP, all subgroups must also make AYP. This means that more diverse schools—those with more students in mandated subgroups—are statistically more likely to miss AYP than less diverse schools, which are not required to meet AYP for subgroups because of small sample sizes....Increased reliance on standardized testing may result in higher dropout rates among LEP and immigrant students who do not perform well on the tests. Additionally, some schools may "push out" students who are low performers into other settings, e.g., for high school equivalency degree programs.[48]

While NCLB does allow for testing accommodations that could result in a more accurate assessment of an LEP student's academic ability (e.g., offering a test in the student's native language, using alternative tests that cover the same material but are less English language-dependent, allowing LEP students to use bilingual language dictionaries during tests),[49] such accommodations vary on a state-by-state basis and are less likely to be found in Midwestern and other non-traditional receiving states where the most recent immigration growth has occurred.[50] In other words, states that need these accommodations the most are the least likely to offer them, placing marginalized students in these states at higher risk of not passing the state test.

Another disadvantage for immigrant and LEP students is the NCLB requirement for students to be taught by highly qualified teachers. While NCLB "does not require current teachers to return to school or get a degree in every subject they teach to demonstrate that they are highly qualified,"[51] it does require that every core content teacher be highly qualified. Consequently, teachers who work with LEP children do not need to be "certified" bilingual or ESL teachers, nor do they need to demonstrate knowledge of how to work with LEP students in their classrooms on an everyday basis; they only need meet the highly qualified criteria for the subject area in which they teach.

Clearly, this puts LEP students at a disadvantage—for these students might be tracked into ESL classrooms with teachers or paraprofessionals who are not highly qualified[52] or they might be taught a core academic subject by someone who is working in a consultative capacity to a regular content teacher. In the latter case, the bilingual teacher or paraprofessional who provides language assistance to LEP students is not recognized as the individual delivering the primary content instruction; therefore, the bilingual assistant does not need to meet the highly qualified criteria as defined by the state.

As such, it is quite possible for LEP students—particularly those who are at the earlier levels of English language proficiency—to receive the majority of their core content instruction in their native language from individuals who are not highly qualified in any particular subject area.[53] In short, the LEP student not only has to learn the subject matter from individuals who may not be qualified or trained to address their linguistic and pedagogical needs, but they are also expected to take the content area assessment along with the rest of their peers in a language they may not understand, perhaps without additional accommodations, and *still* perform to a particular pre-designated standard.[54]

NCLB does allow a one-year grace period before a "recently arrived" LEP student can be tested in reading/language arts.[55] Recently arrived students are those who have attended schools in the U.S. for less than twelve months. The law gives this grace period to schools and districts to avoid testing LEP students in such a language-heavy content area. It is up to the school and the district to determine whether or not they exercise this exemption or test the student in the first year. The law is not as flexible, however, when it comes to granting a similar one-year exemption for assessments in Mathematics and Science; presumably because they are viewed as being less language-dependent.[56] While all recently arrived LEP students must be tested in these content areas, NCLB does allow for language accommodations to be provided to the student, to the extent possible.

Moreover, while all recently arrived LEP students must be tested in Mathematics and Science in the first year (Reading and Language Arts is optional), it is up to the state to determine whether or not the scores of these tests will count towards AYP calculations.[57] In other words, states are allowed some flexibility in the assessment and accountability procedures for recently arrived LEP students. However, NCLB limits that flexibility after an LEP student has been in the United States for three years *regardless* of whether or not a student has mastered the English language during that period of time.[58]

On that note, a school must assess the English language development of LEP students every year *in addition* to testing for student understanding and comprehension of a particular content area. This means that LEP students must not only be tested for English language mastery, but must also be tested for content knowledge mastery every year. Many critics argue that LEP students are not only tested twice as much as other students, but they are expected to master the English language and test for content knowledge mastery in other subjects within that same time frame.[59] This expectation is not placed on other any other students, which leads us to conclude that accountability under NCLB is not only unreasonable but inequitable, especially when it comes to students from language-minority backgrounds.

Undocumented Students and NCLB

NCLB presents unique challenges for both the undocumented student and the schools they attend. For starters, undocumented students must not only navigate the linguistic terrain of schools and the rampant testing regime in force therein, but they must also learn to navigate the psychological demands and pressures they face in being members of an invisible minority.

On top of having to take tests and meet specified performance AYP targets as members of multiple subgroups, they must do so with the added pressure of knowing their lives could be disrupted at any time and for any reason. In fact, research finds that undocumented children not only are at higher risk for economic hardship, but face a unique psychological trauma that is largely driven by fears of family separation, arrest, detention, deportation, or simply being "revealed" as being in the country without the requisite documentation.[60]

With immigration raids on the rise in various communities across the U.S. and with the everyday fear of deportation always looming in the background, the undocumented student must quickly learn to table these fears and "perform" up to par with her/his peers in class and on standardized tests. They must learn to hide an important element of their identity, and be watchful not to reveal details that could potentially uncover their family's immigration status.

Under NCLB, "recently arrived" students must not only be identified and tested by the school to determine LEP eligibility, but the process of identification *itself* is problematic—for it can potentially force students to disclose their immigration status to school officials. Although the identification process is concerned with finding out a student's educational background and LEP designation (and not a student's immigration status per se), students and families must, nevertheless, reveal how long the child has attended schools in the U.S. As such, NCLB not only encourages schools to probe into a child's immigration history, but may encourage students and families to further hide, or even misrepresent, their status in order to protect their family. This has serious implications for both schools and student: schools need to have accurate data in order to make sound pedagogical and curricular decisions for students, and students who misrepresent their educational history may be forced to enter the testing stream prematurely. Clearly, none of these options are ideal.

Conclusion and Implications

Overall, it is clear that NCLB not only impacts a student's educational experience, but structures and shapes student identities by labeling and classifying students, identifying their strengths and weaknesses, and prescribing particular educational interventions and testing options. NCLB sorts students into rigid educational classifications and classifies them according to their "worth" in the testing regime: some onto courses worthy of being taught by "highly qualified" teachers while others are taught by educators with fewer professional qualifications. Moreover, NCLB places enhanced demands on culturally and linguistically diverse students not only to master the English language in an unrealistic amount of time—but to perform well in specific academic content areas *irrespective* of the support or accommodations offered by the school.

Furthermore, NCLB also places demands on schools: forcing them to hastily learn about culturally differences and work across language barriers without the necessary financial support, certified staff, professional development training, or resources to do so. NCLB emphasizes test results over content mastery, and often sacrifices learning in the desperate pursuit to make AYP and avoiding possible state sanctions (including, but not limited to, student transfers, school reconstitution, reconstitution as a charter school, withholding of state funds, and school closure).[61] Indeed, under NCLB, accountability is not only important but is the only thing that is important—and schools will do whatever it takes to ensure that their test scores meet AYP.

In short, NCLB provides a unique opportunity for reflection and analysis. It allows us to see how policy shapes school life and how schools can re-prioritize their missions, goals, and strategies in order to better align themselves with the policy requirements and mandates. It allows us to view how national, state, and local school interests drive the day-to-day decisions of schools, and understand why schools fail to act in the interests of children. As long as schools hold themselves accountable to federal policies, the only ones left behind will be the children, particularly those who come from undocumented and language minority backgrounds.

5

Examining Potential Dangers of the Law in the Schoolhouse

Critical Implications of Racial Privacy Initiatives and Immigration School Raids

Undocumented children and their parents, as well as school district personnel, stand at the center of intense and ongoing efforts in both the educational and immigration law and policy arena. Two potential dangers for the undocumented student can arise in the educational setting. The first one resides in racial privacy initiatives, such as the one that was defeated in California in 2003. These initiatives prohibit states from gathering and classifying information based on race or ethnicity. Among other things, they would make scientific studies of race very difficult. The first part of this chapter examines the effect of such initiatives upon the educational opportunities of undocumented students. While these initiatives are likely to affect all minority students, they especially pose a threat to the undocumented even more, since their irregular immigration status makes them less likely to mobilize politically. This part of the chapter also builds upon the literature analyzing the constitutionality of these initiatives and explores whether they are effective policy.

A second threat for the undocumented student lies in the increase in immigration enforcement, where the implications of potential immigration schoolhouse raids in the United States need to be explored. These raids pose serious concerns for undocumented K–12 students who attend public schools. Some are afraid to attend school because they or their parents believe that immigration officials may raid the school building at any time. While most state laws require students below the age of eighteen to attend school, and *Plyler v. Doe* requires schools to provide educational services to students living in their school districts, undocumented students and their families daily live with concerns about their school attendance. The concerns are: (1) whether immigration agents can conduct school building raids, and (2) whether school personnel can refuse to share student records with these officials. These are important concerns because school should be a safe environment conducive to learning. Because of the potential for chilling classroom attendance, students and their parents should be able to be confident that sending a child to school does not expose the family to deportation. Indeed, *Plyler* implies as much. Thus, the second part of the chapter will examine the ability of *Plyler* to protect students from these raids and other immigration enforcement, and the legal and policy implications of such actions. Let us now turn to first potential danger for undocumented students in the schoolhouse, that of racial privacy initiatives.

Colorblindness and Racial Privacy Initiatives

The current post-*Grutter*[1] and post-*Parents Involved*[2] environment regarding race in education is one in which the Supreme Court has come ever closer to espousing colorblindness. Because of these court decisions and the struggle over state legislation banning consideration of race, such as the proposed Racial Privacy Initiative ("RPI") in California, Ian Haney López has identified the Unites States is as entering an era of "colorblind white dominance."[3] He clarifies that in this era, "a public consensus committed to formal antiracism deters effective remediation of racial inequality, protecting the racial status quo while insulating new forms of racism and xenophobia."[4]

In order to understand how this trend in U.S. society has evolved, it is instructive to begin with the history of "colorblindness."[5] Naturally, the starting point would be the words of Justice Harlan's dissent in *Plessy v. Ferguson*: "Our Constitution is color-blind, and neither knows nor tolerates classes among citizens."[6] Yet it is important to understand the words which contextualize Justice Harlan's famous statement.[7] He asserted that "[t]he white race deems itself the dominant race in this country. And so it is in prestige, in achievements, in education, in wealth and in power. So, I doubt not it will be for all time."[8]

For Justice Harlan, the concern was where to place limits on the government's support for the separation of groups that were unequal. In his view, separation of the races in the social sphere would be acceptable, but not in the context of civic participation. He also made the distinction that:

> [i]t is one thing ... to furnish equal accommodations ... [i]t is quite another thing for the government to forbid ... the black and white races from traveling in the same public conveyance and to punish [those] for permitting persons of the two races to occupy the same passenger coach.[9]

Thus, Justice Harlan objected to the use of race which would "unduly oppress black people," rather than to any and all classifications based on race.[10] Consequently, a colorblind society in which minorities are unduly oppressed would not be consistent with Justice Harlan's sense of justice. When examining the statistics on poverty, such as the fact that African Americans and Latinos have a poverty rate of 21 percent, compared to that of only 8 percent for whites,[11] and that the poverty rate among minority children, 27 percent, is almost three times the rate for white children, 10 percent,[12] it is clear that colorblindness will likely allow a regime to continue where minorities are unduly oppressed.

The evolution of U.S. racial history brings us to *Brown v. Board of Education*, the seminal case which dismantled Jim Crow state segregation laws and yet, ironically, whose legacy has been used by proponents to advocate the Racial Privacy Initiative.[13] The use of *Brown* and of the words used in the case by future Justice Thurgood Marshall, acting as advocate for the plaintiff's case, in support of the RPI do not take into account the racial reality at the time of *Brown*. When Thurgood Marshall stated that: "[d]istinctions by race are so evil, so arbitrary and invidious that a state bound to defend the equal protection of the laws must not involve them in any public sphere,"[14] the reality then was that considerations of race resulted in the oppression of blacks, keeping them in inferior positions and in worse schools, so that separate was in fact not equal. It was the white race that dominated society in the U.S. at the time. At present, the latest incarnation of white dominance has been identified as white privilege.[15]

Thus, the colorblind approach underlying and required by the RPI ignores the roles of racial/ethnic groups in U.S. society, where white supremacy has given way to white dominance. Professor Ian Haney López puts it:

The civil-rights movement changed the racial zeitgeist of the nation by rendering illegitimate all explicit invocations of white supremacy, a shift that surely marked an important step toward a more egalitarian society. But it did not bring into actual existence that ideal, as white people remain dominant across virtually every social, political, and economic domain.[16]

In face of this inability of the civil rights movement and its progeny to bring about a truly egalitarian United States, Professor López concludes that:

[c]olorblindness badly errs when it excuses racially correlated inequality in our society as unproblematic so long as no one uses a racial epithet … To break the interlocking patterns of racial hierarchy, there is no other way but to focus on, talk about, and put into effect constructive policies explicitly engaged with race.[17]

Thus, in the words of Justice Blackmun in *Bakke:* "In order to get beyond racism, we must first take account of race. There is no other way."[18]

Proponents of racial privacy legislation contend that these enactments are the best way to move towards a "colorblind" society; while opponents maintain that these laws would allow governments to ignore the severe inequalities facing people of color in the United States. In fact, the term racial privacy is a misnomer, as it does not seek to protect the privacy of minorities but it would appear to conceal the evidence of racially discriminatory policies on the part of the government. Furthermore, minorities who do not wish to disclose their racial identities can achieve this by refusing to identify themselves as such when asked by the federal, state, and local governments.[19] In addition to the misnomer, then, such initiatives are actually not even necessary. Even so, they have been proposed and are anticipated to be proposed in the future. The proponents are often the same groups that aim to abolish affirmative action and have succeeded in doing so in three states: by initiatives passed in California, Michigan, and Washington.

The best-known initiative regarding racial privacy was California's Proposition 54, the Racial Privacy Initiative. At present, it appears to be the only such legislation to have been proposed. However, it is instructive to analyze this legislation, as its proponents have vowed to continue campaigning for its passage.

California's Proposition 54: Analysis, Constitutionality and Concerns

Proposition 54 appeared on the California ballot on October 7, 2003 and was defeated by 64 percent of the vote.[20] Nearly a million people in the state signed a petition to add the Racial Privacy Initiative to the ballot, even though it had failed to reach the ballot two years earlier.[21] The proposition would have amended the California Constitution to ban state entities from collecting and using certain racial and other data. The California Secretary of State presented the proposition to the voters with a more accurate name: the Classification by Race, Ethnicity, Color, or National Origin Initiative ("CRECNO"). This chapter will continue the use of its more common name, the Racial Privacy Initiative.

The Racial Privacy Initiative sought to prohibit the state from classifying and collecting data on any individual on the basis of race, ethnicity, color, or national origin. The prohibition would have been absolute in the areas of public education, public contracting, and public employment.[22] In all other areas, the prohibition would have applied as a form of "proactive repeal" to prevent any such classifications, unless two-thirds of both chambers of the state legislature and the governor voted to approve a particular classification.[23] The Racial Privacy Initiative also contained limited exemptions to the ban against the collection and use of the racial data, thus allowing for the collection and use of such data (1) to comply with a court order, (2) to comply with federal law, (3) for medical research, (4) to allow law enforcement to use race in the description of suspects, in placing undercover agents, and for placement of inmates at correctional facilities, and (5) to allow the Department of Fair Employment and Housing to collect certain data until 2014.

The campaign against Proposition 54 was helpful in that it brought together unions, the medical profession, law enforcement, and educators to speak out against the initiative.[24] However, it was also instructive to learn how such legislation would have fared if challenged under the Equal Protection Clause.

The Fourteenth Amendment of the Constitution guarantees equal protection under the law. The Equal Protection Clause of the Fourteenth Amendment states that "no State shall ... deny to any person within its jurisdiction the equal protection of the laws."[25] Scholars interpret this constitutional mandate to mean that "similar individuals ... be dealt with in a similar manner by the government."[26] States must have a compelling governmental interest in order to treat individuals differently under the Equal Protection Clause when there are suspect classifications or fundamental rights are involved. To decide whether treating individuals differently violates the Equal Protection Clause, courts will apply a strict scrutiny analysis to determine the existence of a compelling governmental interest. Strict scrutiny is the legal test applied when courts evaluate the importance of the underlying goals of an institution's policy and the necessity of the policy advancing these goals.

Typically, laws that contain racial classifications are subject to strict scrutiny.[27] Racial classifications do not violate the Equal Protection Clause and thus meet the strict scrutiny test if "they are narrowly tailored measures that further compelling governmental interests."[28] Racial classifications can be both "facially racial" and "facially neutral with an invidious intent."[29]

A measure such as the Racial Privacy Initiative would likely survive the application of strict scrutiny analysis. Proponents of the measure would argue that it does not apply to any one race because it bans any act of classification in education, employment, and contracting.[30] Thus, the Racial Privacy Initiative would be unlikely to be seen as a "facially racial" act. Instead, it would be more likely viewed as "facially race neutral," since no racial classification is actually performed. Such neutral provisions must be shown to have an "invidious discriminatory purpose." A court would need to determine if the measure was enacted "because of," not merely in spite of "its adverse effects upon an identifiable group."[31] The notion of colorblindness behind these racial privacy initiatives and prohibitions regarding racial classifications would make it unlikely that this initiative would be determined to have been enacted because of its adverse effects upon any identifiable group. One scholar has predicted that the Racial Privacy Initiative would survive strict scrutiny because: "[a]court likely would fail to discern a racial classification altogether because the Racial Privacy Initiative purports to prohibit the act of racial classification in the areas of public education, employment, and contracting."[32]

Other aspects of equal protection analysis are based on equality of access to the political process. Courts have found violations of the Equal Protection Clause if a provision hinders the enactment of antidiscrimination laws, or allows the political process to be engineered in such a way that such a result will occur.[33] This theory can be applied to laws that negatively impact access to the courts for those seeking to enforce antidiscrimination claims.

In *Hunter v. Erickson*, after a city council passed a fair housing law, voters passed an initiative which amended the city charter to bar ordinances relating to race and religion in the absence of majority support from voters.[34] The Supreme Court held the city charter amendment to be unconstitutional under the Equal Protection Clause, since the initiative had obstructed equal housing by removing only racially fair housing prerogatives from the law-making procedure for all other housing matters. The Court's rationale was that the amendment distinguished between those minorities seeking remedies against discrimination and "those who sought to regulate real property transactions in the pursuit of other ends."[35] The former group was subjected to additional hurdles.[36] While the law was facially neutral, "treating [African Americans] and whites ... in an identical manner, the reality was that the law's [impact] was on the minority."[37] Unlike prior disparate impact cases, the Court did not consider whether the amendment contained an "invidious intent" to discriminate.[38] Thus, the ruling was based on a concern that the amendment in question denied political access to a minority group. It was for this reason that the initiative violated the Equal Protection Clause. In essence, the *Hunter* doctrine allows courts to determine whether a political procedure implicates the Equal Protection Clause when members of a protected racial or ethnic class are burdened more heavily than the majority in their efforts to seek beneficial legislation.[39]

Application of the *Hunter* doctrine to the Racial Privacy Initiative would similarly likely find it unconstitutional—a view that is echoed by scholars who find that:

> If enacted, CRECNO [the Racial Privacy Initiative] could be determined to violate the Equal Protection Clause of the United States Constitution because the state enacting the legislation would be providing less than equal protection to people of color within its boundaries by erecting additional political barriers, in violation of the Hunter Doctrine...Thus, while discrimination still would be outlawed, the state's laws will be rendered virtually ineffective, at least in the areas of monitoring and enforcing fair housing and fair employment laws.[40]

The Supreme Court has further applied the *Hunter* doctrine in the educational context in *Washington v. Seattle School District*.[41] In that case, the Court invalidated an initiative which prohibited school boards from requiring students to attend only the school that was geographically nearest to them, finding that there was little doubt that the initiative was aimed at desegregation busing and had a racial purpose. The Court viewed the practical effect of the initiative as removing the authority to address a racial problem from the existing decisionmaking body in such a way as to burden minority interests, a reallocation of power prohibited by *Hunter*.[42]

However, application of the *Hunter* doctrine has been limited by the lower courts. In *Coalition of Economic Equity v. Wilson*, (*"CEE I"*), the plaintiffs argued under the *Hunter* doctrine that California Proposition 209 violated the Equal Protection Clause.[43] Proposition 209, as enacted, provided that "the state shall not discriminate against, or grant preferential treatment to, any individual or group on the basis of race, sex, color, ethnicity, or national origin in the operation of public employment, public education, or public contracting."[44]

The district court in *CEE I* held that the initiative had a racial focus and denied minorities access to the political process by shifting power from the local bodies to the state constitution, in violation of the Equal Protection Clause.[45] Thus, the lower court granted a preliminary injunction.[46] The Ninth Circuit Court of Appeals vacated the injunction in *CEE II*, formulating the question of whether a burden on achieving a race-based preferential treatment denied individuals equal protection.[47] In doing so, the Ninth Circuit explained that the Equal Protection Clause protects the rights of individuals, not groups, and that it did not find injury to any individual under this law. This court further disagreed with the view espoused by the district court that the law unfairly restructured the political process to the detriment of minorities. Thus, the *Hunter* doctrine did not invalidate Proposition 209 in *CEE II*.

As a result, while a court never ruled on the constitutionality of Proposition 54, there are at least two differing views which a court analyzing similar legislation in the future would need to reconcile.

In order to assert a constitutional challenge to the Racial Privacy Initiative under *Hunter*, the plaintiffs would need to show that the initiative restructures the political process to the detriment of minorities. Such detriment would include hindrance in the enforcement of antidiscrimination laws, prevention of access to court, as well as difficulties in enacting legislation designed to protect minorities.

It is clear that the Racial Privacy Initiative's impact would fall on minorities and people of color. For example, disparate impact discrimination lawsuits in employment and education would be compromised, since these cases normally rely on statistics and data to corroborate other evidence of particular impacts on minorities. Furthermore, because the law denies access to information based on race, public interest groups advocating legislation or policies aimed at to remedying existing discrimination would be unable to formulate the factual/statistical databases for their advocacy work.

This was a concern of those opposing the Racial Privacy Initiative—its effect on plaintiffs trying to show proof of discrimination in civil rights actions. California supporters of the Racial Privacy Initiative believed there is no longer a problem of racism in the country, and characterized it as a positive first step to a colorblind country.[48] However, studies in California show that racism is still quite prevalent, particularly in the housing and job market. For example, in a study of the recognition of voices of people of color: "African-Americans who called about rental units or job openings were told they were no longer available. Yet when a white person called later, suddenly that job opening or unit was available."[49] If the Racial Privacy Initiative had passed, it would be illegal to collect data proving discrimination in these areas.

The experience of France, where the existing legal regime bans the collection of racial data, is also instructive. Law No. 78–17 of 1978 prohibits collecting "any information that shows, directly or indirectly, racial origins, political, philosophical or religious opinions, trade union membership, or moral principles" without either the written consent of the individual or an advance recommendation of the National Commission for Information Technology & Civil Liberties ("CNIL"), which must first be approved by the Conseil d'Etat (Council of State).[50] The conditions which led to the racial riots of 2005 and the severe race-based housing segregation in the country have moved scholars to call for the collection of data, in an effort to be able to measure discrimination and address its ill effects.[51]

What is a Latino Undocumented Student to Do about Racial Privacy Initiatives?

Latino undocumented students live in the contemporary world of public–education—rife with high-stakes testing brought about by the federal mandate of No Child Left Behind (NCLB). Furthermore, they, along with African American students, are heirs of an achievement gap that has persisted nationally since before *Brown*.[52] The educational achievement gap between students is often expressed in the numbers of eighth-graders who will graduate from college with a bachelor's degree, currently 15 percent for Latinos, 17 percent for blacks and 35 percent for whites.[53] In contrast, Latino seventeen-year-olds have math and reading skills that are virtually the same as white thirteen-year-olds.[54] For every 1,000 Latino eighth-grade students, 142 earn a bachelor's degree while 318 white students—more than double the number of Latino students—do so.[55] Without the ability to collect student racial data, schools and children will be operating blindly, unable to direct attention, energy, and resources to closing the achievement gap between undocumented Latino students and other students.

The Racial Privacy Initiative's provisions would frustrate the objectives of the federal NCLB, even though it was designed to not conflict with federal law. Analysts had predicted that:

> Section 32(i) of CRECNO [the Racial Privacy Initiative] allows state and local entities to collect data to comply with federal reporting requirements, although the extent of CRECNO data that states will be allowed to collect under federal laws is unclear.[56]

NCLB mandates that states report testing data on drop-out information by race and ethnicity.[57] However, the California Basic Education Data System that collects enrollment and hiring practice information would be greatly changed by the initiative.[58] Much of the following information would no longer be tracked if the RPI had passed:

(1) High school graduation and drop-out rates by race, ethnicity, color, and national origin for schools not receiving special federal grants under the No Child Left Behind Act;
(2) Student enrollment in AP, honors and special education courses tracked according to race; and
(3) Testing scores disaggregated by race, ethnicity, color, national origin, for tests not required to assess achievement under the No Child Left Behind Act, such as SAT, ACT, and AP exams.

Finally,

> schools and school districts will not be able to use state collected race, ethnicity, color, national origin data in school and classroom integration efforts. ... [It] pushes the constitutional limits further ... because it interferes with a school district's ability to monitor desegregation efforts schools and school districts.[59]

Therefore, even when the Racial Privacy Initiative provided an exception to allow compliance with federal laws, it still could jeopardize efforts to integrate minorities successfully in school systems and close existing achievement gaps where not required by federal law. The prospect that integration will be achieved is even more distant considering that the Supreme Court has recently struck down voluntary school district integration plans, with Chief Justice Roberts asserting a classic colorblind statement that "the way to stop discrimination on the basis of race is to stop discriminating on the basis of race."[60]

Furthermore, some of the problems of a racial privacy initiative would be that there would be no way to know: whether public schools were tracking black or Latino students to remedial classes and white students into Advanced Placement classes; whether there have been any patterns of racial segregation at school or if there has been any school-based law enforcement misconduct based on racial profiling.[61] Thus,

> when deconstructed down to its most basic terms, racial privacy appears to be nothing more than perhaps a strategic label which resonates with sectors of the electorate that find appeal in its superficial promise of a multiracial, yet colorblind, society.[62]

Under a racial privacy initiative, this superficial promise works to the detriment of minority students, who would lose by not being identified when they are tracked in lower or remedial classes when unwarranted. This would be the case since the authorities do not understand "the positive or negative impacts of their policies or programs on ethnic communities including in the area of education, delivery of public services and public assistance."[63] For Latino undocumented students, these ill effects would be further magnified since the students are already part of a "shadow population," which hesitates to identify itself for fear of deportation. Racial privacy legislation would only drive these students further underground, where they would likely not be able to access the education which *Plyler v. Doe* guarantees.

Thus, the answer to the question: What is an undocumented Latino student to do about racial privacy initiatives? is clear—to organize in multiracial coalitions and call attention to the true meaning and intention of these enactments. Similar campaigns have been undertaken with success at the level of individual states regarding the issue of higher education for undocumented students. Similarly, on the issue of racial privacy, parents, teachers, administrators, and others involved in the educational system can also join the students in the struggle to maintain their racial identity to ensure the students' academic success. Scholars have reacted similarly in calling for the government to go in the opposite direction of the Racial Privacy Initiative and actually to "help provide decisionmakers with something that approximates complete data."[64] This endeavor will undoubtedly not be an easy one, as there will likely be resistance to changing the *status quo*. To help elucidate in this endeavor, let us see what Critical Race Theory tells us about such legislation and the motives of its proponents.

Critical Race Theory and Other Theoretical Approaches and Racial Privacy Initiatives

Critical Race Theory ("CRT") is a framework used to examine and challenge the ways that race and racism implicitly and explicitly shape social structures, practices, and discourses. CRT theorists posit that race is a social construct, "a sui generis social phenomenon in which connected systems of meaning serve as the connections between physical features, faces and personal characteristics."[65] Racism is defined as a false belief in white supremacy, a system that holds whites in a higher regard, and maintains the structural subordination of non-white multiple racial and ethnic groups.[66] With its hallmark themes of interest convergence and racial homeostasis, CRT provides a unique tool to analyze race and racism in the United States.[67] Interest convergence holds that the advances of racial minorities only arrive when it is in the interest of the dominant white majority, while racial homeostasis acknowledges the permanence of racism in U.S. society.

Plyler v. Doe was previously analyzed "as a decision embodying the interest convergence covenants in which educational opportunities for minority students exist only when the students' interest and the nation's converge."[68] The educational opportunity afforded to undocumented students by *Plyler* is unfortunately, mostly an inadequate one, which has failed to be a catalyst for change in the lives of these students. The rationale for this view lies in the failure of immigration reform to assure that these students have the opportunity to remain and work legally in this country. This is still the case for undocumented students, who now face colorblindness as a further challenge to their educational achievement in the form of racial privacy initiatives.

As far as the permanence of racism in the U.S., it is implied in the attempted enactment of the California Racial Privacy Initiative, which would have barred consideration of race even in the face of the racial inequalities which still permeate the educational system in this country. As leading Critical Race theorist Cheryl Harris has noted, comparing the intent of the racial privacy initiatives to slavery: "We cannot erase racism by erasing race any more than our eighteenth and nineteenth century predecessors could eradicate the evils of slavery by seeking to eradicate slaves."[69] Similarly, we cannot erase racism against undocumented students by eradicating them via racial privacy legislation.

Furthermore, when analyzing what justice would require under John Rawls' philosophical view, scholar Anita Allen has found that

> in the United States, we may live more proudly and independently precisely because government officials lawfully possess socially, economically and politically relevant race data about individuals. In the present context, barring discrimination based on race, not barring public race data collection, is the way to go.[70]

Thus, Rawls' veil of ignorance should not be applied where there is still inequality and not the perfectly well-ordered and ideal society that his theory requires. In fact, Allen has found that "being discriminated against arbitrarily on the basis of race clearly violates Rawlsian principles."[71] Finally, it is

Allen's view that contemporary society is not a just one for racial minorities: further, "it is pretty clear from reading Rawls that he did not want race to matter in just societies. But I see nothing in Rawls to rule out race-conscious programs that stand to benefit the least advantaged in society."[72]

Finally, the passage of a racial privacy initiative would further the subordination of these students whose demographic profile we have previously identified: poor, Latino, and vulnerable due to their irregular immigration status. Such passage would directly contravene the antisubordination principle, which finds it inappropriate for certain groups in society to have subordinated status because of their lack of power in society as a whole, and under which "both facially differentiating and facially neutral policies are invidious only if they perpetuate racial or sexual hierarchy."[73] This antisubordination principle, coined by Professor Ruth Kolker as a tool for equal protection jurisprudence,[74] and now also part of the Critical Race Theory project,[75] offers an additional lens with which to understand the consequences of the passage of a racial privacy initiative. The erasing of race via the adoption of a racial privacy initiative would perpetuate the existing racial hierarchy where the impoverished Latino undocumented student is found subordinated at the bottom of U.S. society, in a sense, as part of a lower caste.

Therefore, as seen previously, "racial privacy appears to be nothing more than perhaps a strategic label which resonates with sectors of the electorate that find appeal in its superficial promise of a multiracial, yet colorblind, society."[76] In doing so, it reaffirms the Critical Race Theory theme of the permanence of racism, and in particular the permanence of the racialization and inequality of undocumented students. These students experience the permanent inequality in face of substandard school systems which are obligated to educate them but then will not be able to assist them to find any lawful employment to give meaning to their education. This is the case, as the immigration law system has failed to account for the undocumented students' achievements to grant them the opportunity to work legally and become productive members of the U.S. society.

The Fourth Amendment and *Plyler*: Immigration Enforcement at Schools?

Consider now another potential danger after *Plyler* for undocumented children who attend U.S. schools. Of late, undocumented children and their parents nationwide have become apprehensive about the possibility of immigration raids and immigration enforcement inside and in the vicinity of schoolhouses. While this most recent round of immigration enforcement has mostly taken place in the workplace context, undocumented K–12 students and their parents have experienced fear of indiscriminate immigration enforcement, which might lead to raids at schools. Following massive workplace raids in their communities, some parents have been reluctant to send their children to school because they believe that immigration officials may raid the school building at any time. The actions of these parents run afoul of most state compulsory attendance laws, which require students below the age of eighteen to attend school. Whether warranted or not, these concerns need to be analyzed.

This climate of fear of raids appears to contravene the mandate of *Plyler v. Doe* which requires schools to provide education to undocumented students living in their school districts. As a result of this mandate, school officials have a role to play in ensuring that undocumented students are able to attend school free of this fear. Thus, this chapter analyzes: (1) under what circumstances immigration agents can conduct school building raids and not run afoul of the Fourth Amendment, which prohibits unreasonable searches and seizures, and (2) under what circumstances school personnel can decline to cooperate with these raids, even to the point of refusing to share student records with these officials. Thus, this chapter examines the Fourth Amendment as it applies to noncitizens, with all its policy implications, as well as the ability of *Plyler* to protect students from these raids and to afford school officials the opportunity to stay out of any immigration enforcement actions that occur at their schools. This analysis has a real-world impact on undocumented students and their parents to the extent that some courts have curtailed the Fourth Amendment's applicability to some undocumented persons[77] based on the Supreme Court's "substantial connections" test, which we discuss later in this chapter. Furthermore, as a practical matter, undocumented persons are less likely to seek vindication of any applicable Fourth Amendment rights either defensively (through the exclusionary rule) or offensively (through *Bivens* actions), two remedies that we will analyze later on. However, for now let us turn initially to actual cases of immigration enforcement at schools in order to understand the scope of the problem.

Actual Cases of Schools as Locations for Immigration Enforcement: Past Cases of INS and Border Patrol Presence at Public Schools

In 2004, Border Patrol agents detained three Mexican students at Del Norte High School in Albuquerque, New Mexico.[78] An Albuquerque police officer had turned the students over to Border Patrol agents, after he saw them passing keys through the school fence. He made a mistake in judging the perimeters of the school and apprehended the three students. The parents of the three were not detained.[79] Following this experience, the city of Albuquerque implemented an official policy that school grounds should be "safe havens" for undocumented students.[80] The policy prior to 2006 was unofficial, and stated that school employees were not to investigate the immigration status of the students. Under the new policy, school officials are to consult with district lawyers prior to complying with requests from immigration enforcement officials. Officials also are not to make copies of immigration documents.

The official policy was a result of a settlement between the district and the Mexican American Legal Defense and Education Fund ("MALDEF"). MALDEF sued on behalf of the students after the Albuquerque police officer had turned them over to Border Patrol agents, after suspecting their documents were false. However, despite the fact that the boys were seized, interrogated, and searched by the Albuquerque police, while exercising the right guaranteed by *Plyler* to attend school, the Border Patrol deported the students to Mexico.

The need for a classroom safe haven policy is evident from this. The number of juveniles in New Mexico who have had encounters with the U.S. Border Patrol is high. For example, for the 2004 fiscal year, 5,715 juveniles were apprehended in that state.[81] Furthermore, a large number, approximately 2,800 of the students enrolled in the Albuquerque Public Schools, are noncitizens.[82] Given these figures, it is not hard to imagine noncitizen undocumented juvenile students apprehended, and likely finding themselves detained like the ones above, in or nearby the schools they attend. Undocumented students and their families, as well as the educational system itself, would be well served if the policy in Albuquerque, New Mexico would be extended to all schools nationwide.

One of the earliest lawsuits regarding school immigration enforcement took place in El Paso, Texas for activity undertaken in the vicinity of Bowie High School. Immigration agents frequently drove over football fields and the baseball diamond, entered football locker rooms, and used binoculars to watch flag girls practicing on campus.[83] The following is language from the injunction which settled the case in favor of the plaintiff Latinos who had been subjected to school immigration enforcement based on their race:

> The INS has repeatedly and illegally stopped, questioned, detained, frisked, arrested, and searched Plaintiffs and numerous other students from the Bowie High School District. El Paso Border Patrol Agents have subjected Plaintiffs and others to indecent comments, obscene gestures, and humiliation in the presence of their co-workers, friends, family, and relevant community. The proffered evidence strongly supports this Court in its conclusion that the illegal and abusive conduct of the El Paso Border Patrol was directed against Plaintiffs, staff, and residents in the Bowie High School District solely because of their mere immutable appearances as Hispanics.[84]

This has been the experience in the past with school immigration enforcement. In addition, there has been renewed nationwide immigration enforcement following congressional failure at immigration reform and recent immigration raids.

Current Immigration Enforcement at Schools

In Santa Fe, New Mexico, Immigration and Customs Enforcement ("ICE") agents arrested a father while picking up his fourth-grade daughter from school.[85] The state police indicated that ICE had received an anonymous tip that the father had engaged in sexual conduct with a minor. ICE ultimately found that the allegation was unfounded, but during his detention, discovered the father was undocumented. He was later deported, even though he was cleared of the original criminal allegations leading to his arrest. The manner and timing of the arrest were criticized by school and city officials because it was conducted while other parents were picking up their children. School officials also worried that ICE might be expanding the illegal immigration crackdown in Santa Fe to the public schools. The mayor and city police said that ICE should have notified local authorities of its operations.

In Roswell, New Mexico, ICE deported Karina Acosta, a high school senior who was five months pregnant, after a local police officer took her out of class on charges based on a traffic ticket she had received a few days before. Apparently, the young woman never provided proper identification after being cited for a parking violation and for driving without a license.[86] The police officer detained Acosta and contacted U.S. immigration officials about her undocumented status. The police officer who removed Acosta from class was a Student Resource Officer (SRO). SROs are police officers who work within the school to provide safety on school grounds. The assistant superintendent expressed displeasure with the incident and explained that the Acosta was taken into custody without the school's knowledge. Subsequently the local police department and school district agreed to have all SROs removed from Roswell schools.

Finally, schoolhouse immigration enforcement took place in Otero County, New Mexico, when sheriffs took a handcuffed undocumented parent to his children's school in order to seize his five children, ages six to fifteen.[87] This parent was arrested without probable cause outside his own home, as he approached to pick up his wife in order to go to their children's school. Following a civil rights lawsuit, the Otero County Sheriff's office settled the case and entered into an agreement prohibiting sheriff's deputies from detaining, investigating children (under eighteen) at in schools, school parking lots, and on open fields.[88] The language of the agreement provides that:

> All children residing in the United States have the right to attend school. Deputies will not engage in stopping, questioning, detaining investigating or arresting minor children (under 18) on any immigration related

matter while at, in or on church, church property, or a public school ground or property, including adjacent parking lots or open fields.[89]

Immigration Enforcement Current Implications for Undocumented Students Even outside of the School Context

"Will my mother be there when I get home?"[90] This is the question that a young California girl, from a community affected by raids asked recently when leaving for school. It shows the dire consequences for children of increased immigration enforcement, even when outside of the school.

Since early 2006, the United States has experienced an unprecedented increase in immigration raids throughout the nation. New Bedford, Massachusetts; Greeley, Colorado; Contra Costa, California; Postville, Iowa; Grand Island, Nebraska; and Garden City, New York are now familiar names because of immigration raids which have taken place at these locations. There are serious implications for immigration enforcement by federal immigration agents even when such enforcement does not take place at school.

It is common for some undocumented parents in recent times to fear sending their children to school because they believe that immigration officials may raid the school building at any time.[91] Let us consider some real cases that have taken place nationwide.

For example, in 2007, "rumors ... spread about immigration agents coming to the school to conduct raids," in Redwood City, California following early morning raids in apartment buildings and other dwellings.[92] In fact, at least one parent kept her children from school for fear that they would be deported following a raid at school. Greg Land, the principal of a local elementary school, said "we called out and told then, look they haven't been on campus. I even consulted with the district, they are not allowed on campus."[93]

Further immigration enforcement activity has continued in northern California in both the Berkeley Unified School District and the Oakland Unified School District. During a day in May 2008 when students were taking standardized tests, ICE agents were conducting raids in neighborhoods near schools and parking their vehicles for hours across from schools. As a result, "[s]cores of undocumented parents began to panic as early as 7:30 a.m. May 6, as word got around that ICE vehicles were parked near schools in East Oakland and South Berkeley."[94]

In fact, in Berkeley, "[p]arents were so afraid to come to the school, they called family members and neighbors, whoever had papers, to pick up their children."[95] By noon, the district had received so many calls from concerned parents that it acted in response to these concerns by communicating with parents via phone messages both in English and in Spanish.[96] Specifically, Berkeley school district Superintendent Bill Huyet sent out an automated phone message to all parents notifying them that a Latino family had been picked up but he reassured them that the district would "not allow any child to be taken away from the school."[97] ICE reacted by noting "that the agency is mindful of the sensitivities associated with schools"[98] and that "[a] school is not a place we would routinely conduct an enforcement operation for a variety of reasons."[99] The question, of course, remains what exactly ICE consider not to be routine, so that schoolchildren can be directly targeted by ICE.

For students at the Berkeley school district that day, the results of the raids were clearly cause for concern. The undocumented children experienced the stress of not knowing if their families were taken by ICE, of worrying how they were going to get home and if they would be picked up by ICE on their way home. Even for the U.S. citizen children, the experience was noteworthy. Here are some of their stories, both from a student perspective and a parent's perspective:

> Berkeley High senior Chase Stern said he was taking an Advanced Placement test May 6, when he noticed that his classmates were fidgeting in their seats and seemed distracted. He soon found out that the Latino students were receiving text messages and phone calls from family members, warning them that Immigration and Customs Enforcement (ICE) officers were nearby, and that they should be cautious and find their way home because family members could not pick them up.[100]

> Larry Bensky's fifth-grade daughter came home from Berkeley's LeConte Elementary School on Tuesday saying she had no homework because it was "ICE week," which meant "they" were going after the families of the Latino children. "She doesn't know what ICE is," Bensky said. "She doesn't know what targeted is. You can imagine it's very disturbing for children that from one day to the next that a child they sit next to could be kidnapped, arrested and deported."[101]

> School officials also had to take action on the same day in Oakland, once they

> were receiving similar calls from concerned parents and community members that ICE agency vehicles had been spotted near four Oakland schools, including Esperanza Elementary, where parents say they saw agents parked on International Blvd, 98th, 95th, and San Leandro Boulevard, a four block radius surrounding the school.[102] ... [The officials] sent out emails to all school district staff about what was happening and reminding them that the school district's commitment was to educate all students, documented or otherwise. The email also advised staff not to facilitate any immigration enforcement actions.[103]

ICE denied the reports that they were targeting schools on "this" day.[104] ICE's language of "this" day makes a person wonder again, what would happen to undocumented children on all other days. In fact, at least one Oakland school district employee "dismissed ICE's assertion that there was no targeting of any schools, saying: 'They are targeting schools and we are watching them do it.'"[105] Tying the immigration enforcement activity to the failed immigration reform, California state Senator Don Perata, D-Oakland, asserted: "There should be an immediate freeze on ICE raids directed at schoolchildren while legislation aiming to fix immigration is considered."[106]

In May of 2008, ICE raided a meatpacking plant in Postville, Iowa. This left the superintendent of Postville Community School District scrambling to ensure children whose parents were detained had someone to care for them.[107] The next day, approximately 150 Latino students did not attend school. A month before the workplace raid, the Iowa Division of Labor Services served the Postville School District with a subpoena "to provide detailed personal information about Postville students." The subpoena requested Social Security numbers and telephone numbers of all current students and some former ones. It also demanded the names of children working part time at two apartment buildings owned at one time by a school guidance counselor. The school counselor subsequently sold the apartment to the raided plant's CEO. Furthermore, one teacher from Postville was on a field trip at the county courthouse with her students when she was alerted to the raid. The school told her not to come back because some of the students were undocumented. She explained that after a few hours she was allowed to come back, but the school told her to be prepared to be stopped by federal officials. The school expected her to keep any official from boarding the bus.

Another workplace raid that affected school officials and students took place in Grand Island Public Schools District in Nebraska.[108] The school was able to use the district's computerized school record to identify children likely to have both parents arrested by federal agents. Several schools were designated as triage locations where the 165 students concerned could go to receive help. Teachers waited with the students until they were all picked up and accounted for. It took time for the school district to rebuild trust with the families affected by the raid. Eventually, nearly all of the 165 students returned.

In another example, almost 200 students did not attend the first day of school in August 2007 at Kendall-Whittier, an elementary school in Oklahoma.[109] The reason for this significant drop in attendance was House Bill 1804, also known as the Oklahoma Taxpayer and Citizen Protection Act of 2007. It is an anti-illegal immigration statute passed by the state legislature requiring all state and local agencies to verify the citizenship status of job applicants and limiting eligibility for state driver's licenses and ID cards to citizens, nationals, and legal immigrants. While this new legislation does not appear to apply to schools, it has had ripple effects in the undocumented community. Furthermore, the law makes it a felony to "conceal, harbor, or shelter" undocumented residents. There have been instances of teachers being concerned about transporting undocumented students on field trips this law.

Furthermore, rumors spread that immigration agents would be patrolling school grounds waiting to pick up undocumented parents. In an effort to ease tensions, the principal and school staff telephoned parents and visited homes to assure the parents and students that they would be safe on school grounds. By late August, their efforts paid off and attendance was almost 100 percent. However, parents began taking their children out of school and moving away by fall, most likely because House Bill 1804 went into effect in November 2007. Ultimately, school officials reported fewer parents turned out for the annual "Preview Night" in Tulsa, Oklahoma after the passage of House Bill 1804.

Then on March 6, 2007, ICE raided Michael Bianco, Inc., a garment company in New Bedford, Massachusetts.[110] A school district was again confronted with a serious disruption of the educational system. Many of the undocumented workers apprehended had children in the local schools. The superintendent for equity and diversity, Fred Fuentes, had to try to reassure that the remaining families who were not affected that they would not be targeted next.[111] He spoke daily with principals, and worked with community groups. Such a chilling effect would likely have caused some parents to withdraw children from the schools.

Immigration law enforcement officials insist that they would like to avoid immigration enforcement in schools and have policies to that effect. The U.S. Border Patrol Handbook apparently includes a policy which "requires written approval from the chief patrol agent or deputy chief patrol agent prior to any enforcement-related activities at schools or places of worship."[112] It also appears that ICE has a policy of "strongly discouraging arresting fugitives at schools, hospitals, or places of worship, unless the alien poses an immediate threat to national security or the community."[113] Some ICE Service Districts have specific policies indicating that ICE raids on schools are prohibited without specific authorization.[114] However, it is evident that the proscriptions are not followed, as evidenced by the earlier examples in New Mexico and Texas.

Following this examination of the ongoing immigration enforcement as it affects undocumented students, let us now review a hypothetical to help assess the basic contours of the Fourth Amendment's applicability to those who are not United States citizens, in order to ascertain whether undocumented persons, particularly students, can challenge these searches and seizures.

A Hypothetical

Imagine that a principal at East Dakota High School is having trouble communicating with parents of Latino children who are not in the United States lawfully. Letters are often returned to the school because some of the addresses are wrong. Even when letters arrive at their homes, the English language makes them difficult for the parents to understand. After exploring what alternatives are available to improve communication, the principal sends a letter home in Spanish, inviting the Latino parents to a meeting one weekday evening. Somehow another parent in the school gets word of the meeting. This parent does not like the fact there are "all these Mexicans" infiltrating the school district. He often protests illegal immigration, and thinks that "all immigrants are criminals." Thus, driven by his strong feelings, he tips off the Immigration and Customs Service ("ICE") that there are many "illegal aliens" who are coming on that particular night to the school. The night of the parent's meeting, an ICE official arrives at the school and starts to walk around. Sure enough, within a short time, he sees several persons of Latino appearance through the cafeteria windows. He then walks into the building, goes to the cafeteria, and begins asking the parents questions. The principal has not yet arrived at the meeting. During the questioning, one parent admits to being in the country illegally, and another parent claims he is legal, but does not have the documentation in his possession. Both parents are arrested on the spot and taken to a detention center.

If the parents are deported or removed following this encounter, can they move to suppress or exclude the evidence of their unlawful presence if found in violation of the Fourth Amendment? Does the Fourth Amendment even apply to those who are present in the United States without legal authorization?

After concluding the Fourth Amendment does apply to undocumented persons, this part of the chapter analyzes how the opportunity for public education provided in *Plyler* may protect undocumented persons while at school. While *Plyler* has never been used by court in a reported case to limit ICE's power, there are several events in the process of stopping an alien, where *Plyler*'s effect needs to be analyzed, so as to understand how its consideration would fit in to the existing scheme of Fourth Amendment law.

If an ICE agent arrives at a school event, such as a PTA meeting, and asks parents to disclose their immigration status, it is possible that such information could be used to make an arrest if the parent admitted he was unlawfully present in the U.S. or he gave the agent an expired immigration document. Generally, such evidence cannot be suppressed via the exclusionary rule at the deportation or removal hearing.[115] The rule is used to suppress evidence unlawfully obtained by law enforcement in a criminal trial.[116] The Supreme Court has determined that use of the exclusionary rule in a deportation hearing would be a cost rather than a benefit.[117] However, a narrow exception remains, which would allow the exclusionary rule to be invoked to exclude the evidence obtained in violation of the Fourth Amendment.[118] This exception would include "egregious violations" of the Constitution, or violations an immigration agent "know or should know would be in violation of the constitution." It is unclear whether ICE agents would know that the children of undocumented parents have the right to access public education. Further, because only a few cases employ the "egregiousness" standard with respect to seizures, it is unclear whether the denial or deterring of constitutional right derived *Plyler* would reach such a standard. Even without meeting the "egregious" standard, the public policy of the need to educate undocumented children may be strong enough to shift the cost-benefit analysis towards a net benefit that the exclusionary rule would be permitted in the school context.[119]

What remedies lie for undocumented parents and students when immigration agents target schools and commit Fourth Amendment violations? These would include the use of the entrapment by estoppel doctrine, and requests for relief in the form of *Bivens* damages (see pages 158–159) and under the Alien Tort Claims Act ("ATCA"). Let us turn to the question we begin with Does the Fourth Amendment apply to the undocumented?

The Fourth Amendment and the Undocumented

The text of the Fourth Amendment to the U.S. Constitution provides:

> The right of the people to be secure in their persons, houses, papers, and effects, against unreasonable searches and seizures, shall not be violated, and no Warrants shall issue, but upon probable cause, supported by Oath or affirmation, and particularly describing the place to be searched, and the persons or things to be seized.[120]

The Fourth Amendment protects the right of people of the United States, so it would appear to encompass all people, the inhabitants of this country. This would include both lawfully admitted noncitizens and undocumented persons, as well as of course, U.S. citizens. As Fourth Amendment law is largely circumscribed by case law, a textual reading of the Constitution needs to be followed with analysis of court rulings, starting with U.S. Supreme Court precedent, then federal and state court legal rulings as well. While particular state constitutions may afford additional Fourth Amendment protections and state constitutional law may be in some circumstances be relevant to interpreting federal constitutional law, this chapter will only address federal case law and leaves state-by-state Fourth Amendment potential protections of undocumented persons as an area for future research.

The question of whether courts have found that the Fourth Amendment extends to those who are not United States citizens and are present in the country unlawfully is answered initially by considering: Who are the people to whom the amendment refers? This is a question that has not been fully settled by the United States Supreme Court. The closest the Court came to answering this question is the case of *U.S. v. Verdugo-Urquidez*.[121] Let us look at the details and ruling in the case to understand exactly what the Court did and did not say about the Fourth Amendment as it applies to those who are not U.S. citizens.

In *Verdugo-Urquidez*, agents from the federal Drug Enforcement Administration, in cooperation with Mexican law enforcement, made a warrantless search of a home in Mexico and seized documents that established the defendant's involvement in drug smuggling operations.[122] When the defendant Verdugo-Urquidez moved to suppress the evidence because it was obtained in violation of his Fourth Amendment rights, the U.S. Supreme Court ruled that the Fourth Amendment did not apply to him. The Court reasoned that defendant Verdugo-Urquidez was not a member of "the people," who are entitled to the protections against unreasonable searches and seizures.[123] After analyzing the text and history of the Fourth Amendment, the Court concluded that "the people" are "a class of persons who are part of a national community or who have otherwise developed sufficient connection with the country to be considered part of that community."[124] In the Court's view, "[a]liens receive constitutional protections when they have come within the territory of the United States and developed substantial connections with the country."[125]

The defendant in *Verdugo-Urquidez* was involuntarily present in the United States because the Mexican police had turned him over to the U.S. Border Patrol once the drugs were found. It was the Border Patrol then that brought him to American soil. Thus, the Court found that although defendant Verdugo-Urquidez was present in the United States lawfully, his involuntary presence did not "indicate any substantial connection with our country."[126] This is the substantial connection test which courts since have used to determine the applicability of the Fourth Amendment to noncitizens. However, the Supreme Court left open the question of how the *Verdugo-Urquidez* analysis requiring a substantial connection would apply to undocumented persons who live here on a regular basis. Furthermore, the Court did not provide a definition of substantial connection in the opinion itself.

Critiques of *Verdugo-Urquidez*, including Dissent and Concurrence

As *Verdugo-Urquidez* is the only U.S. Supreme Court case on the topic, its rationale regarding the applicability of the Fourth Amendment needs to be fully scrutinized. There are three main criticisms to *Verdugo-Urquidez*: (1) the case by its own facts applies only to extraterritorial searches, which are those take place outside of the U.S. (such as the one which took place in Mexico in *Verdugo-Urquidez);* (2) the Supreme Court did not speak with a united voice on this topic, as the plurality opinion stands for a limited proposition, and there was strong dissent; and (3) the Court's definition of "the people" follows a textual analysis and misses many other factors which would suggest defining the word differently. These critiques are embodied in the dissent and concurrence to the case, and they will be examined in turn.

The initial criticism of *Verdugo-Urquidez* is present in the dissent of Justices William J. Brennan, Jr. and Thurgood Marshall. They espoused a theory of mutuality, and objected to the Court's holding that "although foreign nationals must abide by our laws even when in their own countries, our Government need not abide by the Fourth Amendment when it investigates them for violations of our laws."[127]

Conversely, the Court's plurality opinion focused mostly on a social contract theory, or the view that the greater connection a person shows to the United States by assuming the responsibilities of member of society, the more benefits United States society should grant him or her. The mutuality approach favored by Justices Brennan and Marshall focuses rather on what the government can do to promote good behavior in society. Thus, if the government wishes persons to develop more significant connections to society, then it should extend benefits early on to encourage them to develop those ties. Thus, under this approach, no distinction between "persons" or "people" would exist, and the duty to obey laws in itself would be sufficient enough to trigger the benefit of the protection of the Fourth Amendment. Certainly, unlawfully present noncitizens may be considered as not upholding the law because they are in violation of the federal immigration law by either overstaying their visas or entering the U.S. surreptitiously. Yet the fact remains that they could still be upholding other U.S. state and federal laws. Thus, it is unresolved as to which laws must be followed to acquire enough of a "substantial connection."

The dissenters further argued that noncitizens have constitutional rights, and cited President James Madison's recognition that, "[i]t does not follow, because aliens are not parties to the Constitution, as citizens are parties to it, that, whilst, they actually conform to it, they have no right to its protection ..."[128] The dissent also criticized the significant connection test as ambiguous and unclear by stating that: "[t]he Court articulates a 'sufficient connection' test, but then refuses to discuss the underlying principles upon which any interpretation of that must rest."[129] The dissent rightly points out that there are still many unanswered questions with respect to the substantial connection test. Among these are how "voluntary" is defined and what "significant means."[130] The Court noted that lawful but involuntary presence in the U.S. failed the test, while in dicta it seemed to hint that unlawful but voluntary presence might pass the test.[131] Thus, a noncitizen who has overstayed his or her visa would qualify under the "substantial connection" test, whereas one who surreptitiously crossed the border would not qualify because he or she did not ever avail him or herself of the government's law and accept responsibility as a member of U.S. society. At least one lower federal court has taken this view. In an unpublished opinion in *United States v. Ullah*, a case which will be discussed further below, the court found that a noncitizen who had never been lawfully admitted to the United States could not claim substantial connection under the Fourth Amendment.[132]

Further criticism of *Verdugo-Urquidez* is based mostly on Justice Anthony Kennedy's concurring opinion, in which he asserted that "[i]f the search had occurred in a residence within the United States, I have little doubt that the full protections of the Fourth Amendment would apply."[133] Justice Kennedy was restating what had been understood to be true prior to this case—that the Fourth Amendment applied to those who were unlawfully present in the United States. This assumption came from an earlier case in which the Supreme Court held that the Fourth Amendment's exclusionary rule did not apply in deportation proceedings.[134] If the Fourth Amendment did not apply to noncitizens, then there would have been no need to exclude from deportation hearings evidence seized in violation of this amendment.

Justice Kennedy's concurring opinion is also instructive because he rejected the plurality's interpretation of the word "people." Unlike Justice William Rehnquist, who authored the plurality opinion, Justice Kennedy instead took the view that the "right of the people" phrase in the Fourth Amendment was just a form of diction, meant to underscore the importance of the right.[135] Thus, in his view, it was not intended to restrict the protections of the Fourth Amendment to specific groups of people.[136] Justice Kennedy explained:

> For somewhat similar reasons, I cannot place any weight on the reference to "the people" in the Fourth Amendment as a source of restricting its protections. With respect, I submit these words do not detract from its force or its reach. Given the history of our Nation's concern over warrantless and unreasonable searches, explicit recognition of "the right of the people" to Fourth Amendment protection may be interpreted to underscore the importance of the right, rather than to restrict the category of persons who may assert it. The restrictions that the United States must observe with reference to aliens beyond its territory or jurisdiction depend, as a consequence, on general principles of interpretation, not on an inquiry as to who formed the Constitution or a construction that some rights are mentioned as being those of "the people."[137]

Professor Victor Romero has proposed a framework for understanding and approaching "substantial connections" by pointing out a parallel development in tort premises liability law away from strict categories and toward a rule of reasonableness.[138] He analogizes the connections that different types of aliens can have with the United States to premises liability classifications such as invitee, licensee and trespasser.[139] Invitees are permissibly on the property for the landowner's benefit and to these entrants, the owner would owe a duty of reasonable care. A licensee is a person who is on the property permissibly for his or her own benefit. A trespasser is someone who is on the property without permission. The landowner has a lesser duty towards trespassers and licensees, and is liable only if he acts maliciously towards these last two entrants.

Just as noncitizens vary in their degrees of connection to this country, with a legal permanent resident having the strongest connection to the United States, an invitee would have the strongest connection with the landowner.[140] Just as the landowner would have the strongest duty of care to an invitee, the U.S. government would apply the greatest constitutional protection to the legal permanent resident. A step down from this parallel would be a "licensee" analogous to "legal nonimmigrant." To this lawfully admitted noncitizen that is in the country temporarily, the substantial connection under *United States v. Esparza Mendoza*, a lower federal court ruling which will be discussed in more detail below, would likely be enough to afford Fourth Amendment protections. At the lowest rung would be the "trespasser," and the "undocumented immigrant."[141] At the lowest level no "substantial connection" would exist. Such a person would have to rely on an "egregious" due process exception, if afforded any protection at all.[142] This sliding scale of substantial connection has some drawbacks. Professor Romero acknowledges these distinctions were unworkable and caused excessive complications in premises liability law and were abolished in many states. Thus, states have abolished these distinctions and require that everyone be treated with "reasonable care." Consequently, such distinctions could be just as troubling in the immigration context. Therefore, Professor Romero would apply a unitary approach which would evenhandedly grant Fourth Amendment rights to all noncitizens, whether undocumented, lawfully present, or temporarily in the United States.

Verdugo-Urquidez and its Progeny: Lower Court Findings regarding the Applicability of the Fourth Amendment to the Undocumented and What Will Constitute a "Substantial Connection" to the United States

In the situation where a noncitizen either enters the country by crossing the border without inspection, or overstays a visa, and then works regularly, maintains a home, pays taxes, builds credit, and the like, all within the United States, does he or she have the substantial connections so that the Fourth

Amendment will apply to him or her? Some lower courts have found a substantial connection in the voluntary acceptance of societal obligations during periodic lawful border crossings and lawful temporary entry to the U.S.[143] The case law as far as those present in the United States unlawfully following *Verdugo-Urquidez* will now be analyzed.

To date, only a handful of lower federal courts have addressed the substantial connection of an undocumented noncitizen under the Fourth Amendment. On balance, in two cases the courts have analyzed the substantial connection to find that the Fourth Amendment protects the undocumented and in three cases they have found the opposite. Furthermore, two federal trial courts and two federal courts of appeals have presupposed that undocumented persons possess Fourth Amendment rights.[144] Thus, there is no strong trend either way evidenced in the case law, so the cases will be briefly reviewed in order to understand the courts' rationales.

In *United States v. Esparza-Mendoza*, the Northern District of Utah found against the defendant, who had reentered the United States after being previously deported for cocaine possession and then alleged his Fourth Amendment rights were violated because he was "detained and forced to present his identification without probable cause or even reasonable suspicion."[145] In the court's view, the defendant could not have "sufficient connections" to the United States because the framers of the Constitution would not have treated a criminal noncitizen as part of the community.[146] The court reasoned that "it would be perverse to give greater constitutional rights to those aliens who have most flagrantly flouted the law by unlawfully returning to the United States for the longest periods of time."[147]

When the case was appealed to the Tenth Circuit Court of Appeals, the court expressly left unanswered the question as to whether the Fourth Amendment applied to previously deported felons who reenter the United States.[148] The court held that the police officer's questioning of the defendant's identity was consensual, and therefore, was not a violation of the Fourth Amendment.[149]

Predictably, advocates on both sides of the litigation had opinions as to the court's decision in the case. The ACLU's Immigration Rights Project welcomed the Tenth Circuit's decision, arguing that the opinion confirms that undocumented persons are protected by the Fourth Amendment.[150] In its view, since the court clearly indicated that the defendant's rights were not violated, then the defendant in fact, has Fourth Amendment rights. Others are not as optimistic and saw the decision as posing danger to all. In the words of a practicing attorney in the area: "The Fourth Amendment issue aside ... the 10th Circuit's decision is troubling because it expands the legal standard when determining the legality of police-citizen encounters."[151] This attorney further explained that, "[b]y ruling this way, the court has completely expanded, in what I believe to be an inappropriate manner, somebody's right to terminate a police-citizen encounter by specifically declining to cooperate."[152] In the end, defendant Esparza-Mendoza pled guilty to one count of illegal reentry of a deported alien and was sentenced to seventeen months in prison, to be followed by immediate removal from the United States.[153]

In *United States v. Guitterez,* a lower federal court reversed its initial finding that an undocumented person had no Fourth Amendment rights as he was lacking in significant voluntary connection.[154] Applying a four-factor test, the court held instead that the undocumented person had standing under Fourth Amendment to assert a claim.[155] Among the factors the court considered were the unworkability and unpredictability of the *Verdugo-Urquidez* holding.

In *United States v. Atienzo,* another lower federal trial court, the Central District Court of Utah also confronted the issue as to whether those illegally in the United States are entitled to Fourth Amendment protection.[156] In this automobile stop case, police officers had pulled over the defendant for having a faulty rear license plate light. They conducted a pat-down search of the defendant that produced a wallet with a fake Social Security card. Based on this evidence they then searched another car and a trailer, which produced cash, firearms, and drugs. Judge Paul Cassell, the trial court judge, distinguished this set of facts from *Esparza-Mendoza.* In that case, the defendant was a previously deported felon. In *Atienzo,* the defendant was not a felon. Thus, Judge Cassell found that the holding in *Esparza-Mendoza* only applied to felons.[157] The court buttressed its argument, suggesting that the *Esparza-Mendoza* court had expressly reserved judgment as to aliens who were not felons, but who were in the country illegally.[158] Further, the court explained that because the defendant paid taxes and child support, he had "accepted some societal obligations" and thus had a substantial connection to the U.S., and was entitled to the protection of the Fourth Amendment.[159] Yet, Judge Cassell recognized that the federal government had not fully briefed the substantial connections issue to the court. Thus, the holding in *Atienzo* is limited by this lack of briefing to the court, so that the court ruled with less than complete information. Furthermore, the fact that this is an unpublished opinion also limits its precedential value.

In another unpublished opinion, in *United States v. Ullah,*[160] a lower federal court in New York found that a person who has never been lawfully admitted in the U.S. cannot be found to have the substantial connections required by *Verdugo-Urquidez* and will not be afforded Fourth Amendment protections. No other rationale was adduced in this case, which also lacks precedential value based on its unpublished status.

The Sixth Circuit Court of Appeals has recently found that an undocumented person's Fourth Amendment rights were violated when he was held for an unreasonably long time during a traffic stop. In *United States v. Urrieta,* following a traffic stop on a Tennessee highway while traveling with an expired license plate, the defendant was charged as an illegal alien in possession of firearms and of unlawful identification documents.[161] The district court had denied the defendant's motion to suppress the evidence found in the search of his vehicle conducted while he was detained by a police officer. After pulling the defendant over, the police officer searched a national database to determine whether Urrieta was lawfully present in the United States.[162] The defendant's name did not appear on the database. This absence suggested he was unlawfully present in the country, but it also confirmed that the defendant had not been previously deported. Indeed, at that point, reentry after deportation would have been the only immigration violation that law enforcement had authority to enforce.[163] The police officer subsequently asked the defendant several questions about his immigration status and that of his passengers.[164] Next, the officer asked to search the defendant's car, and once the defendant consented, he recovered the firearms and documents. The Court of Appeals held that the extended detention of the defendant was unlawful and in violation of the Fourth Amendment.[165]

In May 2008, another federal district court decided another case regarding whether an undocumented person had sufficient substantial connections with the United States to make a Fourth Amendment claim. The court in *United States v. Gutierrez-Casada*[166] held that the defendant lacked a reasonable expectation of privacy from governmental intrusion in the residence where he was found. The defendant was convicted for possession of narcotics and ordered deported. Following his deportation, the defendant unlawfully reentered the United States. Some factors the court recognized as important in determining whether an individual has a privacy interest are whether the person was "legitimately on or in possession of the premises, the history of the Fourth Amendment, and society's recognition of permissible conduct in a particular place."

The defendant in *United States v. Gutierrez-Casada* did not have an expectation of privacy even in his own home because he was present unlawfully in the United States. The court stated that "[a]lthough deportation proceedings are not criminal in nature, defendant, by virtue of having been convicted of an aggravated felony rendering him subject to deportation, has a diminished privacy expectation by virtue of his criminal status alone."[167] The court found the defendant could not expect to be free from police intrusion in his home after being "legitimately excluded from that place" via his deportation order.[168] Yet in another case, *United States v. Guitterez*,[169] a lower federal court interpreted *Verdugo-Urquidez* as a plurality opinion, finding that an illegal alien need not demonstrate a "connection" with this country as a prerequisite to asserting the shelter of the Fourth Amendment.

Finally, courts have discussed what constitutes a substantial connection in *Martinez-Aguero v. Gonzalez*,[170] and *American Immigration Lawyers*

Association v. Reno.[171] In these cases two federal trial courts concluded that regular visits to United States would not constitute substantial connection.

Unlike the defendants and noncitizens in these last cases, undocumented schoolchildren are authorized by *Plyler* to attend public school. The children have not been previously excluded from the schoolhouse or indeed, most likely even from the United States. Therefore, arguably they have a greater privacy interest than someone who has been previously deported and convicted of a felony as in *Urrieta* and *Gutierrez-Casada*. They reside in this country, so they would likely be seen as having substantial connections with the U.S. Thus, it would appear that in the case of the average undocumented schoolchildren and their parents, if they have not previously been deported, they will likely have a valid argument that they are the "people" to whom the Fourth Amendment applies.

Next consider the types of violations of the Fourth Amendment which courts may find in the searches and seizures of undocumented children and their parents at schools.

The Importance of the Proper Questioning and Seizing of a Noncitizen

Before any further analysis regarding the potential violations of the Fourth Amendment is possible, the noncitizen has to be "seized" within the meaning of the amendment. If the noncitizen is not seized, then none of the statements can be challenged with the exclusionary rule. The Supreme Court has defined seizure as:

> A person has been "seized" within the meaning of the Fourth Amendment only if, in view of all of the circumstances surrounding the incident, a reasonable person would have believed that he was not free to leave. Examples of circumstances that might indicate a seizure, even where the person did not attempt to leave, would be the threatening presence of several officers, the display of a weapon by an officer, some physical touching of the person ... or the use of language or tone of voice indicating that compliance with the officer's request might be compelled.[172]

Thus, in our example, where the ICE agent enters the cafeteria and questions noncitizen parents of children, many factors mentioned above would need to be analyzed towards a finding on whether the person has been seized. Perhaps the presence of only one officer, who uses soft language while questioning might lead one to believe the aliens were free to leave, and thus not "seized." Conversely, the appearance of an ICE agent in a school in itself might lead a reasonable person to be intimidated and feel that he or she could not leave. Combining this with other factors such as limited English-speaking proficiency and cultural differences would lend support an argument for a "threatening presence," resulting in a potential finding that the noncitizen was seized.

One additional aspect to consider when assessing if a seizure took place is whether the questions asked about a person's immigration status would constitute a seizure under the Fourth Amendment. Generally, "[i]nterrogation relating to one's identity or request for identification by police does not, by itself, constitute a Fourth Amendment seizure ..."[173] This rule comes from *I.N.S. v. Delgado,* a case in which immigration enforcement agents entered a factory and discovered undocumented workers on the premises. Some agents stood by the exits and others questioned employees at their work areas. Nothing in the record suggested what the agents at the door actually did. Yet because the employees "were free to leave" and because questioning a person's identity was not a seizure, the court reasoned that no Fourth Amendment violation occurred. However, the rule in *Delgado* has been criticized for its failure to take language competency and other factors into consideration.[174] Among these factors is race, which will be discussed more fully below.[175] Thus, when the ICE agent in our hypothetical asked a noncitizen for immigration papers as a form of identification, this alone may not have been a seizure because it would be equivalent to a police officer asking for identification.

Questioning beyond mere identification is likely to need a greater protection of the individual's rights before interrogation can proceed. Typically,

[a]bsent consent, an INS agent may not even detain or interrogate a person believed to be an alien unless the agent has a reasonable suspicion based on articulable facts and rational inferences that the person not only is an alien but is illegally in the country.[176]

Thus, the ICE agent proceeding into the cafeteria and interrogating a parent by asking "Are you here legally" may not violate the "reasonable suspicion" test. Here, the agent's receipt of an anonymous tip from a community member might constitute a "reasonable suspicion." However, without detailed information in the tip by a community member, the ICE agent may not have had "specific articulable facts" about the legal status about the particular parent he questioned, and thus he did not have a "reasonable suspicion."

On the other hand, a finding of "reasonable suspicion" is not limited to any one factor. Instead, each case turns on the totality of the specific circumstances, and "the officer is entitled to assess the facts in light of his experience in detecting illegal entry ... ."[177] Therefore, any number of factors can be perceived by the ICE agent to support the reasonableness of the stop. The only limitation is that the agent's actions cannot be based on inarticulate hunches, which rely solely on appearance. Questioning those of Latino appearance solely on that basis would be "unreasonable and violat[e] the Fourth Amendment."[178] In *Farm Labor Organizing Committee v. Ohio State Highway Patrol*, a state police officer pulled over a vehicle for a malfunctioning light. He then asked the passengers questions about their immigration status. When the stop was challenged, the court held that a malfunctioning light did provide a "reasonable suspicion" for asking about immigration status.[179] If the questioning was based on immigration status because some notation on the driver's license clued the police officer about this fact, then such questioning would also have been reasonable.[180] Thus, in the hypothetical scenario where the ICE agent entered the school cafeteria because he saw "Mexican-looking" people, if he or she could show that race or ethnicity alone did not form his "reasonable suspicion," the seizure would not likely violate the Fourth Amendment. As long is race is combined with other factors to form a "reasonable suspicion," then the seizure is likely to be lawful.[181]

Complying with a Warrant/subpoena from an ICE Agent

One other concern for noncitizen children and their parents regarding possible violations of the Fourth Amendment is the issuance of warrants. For example, in Austin, Texas in 2006, school officials sent an email to teachers explaining to them what to do in the event that immigration authorities came into school. It told the parents to: "tell the students they are safe. That they have rights to not answer questions and to request to speak to attorney if they are picked up."[182] The email also stated

> some parents have come and withdrawn their children (students) today. We can't stop a lawful investigation, but we can certainly inquire as to their credentials and to the existence of a lawful investigation. We also must abide by any court orders, such as warrants, they present.[183]

It was not clear whether the email was in response to a legitimate concern or just a knee-jerk reaction to an isolated rumor.[184] However, the previous year, parents in the same school district without Texas or U.S. identification cards had been denied access to the their children's school.[185] The policy has been since reversed. Parents without identification now fill out a form and go through a criminal background check in the event that they do not have identification.[186] That way they can access their children's school.

But the question remains, what should school administrators do when confronted with a warrant to search for undocumented students at school? How are undocumented children and their parents to be assured of the availability of schooling assured by *Plyler?* Practical recommendations include that should the immigration enforcement agent carry a warrant into the school, the principal or ranking school administrator should inspect it carefully. The principal should sequester the immigration enforcement officials in his or her office, immediately inform the attorney for the school district and the superintendent of their presence at school. The principal should also put the children at issue in a safe room, while obtaining legal advice.[187] Only after the advice of an attorney should students be turned over to the immigration law enforcement agents. Should immigration law enforcement agents walk through the school, the principal and a witness should accompany them at all times, and document all proceedings. These practices should be made part of the formal policy of the school.

Other Potential Fourth Amendment Violations

Under the Fourth Amendment, judges may not issue warrants unless based on probable cause. However, most of the recent searches of undocumented persons have been warrantless or based on defective warrants. To challenge such actions under the Fourth Amendment, there must be a state actor, and the search or seizure must impact an individual's privacy interest. The privacy interest requirement arises from the Supreme Court holding in *Katz v. United States*, in which the Court made clear that the Fourth Amendment protects people, not places.[188] In his concurrence in *Katz*, Justice John M. Harlan explained that "a privacy interest is twofold."[189] First, an individual must have an actual, subjective expectation of privacy and second, that expectation of privacy must be reasonable, such that courts are willing to give it Fourth Amendment protections.

However, this expectation of privacy test appears to have been eroded of late for noncitizens, as seen in the *United States v. Gutierrez-Casada* case discussed above. According to the court in that case, the defendant's unlawful presence in the U.S. left him with no reasonable expectation of privacy, not even in his own home. It appears that this is the case, since the undocumented are viewed as fugitives and their mere presence is unlawful.[190] Similarly, immigration scholar Raquel Aldana has recently observed that "immigrants have become so regulated that any *Katz* expectation of privacy to occupy spaces in silence without detection becomes unreasonable."[191] One last example of the diminished expectation of privacy of the undocumented in the U.S. is the Department of Justice (DOJ)'s decision to collect the DNA of any undocumented persons who are arrested.[192] This DNA is included in a database which, prior to the DOJ's decision, only included the DNA of convicted felons.

The standard of reasonableness required in an ordinary search or seizure is more relaxed in the context of immigration law. For example, border searches do not require a warrant or even probable cause.[193] The Supreme Court determined that "the government's fundamental interest in regulating those who enter the country outweighs the rights of an individual, who suffers only a minimal and anticipated invasion of privacy."[194] Thus, in schools located near the border, such searches would likely be subject to this lower standard.[195] Yet, border searches are subject to some limitations.

In *Almeida-Sanchez v. United States*, the Court ruled that roving patrols by the United States Border Patrol could not conduct warrantless searches of vehicles approximately twenty miles north of the border without violating the Fourth Amendment.[196] The Court has also determined that an officer may question a driver and passengers at the border about their citizenship and immigration status or of any suspicious circumstances, but further detention must be based on consent or probable cause.[197] The Court in *U.S. v. Brignoni-Ponce* further explained that in Border Patrol stops "[t]he likelihood that any given person of Mexican ancestry is an alien is high enough to make Mexican appearance a relevant factor, but standing alone it does not justify stopping all Mexican Americans to ask if they are aliens."[198]

Some further exceptions to the warrant requirement that might be applicable in the context of immigration law include consent, and the open fields doctrine. Consent must be voluntary, and not coerced.[199] Factors that are generally considered include the education and intelligence level of the individual. Did the person understand he or she had the right to refuse the search? Was there any type of warning? Consent presents a problem in dealing with undocumented persons because often there is a language barrier. Even in cases where law enforcement officers are bilingual, there may be questions about the linguistic ability of the bilingual officer or the dialect of the foreign language spoken. Furthermore, the individual's educational background may be severely limited. It seems unlikely that a school-aged individual (under eighteen years old) may validly consent because his mental capacity is not considered that of an adult. In contract law, most states require that a person be mentally competent and at least eighteen years old to form a binding contract. Arguably, this standard could be carried over to consenting to a search done by immigration officials or law enforcement officer.

Under the open fields doctrine, law enforcement does not require a warrant for evidence discovered in an open area: for example, a public park, a public street, or a field used to grow crops. An exception to this would be the area immediately surrounding the home. This area is considered curtilage and is afforded the same privacy protection as the home. School grounds are arguably analogous to the area immediately surrounding the home and could be considered curtilage. At common law, curtilage protection was extended to the area which continued the intimate activity associated with a home and the privacies of life.[200] Courts have extended this concept by reference to factors that determine whether an individual has a reasonable expectation of privacy. For example, factors which lead to policies supporting the unfettered reasonable expectation of privacy in the home—such as the protection of the young children likely to be found within—are similarly present in the school-house context. However, as the example regarding the Del Norte High School students demonstrates, in the past, this limitation has not prevented law enforcement from enforcing immigration law in the curtilage of a school.

The Remedy? Use and Non-use of the Exclusionary Rule in Removal Proceedings

When law enforcement conducts warrantless searches of undocumented persons in circumstances such as those described above, what does Fourth Amendment jurisprudence suggest about a remedy for the violations of their rights? If an undocumented child and/or or his or her parents is/are deported following a raid at school, can the exclusionary rule be invoked to prevent their deportation if they are seized in violation of the Fourth Amendment?

One remedy would be for the evidence to be excluded from any subsequent legal action against the undocumented person under the exclusionary rule. The exclusionary rule acts as a deterrent for law enforcement.[201] The rationale behind the exclusionary rule is that law enforcement will be less likely to collect evidence in an unconstitutional manner if such evidence cannot be used in criminal proceedings against a defendant.[202] In the case of a typical undocumented person, the removal hearing which would be the result of being unlawfully present in the United States unlawfully is a civil hearing. The Supreme Court in *I.N.S. v. López-Mendoza* determined that the exclusionary rule does not apply in civil deportation (also known as removal) hearings.[203] "A deportation proceeding is a purely civil action to determine eligibility to remain in this country, not to punish an unlawful entry, though entering or remaining unlawfully in this country is itself a crime."[204] Thus, any evidence discovered in an unlawful search or seizure can be used in a removal proceeding.

However, the Supreme Court has left open the door to a narrow but important exception to this analysis. The Court hinted that it might consider allowing the exclusionary rule in some situations:

> Our conclusions concerning the exclusionary rule's value might change, if there developed good reason to believe that Fourth Amendment violations by INS officers were widespread. Finally, we do not deal here with egregious violations of the Fourth Amendment or other liberties that might transgress notions of fundamental fairness and undermine the probative value of the evidence obtained.[205]

Therefore, the balance of benefits and costs would favor an application of the exclusionary rule. So far only the Ninth Circuit has seized on this exception and has tried to flesh out what might constitute "egregious" behavior that would allow for the use of the exclusionary rule. *Gonzales-Rivera v. INS* was a case where a roving border agent stopped the noncitizen while he was driving on a highway described as a corridor for alien smuggling.[206] The court held that a stop that was made solely on the basis of race was in violation of the Fourth Amendment and was in bad faith. The Ninth Circuit stated:

> [t]he Court has never abandoned its pronouncement ... that in addition to deterrence, the exclusionary rule serves the vital function preserving judicial integrity ... Federal courts cannot countenance deliberate violations of basic constitutional rights. To do so would violate our judicial oath to uphold the Constitution of the United States ... When evidence is obtained by deliberate violations of the Fourth Amendment, or by conduct a reasonable officer should know is in violation of the Constitution, the probative value of that evidence cannot outweigh the need for judicial sanction.[207]

Further, the notion of what is "egregious" and what a "reasonable person should know is in violation of the Constitution" is still a pretty general concept. The Ninth Circuit expanded its idea of an "egregious violation" of the Fourth Amendment, when it moved from targeting based on race to reliance "on a foreign sounding name" as the sole basis of suspicion.[208] In *Orhorhaghe*, the immigration officials relied on the suspect's Nigerian-sounding name, the absence of any record in the INS computer system of his lawful entry into the U.S. and, his suspected involvement in a fraudulent credit card scheme to determine he was in the U.S. illegally. The court rejected the latter two reasons and found that the decision was made mostly on the first factor. The court found that a foreign-sounding name could be used a proxy for race or national origin, and such a suspicion could be used in the same way as race in determining who will be investigated.[209]

The Supreme Court has further defined egregiousness in other Fourth Amendment cases. For example, in *Rochin v. California*, police officers forced the defendant to ingest an emetic solution so that he would vomit drugs he swallowed shortly before.[210] The evidence obtained was not of high probative value, and was obtained through the unreasonable force that "shocked the conscience."[211] Thus, behavior that "shocks the conscience" is one example of "egregious" behavior. The widespread constitutional violations committed during recent nationwide immigration raids are egregious behavior which has led to a call for the reintroduction of the exclusionary rule to removal hearings.[212] Scholars have issued this call for the exclusionary rule to apply to removal proceedings in order to deter immigration law enforcement from further violations.

If one were to apply *Plyler* to standards of "egregious" behavior, then it is possible that a court would find the exclusionary rule may apply in a removal proceeding, depending on the circumstances. On one hand, many undocumented children attend school because education is of "supreme importance" and is the "most vital civic institution for the preservation of a democratic system of government."[213] Its importance in ensuring that education is accessible to everyone and that there is no permanent underclass is a significant policy reason that might overcome the cost-benefit analysis associated with *López-Mendoza*. In other words, the chilling effect that would be created because undocumented workers would no longer send their children to school could be a more significant cost as compared to the judicial administrative costs associated with including an exclusionary rule in deportation proceedings.[214] Thus, under *López-Mendoza's* reasoning, strong public policy would support that allowing parents to be free from arrest on school campus so as to allow the proper implementation of *Plyler*.

It is unclear whether an agent would know that undocumented children have the right to access public education. On one hand, *United States v. López-Mendoza*, would seem to suggest an agent should know. It explained that agents receive education on the Constitution and the Fourth Amendment.[215] This could be construed to suggest knowledge of the constitutional rights of noncitizens in general. Furthermore, with the media attention given to the plight of undocumented children nationwide, it is likely that ICE agents would be aware of *Plyler* and its holding. On the other hand, an ICE agent could be said to have knowledge limited to constitutional issues related to law enforcement, and not with respect to all the constitutional rights of noncitizens. Thus, an ICE agent could not know of *Plyler*, or its importance. On balance, it would appear that immigration law enforcement should be aware that undocumented children have a right to attend school.

However, the Supreme Court granted access to education for undocumented children guaranteed in *Plyler* using a rational basis with a bite or intermediate scrutiny standard. Thus, the question posed becomes whether an arrest of an undocumented parent at a school would be such an unreasonable state interest that would preclude the exercise of that right. Thus, even if an ICE agent "knew or should have known" that such a right exists, the enforcement of the immigration law would still be an important or rational state interest under an intermediate-scrutiny test or rational-scrutiny test. Further, "egregious" behavior is likely to be limited to cases like *Rochin*, where the police misbehavior was overly-harsh or when people of a race are deliberately targeted. While an undocumented Latino parent arrested in a school would seem more as if it was just an event that happened at the wrong place at the wrong time, and would not invoke the same ideas of law enforcement impropriety, it could likely be found egregious if the parent was targeted by race. As to the undocumented children, if they are seized at school, it would likely be egregious behavior. However, the application of the "egregiousness" exception is by no means guaranteed and as noted above, still faces significant challenges with an application that incorporates the access to schooling granted under *Plyler.*

Furthermore, because removal proceedings are considered to be nonpenal, they are not viewed as bearing the social stigma of conviction, which can result in imprisonment.[216] However, one could argue that removal from the U.S. is analogous to imprisonment because individuals may be deprived of their liberty by being sent back to a country against their will, where possibly their lives are in jeopardy or their government seriously curtails their freedom. Even when following a removal or deportation hearing, noncitizens are removed to countries where economic oppression is the norm, this arguably may amount to a deprivation of their liberties as well. Moreover, throughout history, banishment, which is similar to modern removal, was perceived and used as punishment by a country towards its citizens. Banishment is "the transportation or exile by way of punishment for crime; expulsion or deportation by the political authority on the ground of expediency."[217] Yet it is not recognized under U.S. law as cruel or unusual punishment.[218]

Yet the Supreme Court has expressed some understanding of the realities of the life of the undocumented in the U.S. when it has considered the exclusionary rule in the context of deportation hearings. The Court has noted that noncitizens are not just highly regulated; but they are often treated as though they are not humans but rather "hazardous waste or drugs."[219] Justice Sandra O'Connor has interpreted the policy behind the exclusionary rule writing for the majority in *López-Mendoza* as follows:

> Presumably no one would argue that the exclusionary rule should be invoked to prevent an agency from ordering corrective action at a leaking hazardous waste dump if the evidence underlying the order had been improperly obtained, or to compel police to return contraband explosives or drugs to their owner if the contraband had been unlawfully seized. Thus, despite violation of their privacy by the Immigration and Naturalization Service ("INS"), immigrant workers can still be seized and *discarded* because of their illegality. Paraphrasing Justice Benjamin Cardozo's famous quote, Justice O'Connor concludes: "The constable's blunder may allow the criminal go free ... but he should not go free within our borders."[220] (emphasis added)

The concern for the Court in *Verdugo-Urquidez* was that "aliens with no attachment to this country might well bring actions for damages to remedy claimed violations of the Fourth Amendment in foreign countries or in international waters."[221] Yet in the case of the undocumented students and their parents, clearly they have enough attachment to the U.S. since they attend school (the children) or have children who attend school (the parents). Also, many of the parents pay taxes, and both parents and children participate in the life of the country in other various other ways. They should definitely not be discarded or analogized to hazardous waste, contraband explosives, or drugs.

Ultimately, what can we conclude regarding undocumented persons and the Fourth Amendment? The Fourth Amendment's protections have been greatly eroded in recent history, especially in the context of the rights of noncitizens. One might wonder then, about, the situation(s) in which the Fourth Amendment would apply to undocumented persons. The text of the Constitution refers to "the people" not "citizens." The Supreme Court in *Verdugo-Urquidez* concluded that "the people" refers to those "persons who are part of a national community or who have otherwise developed sufficient connection[s] with the country ... ."[222] Imagine a situation where an undocumented person entered this country twenty years ago. He has paid taxes, worked in his local community, attended church, and raised his family. It seems this person would have substantial ties with his community and therefore the United States.

Next, imagine that the local police unlawfully search the outside of a school his children attend based on an unsubstantiated tip that he had committed a crime. The police do not discover any evidence of the crime when they search him and his car, but instead determine he is an undocumented person after asking for identification. He is subsequently arrested and held pending deportation proceedings. Since under current law, the exclusionary rule does not apply in deportation proceedings, it seems that the Fourth Amendment may not be relevant in any situation involving an undocumented person. Once it was discovered that he was illegally in this country, the illegally obtained evidence could be used in a removal proceeding. He could potentially plea bargain by agreeing to be immediately deported and not serve any time for his immigration violation, if he agreed not to contest the illegal search. However, as an undocumented person, he may not even perceive that he has the power to negotiate. While some courts have implied that undocumented persons are protected by the Fourth Amendment and a few actually found this, with others, of course, holding the opposite, it appears that undocumented persons' Fourth Amendment rights are more theoretical than real. Yet, as to the undocumented children who attend schools under *Plyler*, their Fourth Amendment rights at school as students need to be further analyzed in order to assess their scope, particularly in a hypothetical instance where school administrators may involve themselves in the search and seizure of undocumented children.

The Fourth Amendment and Schoolchildren

The Supreme Court first held that the Fourth Amendment applied to school searches in the case of *New Jersey v. T.L.O.*[223] In *T.L.O.*, a school administrator initially searched a student's purse to verify if it contained cigarettes to refute her statement that she was not a smoker. The administrator noticed a package of rolling papers as he removed a pack of cigarettes from T.L.O.'s open purse. This indicated a presence of marijuana, so he could proceed even though he did not initiate the search as a search for marijuana.

The Court adopted the following language:

> Determining the reasonableness of any search involves a twofold inquiry: first, one must consider "whether the ... action was justified at its inception," ...; second, one must determine whether the search as actually conducted "was reasonably related in scope to the circumstances which justified the interference in the first place."[224]

What is reasonable is determined by "balancing the need to search against the invasion which the search entails."[225] In this case, avoiding drug use and maintaining order in the school was a legitimate state interest, as compared with the privacy of the student. Thus, the search was proper. Further, the Court held that a warrant was not needed because such a requirement would be too burdensome.[226] Next, the Court held that the level of suspicion required for a search is just short of probable cause.[227] Interestingly, the Court rejected the state's argument that the school was acting *in loco parentis* in its dealings with the student, finding instead that modern day school administrators are more likely asserting state rather than parental authority.[228] The Court determined that a school search or seizure is reasonable if the school official has

> reasonable grounds for suspecting that the search turn-up evidence that the student has violated or is violating either the law or the rules of the school ... [and] the measures adopted are reasonably related to the objectives of the search and not excessively intrusive in light of the age and sex of the student and the nature of the infraction.[229]

Unlike students who bring illegal substances or weapons on to school grounds, undocumented children have not violated any law or rule of the school.

In later cases, the Supreme Court held that a school can engage in mass drug testing both of athletes and in other non-curricular activities, even if there is no individual suspicion.[230] The Court did not expressly address school administrator cooperation with outside law enforcement in *New Jersey v. T.L.O.* Generally, when an outside law enforcement officer "instigates, directs, participates, or acquiesces in a search conducted by school officials," the officer must have probable cause for the search, even though the school officials acting alone would be subject to the lesser constitutional standard for conducting searches.[231] The reasoning for this rule stems from the agency rule, which prevents law enforcement from circumventing the Fourth Amendment by having a private individual conduct a search or seizure that would have been unlawful if performed solely by law enforcement.[232] For example, in *Colorado v. P.E.A.*, the Colorado Supreme Court declined to find that the school administrators acted as agents of the police when an police officer informed school administrators that several students likely had marijuana on the premises. Even though the searches of the defendant's car and locker were conducted while the police officer was on school grounds, school officials were not acting as his agents because the police officer in no way participated in the search.[233]

Factors that weigh in favor of applying probable cause in a particular search include that police request to be there during the search, and then undertake the following actions: make the decision to search, gather the facts leading to the search, direct the search activities, actually do the searching, and conducting the criminal prosecution which will result from the discovery of any contraband.[234]

However, the greater standard of probable cause does not apply in certain circumstances. One is where there is involvement by which the police provide information which motivates school administrators to undertake the search, but the police do not participate in the search or interrogation. Further, if the nature of police involvement is designed to prevent an incident or danger to school, even more flexibility is present.[235] The need for safety trumps privacy concerns.[236] Another exception is where law enforcement agents are invited in a limited capacity by school officials, and are not acting as police agents.[237] Courts are reluctant to impose a greater burden on schools because they ask for the assistance of trained professionals.[238]

Using this framework, ICE officials would be most likely governed under the same rules as the local police. Hence, any diminished probable cause standard enjoyed by school officials would not be applicable to immigration law enforcement officers. Even if a court were to find that the diminished probable cause standard does apply, the need to enforce immigration laws does not raise the same concerns in terms of providing safety to the school or preventing student drug use. Thus, a student's privacy interest may very well trump the state interest, and a search would thus be unreasonable and not "justified in its inception." Finally, any attempt by ICE to participate in or direct a search by school officials could result in a violation of the agency rule and consequently the Fourth Amendment.

Let us now analyze the specific powers and duties of Immigration and Customs Enforcement ("ICE") under the Fourth Amendment.

ICE and the Fourth Amendment

ICE need not be restrained by the same requirement to show probable cause as other law enforcement entities.[239] Under Title 8 § 1357, immigration law enforcement does have some power to stop and question without a warrant as follows:

(a) Powers without warrant.
Any officer or employee of the Service authorized under regulations prescribed by the Attorney General shall have power without warrant—

(1) to interrogate any alien or person believed to be an alien as to his right to be or to remain in the United States.[240]

Notably, the statute only allows the questioning, not the arrest of the noncitizen, unless the noncitizen in the presence or view of the ICE agent is entering or attempting to enter the United States in violation of any law or if the agent has reason to believe that the noncitizen arrested is in the United States in violation of any law and is likely to escape before a warrant can be obtained for his arrest.[241] In such cases, the arrested noncitizen shall be taken without unnecessary delay for examination before an immigration officer having authority to examine noncitizens as to their right to enter or remain in the United States. So there is some relaxation of the warrant requirement for ICE, but not completely.

Furthermore, courts have reasoned that ICE enforcement actions are closer to administrative inspections.[242] The level of probable cause needed is somewhere between that of a criminal investigation and that of an administrative inspection.[243] Thus, ICE can arrive at a factory with a warrant describing the presence of undocumented workers, and question and arrest any noncitizen, without describing a particular person in its warrant.[244] Using this warrant, ICE can raid a factory and perform person-by-person searches while inside.[245] Yet, public schools are quite different than factories. For one, children have a right to access education, whereas undocumented workers do not have a right to work without legal authorization. The former is legally sanctioned activity while the latter is prohibited. Thus, it would make sense that an ICE law agent conducting a raid on school grounds should need a higher standard of probable cause than that needed for a factory. Finally, such an entry warrant as described above would have little practical effect. Schools typically have hundreds of students. An ICE law agent going student-by-student to apprehend several children of undocumented workers would likely not be efficient in implementing such a strategy. In addition, the ICE agent may use racial profiling of undocumented students when using a general warrant.

The Interplay of *Plyler* with the Rights of the Parents to Raise their Children Without Governmental Interference

Plyler is unique in that the rights of the parents are left undefined. The Supreme Court did not want to punish the children for the actions of the parents. However, a question left unanswered: Is what right to access of public education do the parents have? Can undocumented aliens meet with the teacher/school officials, run for school board, pick up their children, and participate in PTA meetings without danger of reprisal from ICE?

As a starting point, consider laws regarding parental consent for abortion, since they can serve as a tool for understanding the interplay between the constitutional rights of parents and those of their children. Parental consent laws are analogous because they involve a constitutional right enjoyed by a child, which can only be exercised through the parent, after approval for the abortion is given. Similarly, in *Plyler*, the child enjoys the right to education only if the parent enrolls the child in school. One case that outlines the approach towards parental consent is *Bellotti v. Baird*.[246] In *Bellotti*, a minor sought an abortion without parental consent. The Massachusetts statute gave parents absolute authority in the decision.[247] The U.S. Supreme Court rejected the statute's approach in favor of the mature minor doctrine. This doctrine allows courts to determine if the individual adolescent seeking an abortion is mature enough to make the decision, and thus bypass the parental consent.[248] This approach defers to the parents, but allows an escape hatch so the child's still maintains his or her right. The Court held that the Massachusetts statute was unconstitutional because it provided no way for a court to authorize an abortion after finding the minor mature and competent enough to make the decision.[249]

The Court in *Bellotti* explained how children are treated differently under law:

> The Court long has recognized that the status of minors under the law is unique in many respects .... We have recognized three reasons justifying the conclusion that the constitutional rights of children cannot be equated with those of adults: the peculiar vulnerability of children; their inability to make critical decisions in an informed, mature manner; and the importance of the parental role in child rearing.[250]

Adult constitutional rights are also available to minors, albeit in such a way that is sensitive to a parent and family's need to develop the person into a mature adult. The state has a right to "adjust the legal system to account for children's vulnerability."[251] The Court further recognized the important role parents play in this adjustment.

The state commonly protects its youth from adverse government action and from their own immaturity by requiring parental consent to or involvement in important decisions by minors. But an additional and more important justification for state deference to parental control over children is that "[t]he child is not a mere creature of the state; those who nurture him and direct his destiny have the right, coupled with the high duty to recognize and prepare him for additional obligations." (citation omitted) "The duty to prepare the child for 'additional obligations' must be read to include the inculcation of moral standards, religious beliefs, and elements of good citizenship." (citation omitted) This affirmative process of teaching, guiding, and inspiring by precept and example is essential to the growth of young people into mature, socially responsible citizens.[252]

Finally, the Court further suggested a constitutional right to parent without undue adverse interference by the state. It stated "[u]nder the Constitution, the State can properly conclude that parents and others, teachers for example, who have [the] primary responsibility for children's well-being are entitled to the support of laws designed to aid discharge of that responsibility."[253]

Children have special characteristics under the law, especially in the enjoyment of their constitutional rights. Courts have shown deference towards parents in their decisions on how to raise their children.[254] Under *Plyler*, the children of undocumented workers have the right to access public education. However, a child cannot fully enjoy such right unless his parent feels secure in sending him to school. Children can "affect neither their parents' conduct nor their own status."[255] The law has recognized that children may enjoy constitutional rights differently because of their status as minors, and thus the state can "adjust the legal system to account for children's vulnerability." Thus, a court should show deference to parents exercising their right to access education for their children, and afford a level of protection during school functions to undocumented parents, not only to the children.

Further, because a parent has a duty to "prepare a child for additional obligations," the same reasoning should apply in the context of education. This obligation is met when parents enroll their children in school, and show concern for their schooling. The *Plyler* Court recognized education's importance in breaking the cycle of poverty, and integrating new members of United States society.[256] The involvement of undocumented parents in the school system would facilitate the successful and healthy development of immigrant children.

Finally, implicit in the parent's right to parent without overly intrusive state intervention is the right to send a child to school with the same freedom.

Education is vital to the full development of the child. With compulsory education law, states mandate that minor children attend school. Failure to enroll children would be one of many factors in determining parental neglect of a child. Hence, the right of access to public education should be enjoyed by both undocumented parents and children.

Instead, it is law enforcement which has enhanced access to schools, in the form of student resource officers, as seen above, in an effort to prevent school shootings and the like. Thus, school violence has opened the doors to the rise of a law enforcement presence in schools. At present, the schoolhouse appears to be more open to law enforcement than in the past, making the enforcement of immigration law there much more likely. This is likely to be in contravention of the parents' wishes and will result in the school administrators, staff, and teachers being placed in a very uncomfortable and difficult position if the promise of *Plyler* is to become a reality.

School Immigration Enforcement as Disruptive of the School Learning Environment and Violative of Professional Standards for School Leaders

School administrators have a strong interest in maintaining school safety and promoting an effective learning environment. These interests lead to the broad authority school officials have when investigating students. For example, school administrators may stop a minor student and question him without reasonable suspicion "so long as it is not done in an arbitrary, capricious or harassing manner."[257] Generally, school officials are given more leeway in education-related investigations they conduct than are police or law enforcement when they conduct the same investigations. School liaisons, student resource officers, etc. are considered to be law enforcement and to require a higher standard of probable cause when investigating a student.

Law enforcement and school administrators often work together in drug-related or weapons investigations. When student safety is at stake, school administrators can detain a student until the police arrive. Having law enforcement present at school has its own safety concerns. In particular, student safety could be jeopardized by the presence of law enforcement in the school, often carrying weapons. For example, in the case of a weapons investigation, the risk of taking custody of a student carrying a weapon weighs in favor of taking the risk of the presence of law enforcement because other students could be injured. However, most of the time, an undocumented student presents no physical threat to other students. In contrast, if an undocumented student was approached by immigration law enforcement at school and attempted to resist arrest, other students could be injured in the struggle. Thus, the balance does not weigh in favor of allowing immigration law enforcement to pursue undocumented students at school.

Furthermore, in the ordinary context of law enforcement, rarely does the presence of undocumented students in school present a safety risk. In the recent context of enhanced immigration enforcement nationwide, however, there are further concerns about immigration law enforcement, for all students, in addition to the Fourth Amendment concerns for undocumented students.

Recent workplace immigration raids have been conducted in a manner which is extremely disruptive to families[258] and which has caused adverse impact on children.[259] Similar disruptions and adverse impact on children can be expected of any schoolhouse enforcement of immigration law. Recall the case in Roswell, New Mexico, of Karina Acosta, the pregnant teenager who was deported by ICE after a local police officer Student Resource Officer (SRO) took her out of class regarding a traffic ticket she received a few days before. In such a situation, a possible solution would be to allow SROs in the school to enforce safety but prevent them from participating in any kind of immigration enforcement.

Schools are unlikely to be willing participants in immigration enforcement because undocumented students are permitted to be in the schoolhouse. It is a paradox that while public school is compulsory to a certain statutory set age, there is no fundamental right to go to school. Educators generally would prefer that undocumented children attend school and learn than be left uneducated. This was one of the rationales adduced by the Supreme Court in *Plyler*. Furthermore, funding for public schools comes in part from attendance. If schools started turning in undocumented children to immigration officers, they would lose students and in essence, lose much needed dollars that are used to pay teachers' salaries, and the like.

School disruptions such as immigration law enforcement at school contravene the best practices of the school administration profession. These best practices are embodied in the standards for school leaders who are committed to maintaining a safe and supportive learning environment and ensuring that all individuals are treated with fairness, dignity, and respect.[260] Furthermore, other professional standards assert that: "[a]n education leader promotes the success of every student by advocating, nurturing and sustaining a school culture and instructional program conducive to student learning and staff professional growth."[261] In view of these standards and following the unwritten mandate of *Plyler* and the Fourth Amendment jurisprudence, it is apparent that keeping the schoolhouse free from interference by immigration enforcement against both undocumented parents and students is an appropriate course of action for school administrators. So, what approaches can be used by undocumented students to address immigration enforcement on school grounds?

Two Approaches to Preventing ICE Arrests on School Grounds

One approach that is available to noncitizens whose Fourth Amendment rights have been violated entails the filing of so-called *Bivens* lawsuits, named after *Bivens v. Six Unknown Named Agents of the Federal Bureau of Narcotics*.[262] In *Bivens* the court held that a U.S. citizen could recover damages in the federal court from federal agents for violations of the Fourth Amendment. Importantly for our present discussion, in *Sosa v. Alvarez-Machain* the U.S. Supreme Court subsequently extended to noncitizens the same right that was established for U.S. citizens under *Bivens*.[263]

In *Bivens*, the petitioner claimed that federal agents entered his apartment and searched without the necessary warrants. He was never tried for any narcotics crime, so there would have been no reason for the exclusionary rule to be applicable. However, he claimed that there was "great humiliation, embarrassment, and mental suffering as a result of the agents' unlawful conduct, and sought $15,000 damages for each of them."[264] Although the federal government claimed that the violation only allowed for a state law claim for invasion of privacy and that the Fourth Amendment provided no cause of action, the U.S. Supreme Court held that the petitioner had properly stated an action under the Fourth Amendment, and monetary damages were available as a remedy.

The *Bivens* approach is restricted in two ways. First, such causes of action are unavailable where there are "special factors counseling hesitation in the absence of affirmative action by Congress."[265] Second, there can be no damages where there is an alternative specified by Congress.[266] An undocumented person could potentially suffer great humiliation, embarrassment, and mental suffering from an unlawful seizure by an ICE agent and no special factors appear to be present to counsel hesitation in the absence of affirmative action by Congress. In fact, other noncitizens have recovered *Bivens* damages, as will be seen below. Second, undocumented noncitizens have no other congressional alternative. Thus, they appear to satisfy the criteria to bring *Bivens* actions.

Bivens lawsuits have many potential benefits. They allow compensation for unprosecuted violations of the Fourth Amendment. They provide a way to proportionately punish the offending party for the severity of the action.[267] Finally, they impose liability on the offending officer, by specifically targeting the excessive conduct itself, and do not result in the perverse effect of allowing the continuation of unlawful behavior.[268] Law enforcement officers are sued in their individual capacity, and the United States is not a party to the suit.[269] Persons negatively affected by ICE can sue for declaratory and injunctive relief.[270]

The Fifth Circuit Court of Appeals has recently ruled that such a claim is available to a lawfully admitted alien who has been wrongfully detained.[271]

This case involved an angry exchange at the border between an immigration enforcement agent and the plaintiff, who was a Mexican citizen entering the United States.[272] The officer became violent when arresting the plaintiff, who suffered a seizure and had to be administered oxygen.[273] The plaintiff sued for assault, battery, and false arrest. In addition to finding sufficient connections with U.S. so that the protection of the Fourth Amendment would apply, the court also stated that "[i]t follows that she may bring a *Bivens* claims for unlawful arrest and the excessive use of force under the Fourth Amendment."[274]

Thus, even if an ICE agent violates the Fourth Amendment and, as previously discussed,[275] the exclusionary rule cannot be used to prevent the admission of evidence during the deportation or removal proceeding, a noncitizen may be able to bring a *Bivens* claim for violations of the Fourth Amendment. A *Bivens* lawsuit could still provide a deterrent to overly aggressive ICE agents whose conduct on school property may be in contravention of the law. However, the likelihood that undocumented students and their parents would know about redressing Fourth Amendment violations via *Bivens* actions is extremely low, as is the availability of legal counsel to assist with these types of lawsuits. Thus, practically, they may not be very useful for undocumented students and their parents.

A typical defense under *Bivens* is that of qualified immunity of the law enforcement officer. It can be overcome by showing that the right was clearly established and an officer would have reasonably understood that his conduct violated that right.[276] Again, as with the analysis above regarding the applicability of the exclusionary rule in removal hearings, *Plyler* appears to be clearly established law, so that an immigration enforcement officer should have reasonably understood his school-based enforcement actions would have violated *Plyler*.

Another legal defense that may be available for undocumented students seized at school is entrapment by estoppel. The defense of entrapment by estoppel lies where an agent of the government affirmatively misleads a party as to the state of the law and that party proceeds to act on the misrepresentation so that criminal prosecution of the actor implicates due process concerns of the Fifth and Fourteenth Amendments. There must be an "active misleading" by the government agent, and actual reliance by the defendant. Further, the defendant's reliance must be reasonable in light of the identity of the agent, the point of law misrepresented, and the substance of the misrepresentation. [277]

The landmark case in this area is *Raley v. Ohio*.[278] In this case, defendants were convicted for refusing to answer certain questions before the "Un-American Activities Commission of the State of Ohio."[279] The defendants invoked their privilege against self-incrimination after commission members, including the committee chairman, erroneously advised those testifying that the statute protected them against self-incrimination.[280] Afterwards, the defendants were indicted in state court for the exercise of their privilege, and convicted.[281] The Supreme Court found that this practice violated the Fourteenth Amendment.[282] The crime that had been committed was failure to answer, despite the Ohio statute which extended immunity to those testifying. To sustain the conviction "would be to sanction the most indefensible sort of entrapment by the State—convicting a citizen for exercising privilege which the State clearly had told him was available to him."[283] The government cannot also mislead individuals by assurances that activity is legal and then prosecute the individual for the sanctioned conduct.[284]

Thus, when applying this principle to the present set of facts, it is possible that the seizure by an ICE agent of an undocumented parent at a school may be invalidated. Either the school, in terms of enrolling the undocumented child, or official representations by the school, state, or other federal government agencies such as ICE, the Department of Education, which may deal with the inforcement of the *Plyler v. Doe* doctrine, could be deemed "a government agent who affirmatively misleads a party." The misleading statement would be the official representation to the unlawful alien that it is safe to send the child to school. The unlawful alien would "actually rely" on the statement, and attempt to pick up or drop off their child at school, or interact with the school in another fashion which necessitates his or her presence. Thus, if the alien is prosecuted when exercising this "state-sanctioned conduct," then he or she should be able to claim entrapment by estoppel and thus escape conviction of breaking immigration law.

Two complications arise when applying this theory to immigration cases. First, under the current set of facts, the government might argue that the activity, i.e., being unlawfully in the country, is a separate activity than enrolling a child in school. Thus because these activities are separate and unrelated, then entrapment by estoppel would have no application. Second, some courts have been quite restrictive when interpreting the term "government agent" who is able to give statements of the law. For example, in *United States v. Gutierrez-Gonzales*, the defendant claimed entrapment by estoppel when a non-profit agency wrongly advised him of his immigration status.[285] The Tenth Circuit ruled that the non-profit agency could not be considered a "government official or agency responsible for interpreting, administering, or enforcing the law defining the offense."[286] Other courts have been even narrower in their application of the rule.[287] Thus, the government may claim the defense is not applicable because if the parent had relied on a school administrator's representation when deciding to enroll his or her child in school or to travel to the school premises, it is possible that the defense would not be available because the school administrator is part of a local government and not the same federal government as ICE.

However, most cases dealing with this restriction apply to state government representations of federal law, and not local government. It is not absolutely clear that the Tenth Circuit's approach would apply to local governments. For example, the Indiana Department of Education has issued memoranda advising schools to bring them into compliance with *Plyler*.[288] This could be used to argue that an undocumented student has been advised on his or her rights, and thus should be protected by entrapment by estoppel. Despite these challenges, an entrapment by estoppel argument would be attractive because the noncitizen would not have to even address whether the Fourth Amendment applies to noncitizens and avoid the *Verdugo-Urquidez* analysis undertaken above.

The best tools in implementing *Plyler* as a protection for undocumented students against immigration enforcement would be a *Bivens* case or a defense of entrapment by estoppel argument. Despite the uncertainty associated with the application of the Fourth Amendment and to undocumented students, schools should adopt guidelines and policies in the event that immigration officials do make their way on to school premises. Some ideas include a "safe room" for undocumented children and procedures on how to contact the school district's attorney should a warrant be issued.[289]

Critiques of the Fourth Amendment Rights of the Undocumented

The Fourth Amendment protections of the undocumented have been theorized to be legally subordinated because of those individuals' presence in the U.S. in violation of immigration law.[290] The law's construction of the illegality of the undocumented interplays with existing Fourth Amendment doctrine and allows courts to deny them privacy protections.[291] This interplay follows the conception of the undocumented person as a criminal, not deserving of any rights, and the concomitant trend of immigration law becoming increasingly intertwined with criminal law. This convergence of the two areas of law has been termed "crimmigration."[292] Crimmigration is based on membership theory, and thus defines in broad terms who belongs in the U.S., who will be punished, and who will be morally condemned. Furthermore, since the undocumented person is most likely Latino and poor, Critical Race Theory also offers a racial critique of the Fourth Amendment which needs to be examined as follows.

Critical Race Theorist Devon Carbado has analyzed the racial allocation of the burdens and benefits of the Fourth Amendment and found that the material result of this racial allocation is that people of color are burdened more by, and benefit less from, the Fourth Amendment than whites.[293] For Latinos, this racial burden is a function of, and helps to reproduce, the notion of Latinos as outsiders.[294] In particular, Professor Carbado has identified how the Supreme Court's Fourth Amendment jurisprudence constructs race in the experiences that people of color have with the police.[295] In his view, the Court's adjudication of Fourth Amendment cases constructs race neutrally with regard to suspects and police officers.[296] This construction renders African Americans and Latinos as just people and erases their particular racial experiences with, and impressions of, the police, while the white police officers become just police officers—a construction that erases their particular racial impressions of, and social interactions with, African Americans and Latinos.[297] Since

> part of the project of Critical Race Theory has been to illustrate not only the role courts play in constructing racial identities, but also the relationship between the construction of race in judicial opinions and the production and legitimation of racial inequality,[298]

It is necessary to critique the Fourth Amendment case law in order to find the inequality which these opinions engender. The case of *I.N.S. v. Delgado* will be the focus of the discussion.

In *I.N.S. v. Delgado*, the Supreme Court determined that no Fourth Amendment violation took place when immigration agents questioned undocumented workers at their factory work areas while other agents stood by the exits.[299] The Court reasoned that the employees "were free to leave," even though the agents occupied the workplace and in fact, arrested those who left.[300] The Court also found that questioning a person's identity was not a seizure.[301] The questions asked by the agents aimed to ascertain identity, place of birth, citizenship, and whether the workers had legal papers. The Court's seemingly colorblind analysis actually reinforces the view of the Latino as an outsider, "always living on the border."[302] This message contradicts the antisubordination principle[303] of Critical Race Theory as well.

We live in critical times during which a careful analysis of the rights afforded to the undocumented under *Plyler* and under the Fourth Amendment is necessary and warranted in order to elucidate the current situation for all the stakeholders involved. This chapter has endeavored to advance the existing knowledge in this evolving area and to initiate deeper inquiry into the current discourse.

Further areas of inquiry should revolve around the involvement of state law enforcement agencies in federal immigration law enforcement, an area of traditional preeminent federal jurisdiction. Such involvement can further weaken the expectation of privacy of those who are not U.S. citizens as outlined above and may cause distrust of local police to the detriment of undocumented persons who are victims of crime.

Having examined the two potential dangers for undocumented students in the schoolhouse, racial privacy initiatives and immigration enforcement, this chapter has shown the continued vulnerability of these students in the U.S. legal and educational systems. The two areas of vulnerability, their race and their unlawful immigration status, make undocumented students more likely to have decreased educational achievement. This happens either because the undocumented students drop out of school because of racially blind school policies or fail to attend school because of fear of the immigration authorities. In addition to being unfortunate and unnecessary, either of these scenarios is likely to directly contravene the letter and spirit of *Plyler*, a Supreme Court case that is still the law of the land in the United States today.

Conclusion

Undocumented students, who are present in the United States in the classic words of the Supreme Court "through no fault of their own,"[1] find that their immigration status severely restricts their future opportunities. Despite the myriad efforts undertaken in the litigation, legislation, and policy arenas, the current situation for the undocumented student in the U.S. educational system unfortunately remains bleak. Those select few students who successfully navigate the obstacles in the educational system are likely to become members of the working poor who—despite having the intellectual capacity and skills necessary to graduate from high school, attend a university, and become productive members of society—must wait until comprehensive immigration reform is enacted to help regularize their immigration status. The rest of the undocumented student population is ravaged by the systemic persistent inequality we have identified in this book.

The immigration laws that act as obstacles, as well the educational policies that aim to fix the problem of educating undocumented students, highlight a further fundamental systemic flaw: that most of these policies fail to address the educational, living, and working conditions of undocumented Latino students. Such conditions, in fact, may likely not be much different from the problems of the U.S. citizen and legal resident Latino children, many of whom live in marginalized communities and are not reaching their full educational potential. For example, Latino undocumented children are part of the minorities who continue to live in the achievement gap of No Child Left Behind.[2] What accounts for this systemic flaw? We posit that the answer lies in the racial composition of the undocumented Latino student population. This undocumented student population, like most of the Latinos who are U.S. citizens and lawful residents, is comprised of people of color, even of indigenous background, and thus are considered minorities under the prevailing U.S. the racial hierarchy. Therefore, in addition to the immigration status barriers they face, these students must also live with the racial realities of being minorities in the United States. They must face negative stereotypes, such as being called "dirty Mexicans," face and in daily microaggressions such as being told to "go back to Mexico." These sentiments don't necessarily come from evildoers in white robes or skinheads, but more often come from neighbors, teachers, newscasters, radio talk show hosts, and other seemingly innocuous individuals. Indeed, it is telling that of late, the media has focused with laserlike precision on the U.S.–Mexico border and those who cross it as carriers of the H1N1 ("swine") flu, and this has caused rampant racially motivated outbursts.[3] Such is the atmosphere in which the undocumented student has to live and try to thrive, against all odds.

In the current, seemingly post-racial climate following the historic election of President Barack Obama, other than Arab/Muslims whose discrimination continues in the wake of the tragic events of 9/11, the only group to which it appears acceptable to openly show racial animus are the undocumented, the so-called "illegal aliens." Of course, the vast number of these are Latinos, mostly Mexican. The U.S.–Mexico border is the locus and focus of the fears of an "immigrant invasion." It is no coincidence that the only substantive immigration legislation which Congress has been approved of late is the border fence, as if to keep out the outsider, the Mexican. This exclusion serves to emphasize the "otherness" and increase the stigma against Mexicans and other Latinos.

Scholar Ediberto Roman's research has shown that the United States is currently experiencing heightened stigmatization and even demonization of the Latinos.[4] Such demonization has led local law enforcement to encourage their agents to ask schools to identify undocumented students, to later deport them and their parents, all in violation of *Plyler*.[5]

Despite the anti-immigrant backlash and racial hatred, it is inescapable that *Plyler* is still good law and it stands for the proposition that education, although not a fundamental right, is an integral aspect of membership in our community. And the students who are able to attend school under its aegis deserve the opportunity that the U.S. Supreme Court found under the Equal Protection Clause of the Constitution in 1982. Thus, *Plyler* is still a vital opinion even in the face of the current "immigration crisis" because *Plyler* stands for abolition of castes and an affirmation of equality—two precepts which should still be bedrock principles of the critical post-racial democratic moment in which we live.

These two propositions for which *Plyler* stands are dead letter law in the face of the reality of the undocumented student. The unwelcome but inescapable reality for undocumented students is that, without the prospect of normalizing their immigration status, the education they receive may limited to only being useful individually for personal growth. However, it is of little or no consequence for the betterment of the overall condition of Latinos in the United States because the undocumented remain unable to participate in our democratic society. In that sense, *Plyler v. Doe* may join *Brown v. Board of Education*[6] as a decision embodying the interest convergence covenants in which educational opportunities for minority students exist only when the students' interests and the nation's interests converge.[7] Analyzing *Plyler* under an interest convergence lens demonstrates that the nation's interest is the maintenance of an underclass of undocumented, low-wage earners who fuel the nation's economy by performing work that is undesirable to many United States natives, even in this economic recession. The continued existence of this underclass must be related to the limited educational attainment of those in the group, a result perpetuated by the lackluster effect of *Plyler* as a catalyst for further educational gains for Latino undocumented children.[8]

What can be done about this current state of affairs? What should be done in the face of this persistent inequality? Based on their view that colorblindness in our society has failed, scholars Lani Guinier and Gerald Torres have called for all those concerned about social justice in our midst to embrace the concept of political race.[9] Political race "confronts the social and economic consequences of race in a 'third way' that offers a multi-layered political strategy rather than a set of public policy or primarily legal solutions to issues of racial justice."[10] In view of the inability of the current policy and legal regimes to fully address the needs of undocumented students, indeed of so many Latino and minority students, it would appear that political race, with its use of political coalitions, would be a hopeful start to the exercise of erasing the persistent inequality for undocumented students that continues unabated in our midst. There is evidence to point to the success of coalition building in both the educational and immigration law arena. The immigrant rights marches of 2006 are vivid examples of this phenomenon, where organized labor, immigrants' rights groups, the clergy, the business community, educators and others joined forces to decry draconian congressional immigration proposals. Ultimately, these legislative proposals failed and have not resurfaced.

The coalition building which took place during the immigration marches of 2006 highlights the desperate need in the educational policy arena, for visionary and transformative leadership. Take for instance, the actions of Kent Paredes Scribner, then Isleta, Arizona School District Superintendent. In Spring 2006, at the time when students in his school district sought to support the marches taking place all over the country, Superintendent Scribner made it possible for the students in his school district to join the marches safely, rather than opposing them, as others throughout the nation had done. In fact, Scribner had the cafeteria prepare sack lunches for the student marchers so they would have sustenance while showing his solidarity in their cause. It is this type of courageous leadership that is precisely needed during these times of rampant repressive policies against the undocumented student.

Consider an alternate vision of the U.S. and its immigration and educational system in the not too distant future. Imagine that every morning, the major news outlets, along with reporting the Dow Jones industrial averages, the NASDAQ and Nikkei numbers, also report the major educational indices in the country. Consider for example this hypothetical news report:

Today the sixth grade students at Short Ridge Middle School in Indianapolis, Indiana are attending a summit they have designed to study Critical Race Theory and how it affects their lives. As a result of such innovative curriculum design in the Indianapolis Public Schools ("IPD"), the largest school district in Indiana, the drop out rate in the state has now reached an all time low ...,

the National Public Radio's announcer will say, with the same enthusiasm and interest as she reads the Wall Street numbers. Furthermore, the announcer will add

In other news, 100 U.S. citizens were naturalized in Los Angeles, having completed the educational and good moral character requirements of the DREAM Act. These new citizens have lived as lawful permanent residents for the period required by law and now join this country's political community. ...

Only when such an alternative future becomes a reality will the persistent inequality for undocumented students end. And with it would come better educational opportunities for all in the U.S. public schools and a more fair and humane immigration system. These undoubtedly are two goals that we can all aspire to make realities in our lifetimes. This book is a call to do so. The sooner, the better. Neither the children, nor the country, can wait.

Notes

Introduction

1 These are the words of the U.S. Supreme Court in *Plyler v. Doe*, 457 U.S. 202, 226 (1982).

2 Sam Dillon, *No Child Law Is not Closing a Racial Gap*, N.Y. TIMES, April 29, 2009 at A1 (noting that despite the focus of No Child Left Behind on improving the test scores of African Americans and Latino students, the achievement gap has not narrowed).

3 *Parents Involved in Community Schools v. Seattle School District No. 1*, 551 U.S. 701 (2007).

4 PATRICIA GANDARA & FRANCES CONTRERAS, THE LATINO EDUCATION CRISIS: THE CONSEQUENCES OF FAILED SOCIAL POLICIES (2008).

5 *See* Nina Bernstein, *Leaning on Jail, City of Immigrants Fills Cells with its Own*, N.Y. TIMES, December 2, 2008 at A 1 (discussing parents who hide and do not send children to school because of fear of raids).

6 *See* Erik Camayd-Freixas, Interpreting after the Largest ICE Raid in U.S. History, A Personal Account, June 13, 2008, *available at* http://graphics8. nytimes.com/images/2008/07/14/opinion/14ed-amayd.pdf?scp=2&sq=Camayd&st=cse.

7 Immigration and Naturalization Act, 8 U.S.C. § 1101(a)(3) (2004).

8 Kevin R. Johnson, *"Aliens" and the U.S. Immigration Laws: The Social and Legal Construction of Nonpersons*, 28 U. MIAMI INTER-AM. L. REV. 263, 268 (1997).

9 *E.C. v. Obergfell*, Case No. CV-0359-DFH-WTL, filed March 2, 2006 (U.S. Dist. Ct. S.D. In), *see also* Diana Penner, *Indiana Relents on College Aid Program*, INDIANAPOLIS STAR, January 8, 2007.

10 *Id.*

11 Editorial, *Targeting Immigrants*, L.A. TIMES, May 9, 2009.

12 *See generally* TARA J. YOSSO, CRITICAL RACE COUNTERSTORIES ALONG THE CHICANA/CHICANO EDUCATIONAL PIPELINE (2006).

13 457 U.S. 202 (1982).

14 Two of the earliest recorded cases in the struggle for equality in education for Latino students are *Alvarez v. Owen*, No. 66625 (Cal. Sup. Ct. San Diego County filed Apr. 17, 1931), and *Westminster School District v. Mendez*, 161 F.2d 774, 781 (9th Cir. 1947). *Alvarez* took place in the 1930s in the Lemon Grove community in San Diego County, California. It was the first successful school desegregation case in the United States. The community's attempt to exclude Mexican students from grammar school was unsuccessful, as the lower court ordered school officials to admit the Mexican students to the school. The court also indicted school board members for illegal segregation. *See* Robert R. Alvarez, Jr., *The Lemon Grove Incident: The Nation's First Successful Desegregation Court Case*, 32

J. San Diego Hist. 116 (Spring 1986), *available at* http://sandiegohistory.org/journal/86spring/lemongrove.htm (last visited July 6, 2008). In *Westminster*, a federal court found that the segregation of school children of Mexican descent was a violation of the Fourteenth Amendment. In this sense, *Alvarez* and *Westminster* are precursors to the landmark Supreme Court desegregation decision of *Brown v. Board of Education.*

15 347 U.S. 483 (1954).

16 *See generally* Carlos Suárez-Orozco & Marcelo Suárez-Orozco, Transformations: Immigration, Family Life, and Achievement Motivation among Latino Adolescents (1996).

17 *See e.g.* Alejandro Portes & Rubén J. Rumbaut, Legacies: The Story of the Immigrant Second Generation, 276–80 (2001) (explaining the downward assimilation among future generations of Mexican immigrants).

18 Rubén Rumbaut, *The New Californians: Comparative Research Findings on the Educational Progress of Immigrant Children*, in California's Immigrant Children: Theory, Research, and Implications for Educational Policy 52 (Wayne Cornelius & Rubén Rumbaut, eds., 1995).

19 Michael Fix & Jeffrey S. Passel, "U.S. Immigration—Trends & Implications for Schools" The Urban Institute, Jan. 28–29 2003, *available at* Educational Resources Information Center, U.S. Dep't of Educ., http://www.eric.ed.gov/, document no. ED474609.

20 *Id.* at 7.

21 Nat'l Ctr. for Educ. Statistics, U.S. Dep't of Educ., *Status and Trends in the Education of Hispanics, available at* http://nces.ed.gov/pubsearch/pubsinfo. asp?pubid=2003008 (Apr. 15, 2003).

22 *Id.*

23 *Id.*

24 Richard Fry, *The Changing Landscape of American Public Education: New Students, New Schools*, at 1 (Pew Hispanic Center, 2006).

25 *See generally* Nat'l Ctr. for Educ. Statistics, *supra* note 21.

26 *Id.* at 8.

27 U.S. Gen. Accounting Office, Report to the Chairman, Committee on the Judiciary, House of Representatives: Illegal Alien Schoolchildren—Issues in Estimating State-by-State Costs, *available at* http://www.gao.gov/new.items/d04733.pdf (June 2004).

28 Jeffrey S. Passel et al., *Undocumented Immigrants: Facts and Figures, available at* Urban Institute, http://www.urban.org/url.cfm?ID=1000587 (Jan. 12, 2004).

29 Jeffrey S. Passel & D'Vera Cohn, *A Portrait of Unauthorized Immigrants in the United States*, Pew Hispanic Center, April 14, 2009, at ii.

30 Roberto G. Gonzalez, *Left Put but not Shut Down: Political Activism and the Undocumented Student Movement*, 13 Northwestern J. L. & Pol. 220, 223 (2008).

31 Jeffrey S. Passel, *Background Briefing Prepared for Task Force on Immigration and America's Future*, Pew Hispanic Center, June 14, 2005, at 29.

32 *Id.*

33 Nat'l Ctr. for Educ. Statistics, U.S. Dep't of Educ., *Status and Trends in the Education of Hispanics, available at* http://nces.ed.gov/pubsearch/pubsinfo. asp?pubid=2003008 (Apr. 15, 2003).

34 *Id.*

35 Angelina KewalRamani, Lauren Gilbertson, Mary Ann Fox, and Stephen Provasnik, *Status and Trends in the Education of Racial and Ethnic Minorities*

(NCES 2007–039). National Center for Education Statistics, Institute of Education Sciences, U.S. Department of Education (2007) at 6.

36 *Id.*

37 Bd. on Children & Families et al., *Immigrant Children and Their Families: Issues for Research and Policy*, 5 Critical Issues for Children & Youths 72 (1995), *available at* http://www.futureofchildren.org/information2826/information_show.htm?doc_id=71141 [hereinafter *Immigrant Children*].

38 Angelina KewalRamani, et al. *supra* note 35.

39 *Id.*

40 Nat'l Ctr. for Educ. Statistics, *supra* note 12.

41 Michael Fix & Jeffrey S. Passel, "U.S. Immigration—Trends & Implications for Schools" The Urban Institute, Jan. 28–29 2003, *available at* Educational Resources Information Center, U.S. Dep't of Educ., http://www.eric.ed.gov/, document no. ED474609, at 11.

42 *Id.*

43 *See generally Immigrant Children supra* note 37.

44 *Id.*

45 *Id.*

46 *See generally* Stanton Wortham, Enrique G. Murillo & Edmund T. Hamman, Education in the New Latino Diaspora: Policy and the Politics of Identity (2001).

47 *See generally Immigrant Children supra* note 37.

48 Memorandum from Alison P. Landry, Assistant Attorney General, to Presidents, Chancellor, Rectors, Registrars, Admissions Directors, Domicile Officers and Foreign Student Advisors (INS Designated School Officials) and the Executive Director of the State Council for Higher Education in Virginia (Sept. 5, 2002), *available at* http://www.steinreport.com/va_colleges_11152002.htm.

49 Maree Sneed, *Questioning Immigration Status When Students Enroll*, 64 School Administrator 10, 12 (November 2007), *available at* http://www.aasa.org/publications/content.cfm?ItemNumber=9481.

50 Raam Wong, *ICE Picks Up Dad at School District*, Albuquerque J., March 29, 2007 at 1.

51 The invitation to local sheriffs, highway patrols, and police agencies to enforce immigration law raises Tenth Amendment federalism issues under *New York v. United States*, 505 U.S. 144 (1992). At least one immigration scholar has concluded that the form in which the federal government has obtained the cooperation of local law enforcement, through an invitation, rather than a mandate, avoids Tenth Amendment concerns. *See* Huyen Pham, *The Inherent Flaws in the Inherent Authority Position: Why Inviting Local Law Enforcement to Enforce Immigration Law Violates the Constitution*, 31 Fla. St. U. L. Rev. 965, 975–76 (2004).

52 *Id.* at 970–71 (citing Memorandum of Understanding Between the INS and the State of Florida (July 26, 2002), *reprinted in* 79 Interpreter Releases 1138, app. II, at 1120 (2002)).

53 These states have entered into these agreements under Immigration and Nationality Act section 287(g). For a full listing of the states and localities that are partners with Immigration and Customs Enforcement ("ICE"), see http://www.ice.gov/partners/287g/Section287_g.htm.

54 *Cf.* Plyler v. Doe, 457 U.S. 202, 223 (1982) (remarking on the stigma of illiteracy).

55 *See e.g.* Missouri v. Jenkins, 515 U.S. 70 (1995); Freeman v. Pitts, 503 U.S. 467 (1992); Bd. of Educ. of Okla. City Pub. Schs. v. Dowell, 498 U.S. 237 (1991). *See*

generally Joseph R. McKinney, Commentary, *The Courts and White Flight: Is Segregation or Desegregation the Culprit?*, 110 EDUC. L. REP. 915 (1996).

56 The 2000 Census data showed increasing residential segregation for Latinos in almost all parts of the country. This, along with migration, explains much of the increased segregation in schools. *See* Gary Orfield & Chungmei Lee, Brown *at 50: King's Dream or Plessy's Nightmare*, *at* http://www.civilrightsproject.harvard.edu/research/reseg04/resegregation04.php (Jan. 2004); *see also* Erica Frankenberg et al., *A Multiracial Society with Segregated Schools: Are We Losing the Dream*, *at* http://www.civilrightsproject.harvard.edu/research/reseg03/resegregation03.php (Jan. 2003) (describing patterns of resegregation in the United States in the last twelve years).

57 *See, e.g.*, Keyes v. Cong. of Hispanic Educators, 902 F. Supp. 1274 (D. Colo. 1995). In Colorado, for example, in 1991, only 1 percent of Latino students were in intensely segregated minority schools (more than 90 percent minority enrollment), while in 2001, 17 percent of Latino students were in intensely segregated minority schools.

58 Grutter v. Bollinger, 539 U.S. 306, 345 (Ginsburg, J., concurring).

59 Orfield & Lee *supra* note lvi, at 20 & 21 table 9.

60 *Id.* at 20.

61 GARY ORFIELD ET AL., DISMANTLING DESEGREGATION 65–67 (1996).

62 *Id.*

63 411 U.S. 1 (1973).

64 *Id.* at 54–55. This result is precisely the opposite of what had been found by the California Supreme Court in *Serrano v. Priest*, 487 P.2d. 1241 (Cal. 1971), a decision in which the California school funding system was found in violation of the state and federal equal protection clauses.

65 *See* James E. Ryan, *The Influence of Race in School Finance Reform*, 98 MICH. L. REV. 432, 435 (1999).

66 Watson Scott Swail et al., *Latino Youth and the Pathway to College* vii, *available at* http://www.educationalpolicy.org/pdf/Latino_Youth.pdf (June 2004). The higher risk factors faced by Latinos in higher education were brought to the attention of the Supreme Court in *Gratz v. Bollinger*, 539 U.S. 234 (2003). *See* Brief of Latino Organizations as Amici Curiae in Support of Respondents, Gratz v. Bollinger, 539 U.S. 234 (U.S. 2003) (No. 02–516), *available at* 2003 WL 536740.

67 Watson Scott Swail et al., *supra* note 66 at 28.

68 *Id.* at 32.

69 Wayne A. Cornelius at the Center for Comparative Immigration Studies at the University of San Diego has done important longitudinal research on the dynamics of the U.S. Mexico migration and the effect of U.S. immigration policy on Mexican migration patterns. *See e.g.*, WAYNE A. CORNELIUS & JESSICA M. LEWIS, IMPACTS OF BORDER ENFORCEMENT ON MEXICAN MIGRATION: THE VIEW FROM THE SENDING COMMUNITIES (2007).

70 Alejandro Portes, of Princeton University, has conducted groundbreaking longitudinal studies of the assimilation of the children of immigrants. *See e.g.* PORTES & RUBÉN RUMBAUT, *supra* note 17.

71 Yosso, *supra* note 12 at 5.

72 RICHARD DELGADO & JEAN STEFANCIC, CRITICAL RACE THEORY: AN INTRODUCTION 16 (2001).

73 *Id.* at 51.

74 *Id.*

75 Yosso, *supra* note 12 at 6.

76 *Id.* at 8.

77 *Id.*

78 Richard Delgado, Critical Race Theory: The Cutting Edge xiv (1995).

79 Derrick Bell, *Property Rights in Whiteness: Their Legal Legacy: Their Economic Costs*, in Critical race theory: The cutting edge, 75–83 (Richard Delgado, ed.) (1995).

80 Yosso *supra* note 12 at 10.

81 *Id.* at 12.

82 *Id.* at 13.

83 *Id.* at 15.

84 *Id.* at 9.

Chapter 1

1 Michael A. Olivas, *Plyler v. Doe, the Education of Undocumented Children, and the Polity*, in Immigration Stories 213 (David A. Martin & Peter H. Schuck, eds, 2005).

2 Plyler v. Doe, 457 U.S. 202 (1982).

3 In Re Alien Children Litigation, 501 F.Supp. 544, 554 (D.C. Tex. 1980).

4 *Id.* at. 554–5.

5 Phillip J. Cooper, "*Plyler at the Core: Understanding the Proposition 187 Challenge*," 17 Chicano Latino L. Rev. 64 (1995).

6 *Id.*

7 *Id.*

8 Doe v. Plyler, 458 F. Supp. 569, 572 (E.D. Tex. 1978).

9 *Id.*

10 *Id.* at 575–75.

11 Cooper, *supra* note 5 at 64.

12 Doe v. Plyler, 458 F. Supp. 569, 577 (E.D. Tex. 1978).

13 *Id.* at 575.

14 *Id.* at 585.

15 *Id.* at fn. 28, 585.

16 Doe v. Plyler, 458 F. Supp. 569, 592 (E.D. Tex. 1978) (*citing* Tr. 12/12 at 164).

17 *Id.*

18 *Id.* at 592.

19 Article 47, Buenos Aires Protocol, 21 U.S.T. 607, T.I.A.S. No. 6847 (1970) cited in Doe v. Plyler, 458 F. Supp. 569, 592 (E.D. Tex. 1978).

20 In Re Alien Children Litigation, 501 F.Supp. 544 (D.C. Tex. 1980).

21 *Id.* at 598.

22 *Id.* at 596–97.

23 *Id.* at 590.

24 Doe v. Plyler, 628 F.2d 448 (5th Cir. 1980).

25 *Id.* at 461.

26 Cooper, *supra* note 5 at 76.

27 *Id.*

28 *Id.* at 79.

29 *Id.* at 80.

30 304 U.S. 144, 152, n.4 (1938).

31 *Id.* at 82 (*citing* Letter from Harry A. Blackmun, U.S. Supreme Court Justice, to William J. Brennan, Jr., U.S. Supreme Court Justice, T.M.P., (Mar. 10, 1982) at 2).

32 *Id.* at 83.

33 *Id.*

34 Lucy Hood, *Educating Immigrant Students,* 4 CARNEGIE REPORTER, Vol. 4, No. 2 (Spring 2007), *available at* http://carnegie.org/reporter/14/immigrant/index.html.

35 457 U.S. 202 (1982).

36 347 U.S. 483 (1954); *see also* Kevin R. Johnson, *Civil Rights and Immigration: Challenges for the Latino Community in the Twentieth Century,* 8 LA RAZA L.J. 42, 44 (discussing *Plyler* as a high-water mark for Latinos before the Supreme Court and comparing it to *Brown*).

37 438 U.S. 265 (1978).

38 *See, e.g.,* Halle Butler, Note, *Educated in the Classroom or on the Streets: The Fate of Illegal Immigrant Children in the United States,* 58 OHIO ST. L.J. 1473, 1490–91 (1997) (discussing data regarding the contributions of noncitizens to the United States economy). Even President George H.W. Bush has recognized "a basic fact of life and economics: some of the jobs being generated in America's growing economy are jobs American citizens are not filling." Press Release, President Bush Proposes New Temporary Worker Program (Jan. 7, 2004), *available at* http://www.whitehouse.gov/news/releases/2004/01/20040107-3.html.

39 UNDERGROUND UNDERGRADS:UNDOCUMENTED IMMIGRANTS SPEAK OUT (UCLA Center for Labor Research and Education 2007) is a recent volume written by undocumented students, in which these students showcase their talents in the arts, as well as their academic achievements. They also very strongly state their views regarding their inability to work and obtain legal status in the U.S. and chronicle their struggles to achieve reform in these areas.

40 *Plyler,* 457 U.S. 202 at 213; *see also* Michael A. Olivas, *IIRIRA, The DREAM Act, and Undocumented College Student Residency,* 30 J.C. & U.L. 435, 443 (2004) (discussing how "[p]rior to *Plyler,* the Supreme Court had never taken up the question of whether undocumented aliens could seek Fourteenth Amendment equal protections").

41 *See* Olivas, *supra* note 40 at 443.

42 *Plyler,* 457 U.S. at 210.

43 *Id.*

44 118 U.S. 356 (1866).

45 *Id.* at 369.

46 *Plyler,* 457 U.S. at 212, n.10.

47 U.S. CONST. amend. XIV.

48 *Plyler,* 457 U.S. at 210.

49 *Id.* at 214 (*quoting* CONG. GLOBE, 39th Cong., 1st Sess. 1090 (1866) (remarks of Rep. Bingham)).

50 Kotch v. Board of River Pilots, 330 U.S. 552 (1947).

51 Nguyen v. I.N.S., 533 U.S. 53 (2001).

52 *Plyler,* 457 U.S. at 223.

53 *Id.* (*citing* San Antonio Indep. Sch. Dist. v. Rodriguez, 411 U.S. 1, 28–39 (1973) (holding that education is not a fundamental right and that "a State need not justify by compelling necessity every variation in the manner in which education is provided to its population")).

54 411 U.S. 1 (1973).

55 *See Plyler,* 457 U.S. at 230–31. Article 28 of the Convention on the Rights of the Child states that "Parties recognize the right of the child to an education." Convention on the Rights of the Child, Nov. 20, 1989, art. 28, 28 I.L.M. 1448, 1467. Subsection (a) of that article requires Parties to the Convention "make primary education compulsory and available free to all." *Id.* art. 28(a), 28 I.L.M. at 1467; *see also* Charter of Fundamental Rights of the European Union, Dec. 7, 2000, art. 14, 2000 O.J. (C 364) 1, *available at* University of Minnesota Human Rights Library, http://www1.umn.edu/humanrts/instree/europeancharter2.html (stating that everyone has a right to education including the possibility of receiving a free compulsory education) (last visited August 17, 2008).

56 *See generally* Mark Tushnet, *Justice Lewis F. Powell and the Jurisprudence of Centrism,* 93 MICH. L. REV. 1854, 1862–74 (1995) (discussing the deliberations that took place during the drafting of the *Plyler* decision).

57 *Rodriguez,* 411 U.S. at 62 (Brennan, J., dissenting).

58 *Id.* at 62–63 (Brennan, J., dissenting) (*quoting Rodriguez,* 411 U.S. at 102–03 (Marshall, J., dissenting)).

59 *Rodriguez,* 411 U.S. at 63 (Brennan, J., dissenting).

60 *Id.* (Brennan, J., dissenting).

61 This application of heightened scrutiny under the rational basis standard of review seems stronger than traditional rational basis because under traditional rational basis the classification only needs to be rationally related to a legitimate government interest. *See* Robert C. Farrell, *Successful Rational Basis Claims in the Supreme Court from the 1971 Term Through* Romer v. Evans, 32 IND. L. REV. 357, 382 (1999); *see also* Rebecca E. Greenlee, Note, *Equal Protection Analysis Bite Grows Stronger:* Plyler v. Doe, 17 REV. JUR. U.P.R. 335 (1983).

62 *Plyler,* 457 U.S. at 222 (*quoting* Brown v. Bd. of Educ., 347 U.S. 483, 493 (1954)).

63 *Id.* at 224.

64 *Id.*

65 *Id.* at 223 (*quoting* Brown, 347 U.S. at 493).

66 *Id.* (*quoting* Brown, 347 U.S. at 493).

67 *Id.* at 220.

68 *Plyler,* 457 U.S. at 220 (*quoting* Trimble v. Gordon, 430 U.S. 762, 770 (1977)).

69 *See id.*

70 Immigration and Naturalization Act section 212(a)(9)(B)(iii) (2000).

71 *Plyler,* 457 U.S. at 219.

72 *Id.* at 218 n.14.

73 *Id.* at 223.

74 *Id.* at 219.

75 *Plyler,* 457 U.S. at 218–19.

76 *Id.* at 228.

77 Doe v. Plyler, 458 F. Supp. 569 (E.D. Tex. 1978).

78 Elizabeth Hull, *Undocumented Aliens and the Equal Protection Clause: An Analysis of* Doe v. Plyler, 48 BROOK. L. REV. 43, 59 (1981); *see also Plyler,* 458 F. Supp. at 588–89.

79 *Plyler,* 457 U.S. at 229–30.

80 *Id.* at 230.

81 *Id.*

82 See María Pabón López, *The Education of Latino Undocumented Children: Reflections on Plyler v. Doe and Beyond,* 35 SETON HALL L. REV. 1373, 1377 (2005).

83 Plyler, 457 U.S. at 230 (Marshall, J., concurring).

84 *Id.* at 231 (*quoting* San Antonio Indep. Sch. Dist. v. Rodriguez, 411 U.S. 1, 99 (1973)).

85 *Id.*

86 *Plyler*, 457 U.S. at 231 (Blackmun, J., concurring).

87 *Id.* at 234 (Blackmun, J., concurring).

88 *Id.* at 236 (Blackmun, J., concurring).

89 *Id.* at 236 (Blackmun, J., concurring).

90 *Id.* at 237–38 (Powell, J., concurring).

91 *Id.* at 240 (Powell, J., concurring).

92 Tushnet, *supra* note 56, at 1866–73.

93 *Id.* at 1873.

94 *Id.*

95 *Id.*

96 *Plyler*, 457 U.S. at 244 (Burger, C.J., dissenting).

97 *Plyler*, 457 U.S. at 244 (Burger, C.J., dissenting).

98 *Id.* at 253–54.

99 *Id.* (internal quotation marks omitted).

100 R. Jeffrey Smith, Jo Becker and Amy Goldstein, *Documents Show Roberts Influence in Reagan Era*, WASH. POST, July 27, 2005, at A01.

101 *Plyler*, 457 U.S. at 254 (Burger, C.J., dissenting).

102 *Id.*

103 *Id.*

104 *See Plyler*, 458 F. Supp. at 571 & n.1 ("Prior to the trial of this case on the merits, the court ordered that the action be maintained as a class action on behalf of all undocumented school-aged children of Mexican origin residing within the boundaries of the Tyler Independent School District").

105 *Plyler*, 457 U.S. at 229–30.

106 *Id.* at 230.

107 *Id.* at 230.

108 *See* U.S. Census Bureau, Current Population Survey, Annual Social and Economic Supplement, 2004, Table 2.6 Foreign-Born Population by World Region of Birth, U.S. Citizenship Status, and Year of Entry: 2004, *available at* http://www.census.gov/population/socdemo/foreign/ppl-176/tab02-6.pdf (last visited August 17, 2008).

109 *Id.*

110 *Id.*

111 *Id.*

112 Paul Feldman, *Texas Case Looms Over Prop. 187's Legal Future*, L.A. TIMES, Oct. 23, 1994, at A1.

113 *Id.*

114 *Id.*

115 *Id.*

116 *Id.*

117 *Id.*

118 T. Alexander Aleinikoff & Rubén G. Rumbaut, *Terms of Belonging: Are Models of Membership Self-Fulfilling Prophecies?*, 13 GEO. IMMIGR. L.J. 1, 10 (1998).

119 Rebecca A. Maynard & Daniel J. McGrath, *Family Structure, Fertility, and Child Welfare*, *in* THE SOCIAL BENEFITS OF EDUCATION 125 (Jere R. Behrman & Nevzer Stacey, eds., 1997).

120 *Id.*

121 *Plyler*, 457 U.S. at 244 (Burger, C.J., dissenting).

122 Phillip B. Kurland & Dennis J. Hutchinson, *The Business of the Supreme Court, O.T. 1982*, 50 U. Chi. L. Rev. 628, 650 (1983). In fact, Professor Hutchinson took his critique further, stating that that "*Plyler* cut a remarkably messy path through other areas of the Court's jurisprudence." Dennis J. Hutchinson, *More Substantive Equal Protection? A Note on* Plyler v. Doe, 1982 Sup. Ct. Rev. 167, 184.

123 López, *supra* note 82 at 1396.

124 H.R. 4134 104th Congress. 1 (1996). The amendment was also introduced in 1995, see 104th Cong. (1995).

125 *Id.*

126 Jaclyn Brickman, *Educating Undocumented Children in the United States: Codification of Plyler v. Doe Through Federal Legislation*, 20 Geo. Immigr. L. J. 385, 391 (2006).

127 *Id.*

128 *Id.*

129 López, *supra* note 82 at 1396.

130 Julia Preston, *7-Year Immigration Rate is Highest in U.S. History*, N.Y. Times, November 29, 2007 at A20.

131 Lora Grandrath, *Illegal Immigrants and Public Education: Is there a Right to the 3Rs?*, 30 Val. U.L. Rev. 749, 790–93, (1996).

132 *League of United Am. Citizens v. Wilson*, 908 F. Supp. 755, 763 (C.D. Cal. 1995).

133 *See* Kevin R. Johnson, *Public Benefits and Immigration: The Intersection of Immigration Status, Ethnicity, Gender, and Class*, 42 UCLA L. Rev. 1509 (1995).

134 *Id.*

135 *League of United Am. Citizens*, 908 F. Supp. 755 at 774.

136 997 F. Supp. 1244 (C.D. Cal. 1997); 908 F. Supp. 755 (C.D. Cal. 1995) [hereinafter *LULAC*].

137 *LULAC*, 997 F. Supp. 1244, 1255 (C.D. Cal. 1997) (citation omitted).

138 Janice Alfred, Note, *Denial of the American Dream: The Plight of Undocumented High School Students Within the U.S. Educational System*, 19 N.Y.L. Sch. J. Hum. Rts. 615, 626 & n.62 (2003).

139 *See* Tanya Broder, *State and Local Policies on Immigrant Access to Services: Promoting Integration or Isolation?* May 2007, at 2 n.6. National Immigration Law Center, *available at* www.nilc.org (last visited August 19, 2008).

140 Abigail Johnson, *Pair of Contentious Bills Die Early*, Indiana Lawyer, Feb 8, 2006.

141 *Id.*

142 *Id.*

143 *See* Broder, *supra* note 139, at 4 n.15.

144 *Id.* at 4.

145 *Yes on Proposition 200 v. Napolitano*, No. CV2004–092999 (Maricopa County Sup. Ct., order issued Mar. 14, 2005); AZ Court of Appeals Div. One, CA-CV 05–0235.

146 *See* Broder, *supra* note 139 at 4.

147 *Id.*

148 *Id.* at 10 (*citing* Mary Vandeveire, *Prop 200 Confusion Being Lamented: Participation Drop Seen in Services Not Affected by New Law*, Arizona Daily Star (Tucson ed.), April 4, 2005; Elvia Diaz and Robert Sherwood, Prop. *200's Effect Minimal: Political Fallout May Loom Large in '06 Races*, Arizona Public, June 5, 2005 (immigrants are missing medical appointments and are delivering babies elsewhere).

149 *Plyler*, 457 U.S. at 229.

150 *Id.* at 220.

151 *Id.* at 238.

152 Yoder v. Wisconsin, 406 U.S. 205, 232 (1972) (holding that the State could not compel Amish children to attend school beyond eighth grade in contradiction of their parents' wishes).

153 Alien is the term in the Immigration and Nationality Act for "any person not a citizen or national of the United States." 8 U.S.C. 1101(a)(3) (2000) It is used interchangeably with its synonym "noncitizen," another term with the same meaning, yet having less negative connotations.

154 *Plyler*, 457 U.S. at 212 ("In concluding that 'all persons within the territory of the United States,' including aliens unlawfully present, may invoke the Fifth and Sixth Amendments to challenge actions of the Federal Government, we reasoned from the understanding that the Fourteenth Amendment was designed to afford its protection to all within the boundaries of a State").

155 262 U.S. 390 (1923).

156 *Id.*

157 William G. Ross, *A Judicial Janus:* Meyer v. Nebraska *in Historical Perspective*, 57 U. Cin. L. Rev. 130, 155 (1988–89).

158 Brief of defendant in error, Meyer v. Nebraska, 1923 U.S. LEXIS 2655 (1923).

159 262 U.S. at 402.

160 *Id.* at 400.

161 268 U.S. 510 (1925).

162 *Id.* at 534.

163 *Id.* at 530.

164 *Id.* at 537.

165 *Id.* at 532.

166 *Id.*

167 *Id.* at 533.

168 *Id.* at 534.

169 *Plyler*, 457 U.S. at 221.

170 *Yoder*, 406 U.S. at 233 (1972).

171 *Id.*

172 *Id.* at 236.

173 *Id.* at 213–215.

174 *Id.* at 215.

175 530 U.S. 57, 66 (2000).

176 *Id.* at 66.

177 *Id.* at 73.

178 *Id.* at 61.

179 *Id.*

180 *Id.* at 63.

181 *Id.* at 73.

182 *Id.* at 68–69.

183 Immediato v. Rye Neck Sch. Dist., 73 F.3d 454, 461–62 (2d Cir. 1996); Hubbard v. Buffalo Indep. Sch. Dist., 20 F. Supp. 2d 1012, 1017 (W.D. Tex. 1998); Cornwell v. State Bd., 314 F. Supp. 340, 344 (D.C. Md. 1969), *aff'd*, 428 F.2d 471, 472 (4th Cir. 1970) (per curiam).

184 There is some disagreement as to whether a heightened form of scrutiny should always be used with respect to parental rights and education. Immediato v. Rye Neck Sch. Dist., 73 F.3d 454, 461 (2d Cir. 1996) (applying rational-basis review);

see also, Brown v. Hot, Sexy, and Safer Productions, Inc., 68 F.3d 525, 533 (1st Cir. 1995) ("the Supreme Court has yet to decide whether the right to direct the upbringing and education of one's children is among those fundamental rights whose infringement merits heightened scrutiny").

185 *Cf. Yoder,* 406 U.S. at 238. (*quoting* Brown v. Board of Education, 347 U.S. 483, 493 (1954)); *Plyler,* 457 U.S. at 222–23.

186 *See* Anne T. Henderson and Karen L. Mapp, National Center for Family and Community Connections with Schools, Southwest Educational Development Laboratory (SEWL), A New Wave of Evidence: The Impact of School, Family, and Community Connections on Student Achievement 7 (2000). (*available at* http://www.sedl.org/connections/resources/evidence.pdf (last visited March 11, 2008).

187 *Id.*

188 *Plyler,* 457 U.S. at 219.

189 Jane Rutherford, *Community Accountability for the Effect of Child Abuse on Juvenile Delinquency in the Brave New World of Behavioral Genetics,* 56 DePaul L. Rev. 949, 991 (2007).

190 *Id., see also,* Christopher A. Bracey, *Getting Back to Basics: Some Thoughts on Dignity, Materialism and a Culture of Racial Equality,* 26 Chicana/o-Latina/o L. Rev. 15, 34 (2006).

191 Jennifer L. Sabourin, *Parental Rights Amendments: Will a Statutory Right to Parent Force Children to "Shed Their Constitutional Rights" at the Schoolhouse Door?,* 44 Wayne L. Rev. 1899 (1999).

192 *Id.* at 1902.

193 *Id.* at 1906.

194 *Id.* at 1901 n. 14.

195 Ross, *supra* note 157 at 186.

196 Parents in Texas have the right to review all teaching materials used in the classroom, a right to remove the child from lessons that are objectionable moral or religious reasons, a right of prior consent before a child may be videotaped by a school employee, and the right to file a grievance before the school board. Tex. Educ. Code § 26.001–26.012 (West 2007); *see also* Tex. Fam. Code § 151.001. (West 2007) (Recognizing a parent's right to direct education).

197 Ross, *supra* note 157 at 186.

198 *Id.*

199 *Id.*

200 868 S.W.2d 306 (Tex. 1993).

201 *Id.* at 308.

202 *Id.* at 314.

203 *Id.* at 316.

204 *Id.* at 309. Other findings included that about 54 percent of the public university students in the border area were Hispanic, as compared to 7 percent in the rest of Texas; that the average public college or university student in the rest of Texas had to travel 45 miles from his or her home county to the nearest public university offering a broad range of masters and doctoral programs, but the average border area student had to travel 225 miles; that only three of the approximately 590 doctoral programs in Texas were located at border area universities; that about 15 percent of the Hispanic students from the border area who attended a Texas public university were at a school with a broad range of masters and doctoral programs, as compared to 61 percent of public university students in the rest of Texas; that the physical plant value per capita and number of library

volumes per capita for public universities in the border area were approximately one-half of the comparable figures for non-border universities; and finally, that these disparities existed against a history of discriminatory treatment of Mexican Americans in the border area (with regard to education and otherwise), and against a climate of economic disadvantage for border area residents. *Id.*

205 *Id.*

206 *See id.* at 310. The applicable Texas state constitutional provisions are as follows. Article 1 § 3 of the state Equal Protection Clause of the Texas Constitution provides "All free men, when they form a social compact, have equal rights, and no man, or set of men, is entitled to exclusive separate public emoluments, or privileges, but in consideration of public services." Tex. Const. art. I § 3. Article I § 3a provides: "Equality under the law shall not be denied or abridged because of sex, race, color, creed, or national origin. This amendment is self-operative. Tex. Const. art. I § 3a."

207 Richards, 868 S.W.2d at 310.

208 *Id.* at 317.

209 *Id.* at 311.

210 *Id.*

211 *Id.*

212 *Id.* at 312.

213 *Id.* at 314.

214 *Id.* at 313–14.

215 *Id.* at 314–17.

216 *Id.* at 311, 312 & n.6.

217 *Id.* at 312 n.6 (internal citations omitted).

218 Plyler v. Doe, 457 U.S. 202 at 219 n.19.

219 Richards v. League of United Latin Am. Citizens, 868 S.W.2d 306, 312 n.6 (Tex. 1993).

220 *Id.* at 314–15 (*quoting* Stout v. Grand Prairie Indep. Sch. Dist., 733 S.W.2d 290, 294 (Tex. App. 1987).

221 Tex. Const. art. VII § 1.

222 *Richards*, 868 S.W.2d at 311.

223 *Plyler*, 457 U.S. at 238 (Powell, J., concurring) ("I agree with the Court that their children should not be left on the streets uneducated.").

224 *Id.* at 218–19.

225 *Cf. id.* at 205–06 with *Richards*, 868 S.W.2d at 308.

226 *Plyler*, 457 U.S. at 228–29.

227 Hernandez v. Houston Indep. Sch. Dist., 558 S.W.2d 121 (Tex. App. 1977).

228 *Id.* at 122–23.

229 *Id.* at 122–124.

230 *Id.* at 124–25.

231 *See* Cooper, *supra* note 5 at 70 n.25 ("A state case was decided while the *Doe v. Plyler* suit was pending but there was no attempt to challenge the federal action on that ground.").

232 *Cf.* Kirby v. Edgewood Indep. Sch. Dist., 761 S.W.2d 859, 861 n.4 (Tex. App. 1988) ("The precise holding in *Hernandez*, that the state need not provide a tuition-free education to illegal alien children, was overruled by *Plyler*.").

233 *School Is Accused of Barring Student*, Chicago Trib., Northern Edition, Aug. 10, 2007, at 3.

234 *Id.*

235 Letter from Mexican American Legal Defense Fund (MALDEF) to Dr. Sandra Ellis Superintendent Northern Chicago Community Unit Schools August 9, 2007. *Available at* www.maldef.org, last visited August 26, 2007.

236 *Id.*

237 *Id.*

238 *Id.*

239 *Id.*

240 *School Is Accused of Barring Student*, Chicago Trib., Northern Edition, Aug. 10, 2007, at 3.

241 *See* Email from Ricardo Meza, MALDEF to María Pabón López (July 21, 2008, 3:22pm) (on file with author).

242 See Executive Order No. 10, Creating New Americans Immigrant Policy Council (2005), *available at* http://www.illinois.gov/gov/execorder.cfm?eorder=43 (last visited August 19, 2008).

243 *Id.*

244 *See* Joel R. v. Manheim Middle School, 686 N.E.2d 650, 653 (Ill. App. 1997).

245 *See* Superintendents Memorandum No.92 from Jo Lynne DeMary to Division Superintendents, May 30, 2003, *available at* http://www-prod.pen.k12.va.us/VDOE/suptsmemos/2004/inf170.htm) (last visited August 19, 2008).

246 *See e.g.,* 23 Ill Admin Code § 1.240(2005) Equal Opportunities for All Students, *available at* http://www.icsps.ilstu.edu/ocr2/quickview/23cfr1_240.pdf (last visited August 19, 2008).

247 *See* Indiana Department of Education, "Public School Attendance of Undocumented Students," *available at* http://www.doe.state.in.us/lmmp/pdf/lmmp_brochure.pdf (last visited August 19, 2008); Tennessee Department of Education, Attendance Manual at 4, *available at* http://tennessee.gov/education/schapproval/attendancemanual/doc/AttManualSectionC.pdf (last visited August 19, 2008).

248 Missouri Department of Education, Guidelines Regarding the Use of Social Security Numbers and the Attendance at School of Undocumented Students, *available at* http://www.dese.mo.gov/schoollaw/freqaskques/undocumented-students.htm (last visited August 19, 2008).

249 María Pabón López, *More Than a License to Drive: State Restrictions on the Use of Driver's Licenses*, 29 S. Ill. U. L.J. 89 (2004).

250 Susan C. Morse and Frank S. Ludovina, *Responding to Undocumented Children in the Schools*, http://www.eric.ed.gov/ERICDocs/data/ericdocs2sql/content_storage_01/0000019b/80/29/c2/f0.pdf ERIC Identifier: ED433172.

251 *Id.*

252 *Id.*

253 *Id.*

254 Mary Ann Zehr, *High Court's School Access Ruling Endures as a Quiet Fact of Life*, Education Week, June 6, 2007.

255 *See* Email from Gaylon Nettles, Director, Office of Student Services, Indiana Department of Education (July 14, 2008, 10:41:34 AM EDT) (on file with author).

256 Foreign Students Enrolled in Public School Districts, Michigan Dept. of Education, Bureau of School Finance and School Law (February 15, 2005), *available at* http://wash.k12.mi.us/files/pupilacct/Foreign_Feb05.doc. (last visited October 1, 2008).

257 *Id.*

258 *Id.*

259 James Rapp, 3–8 Education Law Section 8.04 [7][d] (1984 & Supp. 2008).
260 *See* 8 C.F.R. 214.3 (2008) (Approval of schools for enrollment of F-1 and J-1 nonimmigrants).
261 *See* INS General Counsel Op. No. 93–74, 1993 WL 1504021 (INS).
262 *Id.* (*quoting* Plyler v. Doe, 457 U.S. at 229, the Supreme Court recognized that school districts "are free to apply undocumented children established criteria for determining residence as they are to apply those criteria to any other child who seeks admission." ... "a school district may require that illegal alien children, like any other children, actually reside in the school district before admitting them to the schools. A requirement of de facto residency, uniformly applied, would not violate any principle of equal protection." *Id.* at 240, n. 4 (Powell, J., concurring).)
263 Rapp, *supra* note 259 at Section 8.04[7][d].
264 U.S. Gen. Accounting Office, Report to the Chairman, Committee on the Judiciary, House of Representatives: Illegal Alien Schoolchildren—Issues in Estimating State-by-State Costs, *available at* http://www.gao.gov/new.items/d04733.pdf (June 2004) p 14 n. 32. (*citing* LULAC v. Wilson, 907 F. Supp. 1244 (C.D. Cal. 1997).
265 *Id.*
266 Statutory law, federal regulations, and case law are all silent as to whether FERPA applies to undocumented students; *see also* 8 U.S.C 1372 § (c)(2) (2000) ("[t]he Family Educational Rights and Privacy Act of 1974 [20 U.S.C. § 1232g] shall not apply to aliens [nonimmigrant foreign students] described in subsection (a) to the extent that the Attorney General determines necessary to carry out the program under subsection (a).").
267 20 U.S.C. § 1232g(b)(1) (2000).
268 34 C.F.R. § 99.3 (2008).
269 20 U.S.C. § 1232g(b)(2) (2000).
270 John Willshire Carrera, *Immigrant Students, Their Legal Right to Access Public Schools, A Guide for Advocates and Educators*, p 13 1992, National Coalition for Advocates for Students. ED 381 588 p 14 (explaining why non-communication is important with the exception of F-1 and J-1 visas).
271 *Id.* at 15.
272 *See* Rapp, *supra* note 259 at Section 8.04[7][d].
273 Letter of Gaylon J. Nettles, Director, Office of Student Services, Indiana Department of Education dated September 18, 2008, *available at* http://www.doe.state.in.us/lmmp/pdf/immigrant_ltr.pdf (last visited October 1, 2008).
274 Broder, *supra* note 139 at 21.
275 Stephen Dinan, *States pay $7.4 Billion to Educate Illegals; Report Notes Drain on U.S. Children*, Wash. Times, August 21, 2003, at A04; *see also* Michael E. Fix and Jeffrey S. Passel, *U.S. Immigration: Trends and Implications for Schools*, Urban Institute, Jan. 2003, at 9.
276 *Id.*
277 *Id.*
278 *Id.*
279 *Id.*
280 *See generally* U.S. Gen. Accounting Office, Report to the Chairman, Committee on the Judiciary, House of Representatives: Illegal Alien Schoolchildren—Issues in Estimating State-by-State Costs, *available at* http://www.gao.gov/new.items/d04733.pdf (June 2004).

281 *Id.*

282 Julian L. Simon, *Errors about Immigrants: The Government Spends more on the native born*, The Cato Institute, June 25, 1997, *available at* http://www.cato.org/dailys//6–25–97.html (July 25, 2007).

283 *See* CARLOS SANDOVAL & CATHERINE TAMBINI, FARMINGVILLE (2004).

284 Lisa Richardson, *High School District Mulls Suing Mexico; Restitution: Proposal under Debate Would Demand $50 Million for Education of Mexican Children in Anaheim. Racism is Charged*, L.A. TIMES, May 28, 1999, at 11.

285 *Id.*

286 *Id.*

287 Matthew Ebnet, *Debate Over Educating Immigrants Stirs Passions; Schools: Pickets Warn of Ethnic Bashing As Anaheim School Board Talks of a Plan To Bill the U.S. Government or Other Nations for the Costs of Teaching the Undocumented*, L.A. TIMES, August 1, 1999, at 3.

288 *Id.*

289 *See* Richardson, *supra* note 284.

290 *Id.*

291 *Id.*

292 Lisa Richardson, *School Board Moves Closer to Mexico Suit; Education: Anaheim District Orders Resolution Drawn Seeking Payment for Teaching Mexican Students*, L.A. TIMES, May 29, 1999, at 3.

293 *Id.*

294 Maria Elena Fernandez, *Trustees Redirect Efforts on Illegal Immigrant Costs; Schools: Two Anaheim Board Members, Saying Other Nations Can't Be Sued, Now Want to Bill Feds*, L.A. TIMES, July 31, 1999, at 1.

295 *Id.*

296 *See* Ebnet, *supra* note 287.

297 H.G. Reza, *District Loses Immigrant School Case; Anaheim Union High Tried to Get U.S. Help Paying Education Costs of Students Illegally in Country*, L.A. TIMES, May 13, 2000, at 3.

298 Claire Luna, *Trustee's Loss Part of a Centrist Trend?; The Controversial Anaheim High School Board Member Was Too Extreme to Win a Third Term, Observers Say*, L.A. TIMES, November 7, 2002, at 15.

299 Danil Yi, *Anaheim Faces Immigration Battle; Group Wants the City Council to Seek First-In-The-Nation Permission for Local Police to Arrest Illegal Immigrants under Federal Law. Opposing Side Fears Racial Profiling. Both Groups Vow to Pack Meeting*, L.A.TIMES January 23, 2001, at 3.

300 *Id.*

301 Steven Barnett, The State of Preschool: 2003 State Preschool Yearbook 8 (2003) National Center for Education Statistics, U.S. Department of Education, http://nces.ed.gov/pubs2003/2003060.pdf.

302 See Betty Waters, *Tyler Independent School District Trustees Urged to Create Service Center*, TYLER MORNING TELEGRAPH, December 8, 2005.

303 *See* PRA, Pub. L. No. 104–193, 403(a), 110 Stat. 2105, 2265 (1996); 403(c)(2), 110 Stat. at 2226.

304 RICHARD ROTHSTEIN, CLASS AND SCHOOLS 141 (2004).

305 *Id.*

306 *Id.*

307 James Ryan, *A Constitutional Right to Pre-School*, 94 CALIF. L. REV. 49 (2006).

308 *Id.* at 50.

309 *Id.* at 66.

310 *Id.* (*citing,* Art Rolnick and Rob Grunewald, *Early Childhood Development: Economic Development with a High Public Return,* Federal Reserve Bank of Minneapolis, December 2003).

311 See Robert G. Lynch, Exceptional Returns, Economic, Fiscal, and Social Benefits of Investment in Early Childhood Development, Economic Policy Institute, 2004, *available at* http://www.earlylearningillinois.org/EPIExceptionalReturns. pdf (last visited at November 9, 2007).

312 William Dickens, Isabel V. Sawhill, Jeffrey Tebbs, *The Effects of Investing in Early Education on Income Growth,* The Brooking Institution, April 2006, http://www.brookings.edu/comm/policybriefs/pb153.htm; *see also,* Isabel V. Sawhill, *Kids Need an Early Start: Universal Preschool Education May Be the Best Investment Americans Can Make in our Children's Education—and our Nation's Future,* Blueprint (http://www.ndol.org/blueprint/fall/99/solutions10.html) (Fall 1999).

313 Press Release, Governor Blagojevich's Preschool for All Plan and College Tuition Relief Plan win Legislative Approval, May 4, 2006, *available at* http://www.illinois.gov/PressReleases/ShowPressRelease.cfm?SubjectID=1&R ecNum=4827 (last visited October 7, 2008).

314 Ryan, *supra* note 307 at 69–71.

315 Peter Enrich, *Leaving Equality Behind: New Directions in School Finance Reform,* 48 Vand. L. Rev. 101, 105–110 (1995).

316 Indiana Dep't of Educ. v. Evansville-Vandenburgh Sch. Corp., 844 N.E.2d 481 (Ind. 2006).

317 Abbott v. Burke, 748 A.2d 82 (N.J. 2000); Abbott v. Burke, 693 A.2d 417, 436 (N.J. 1997).

318 Lake View Sch. Dist. v. Huckabee, 91 S.E.3d 472, 500–02 (Ark 2002); Hancock v. Comm'r of Educ., 822 N.E.2d 1134, 1156–57 (Mass. 2005); Hoke County Bd. of Educ. v. State, 599 S.E. 365 393–94 (N.C. 2004).

319 Hancock v. Driscoll, No. 02–2978, 2004 WL 877984 (Mass. Super. Ct. Apr 26, 2004) at 137; *see also* Hoke County Bd of Educ. v. State, No. 95CVS1158, 2000. (N.C. Super. Ct. Oct. 12, 2000).

320 *Id.*

321 *Plyler,* 457 U.S. at 225.

322 *Id.* at 226.

323 *Id.*

324 Plyler, 457 U.S. at 230.

325 *Id.* at 223.

326 See Ryan *supra* note 307 at 66.

327 Luke van Houwelingen, *Tuition-based All-Day Kindergartens in the Public Schools: A Moral and Constitutional Critique,* 14 Geo. J. on Poverty L. & Pol'y 367, 376 (2007).

328 "[A]n alien who is not a qualified alien [i.e. not a lawful permanent resident, or lawfully admitted as a refugee or asylee or alien lawfully present in the U.S. under two other laws] is not eligible for any public benefit ..." 8 U.S.C. §§ 1611 and 1641(a) (2000).

329 *Id.*

330 European Commission (Directorate-General for Education and Culture), Integrating Immigrant Children into Schools in Europe, June 2004 ISBN 2–87116–376–6, *available at* http://www.okm.gov.hu/doc/upload/200701/ eurydice_migrants_en_070104.pdf (last visited: October 1, 2008).

331 *Id.*

332 Universal Declaration of Human Rights, G.A. Res. 217A (III), U.N. GAOR, 3d Sess., 1st plen. mtg., U.N. Doc. A/810 (Dec. 10, 1948). Art. 26; see also United Nations Convention of the Rights of the Child, G.A. Res. 44/25, Art. 1, Annex, at 167, U.N. GAOR 44th Sess., Supp. No 49, U.N. Doc. A/44/49 (Nov. 20, 1989) (entered into force Sept. 2, 1990) (signed by the United States on Feb. 16, 1995, but not ratified). Art. 28.

333 *See* International Covenant on Economic and Social Rights Dec. 16, 1966, 993 U.N.T.S. 3., Arts. 13, 14.

334 2000 O.J. (C 364) 9, Art. 14 *available at* http:// www.europarl.europa.eu/charter/pdf/text_en.pdf.

335 *See* Council Directive 2003/43, Art. 2(2)(b), 2000 O.J. (L 180/22): "Indirect discrimination shall be taken to occur where an apparently neutral provision, criterion or practice would put persons of a racial or ethnic origin at a particular disadvantage compared with other persons, unless that provision, criterion or practice is objectively justified by a legitimate aim and the means of achieving that aim are appropriate and necessary."

336 6 Eur. Ct. H.R. Series A, No. 6. 1 E.H.R.R. 252 (1968). (the "Belgian Linguistics Case").

337 *Id.*

338 *Id.*

339 Third-country nationals can achieve the status of long-term residents following continuous legal residence within the member state of at least five years. Council Directive 2003/109/EC, EC of Nov. 25 2003, Arts. 4 and 5.

340 *See* Directive 2003/9/E C, Art. 11. Denmark, Ireland and the United Kingdom have not adopted this Directive.

341 *See* Integrating Immigrant Children into Schools in Europe *supra* note 329 at 33, *see also* Belgium: Constitution, Art. 24 para. 3, Czech Republic: Regulation No. 21 836/2000–11, Greece: Art. 40 of L. 2910/2001, France: Ordonnance n° 2000–549, Art. L.131–1, Ireland: Education Act 1998, Italy: 1995, legislation that overturned the 1991 Ministerial Circular No. 400, which denied compulsory education for immigrant students unless their parents held valid residency status, Luxembourg: July 2003 Regulation, Netherlands: the Constitution, Austria: the Constitution and the *Schulpflichtgesetz*, Portugal: Constitution of the Portuguese Republic.

342 *See* Integrating Immigrant Children into Schools in Europe *supra* note 330 at 33.

343 *Id.* at 34.

344 *Id.* at 35.

345 *Id.* at 36.

346 *Id.* at 37.

347 *Id.* at 38.

348 *Id.*

349 *Id.* at 39.

350 *Id.*

351 *Id.*

352 *Id.* at 43.

353 *Id.* at 44.

354 *Id.* at 45.

355 *Id.* at 49.

356 *Id.*

357 *Id.* at 52.

358 *Id.* at 45.

359 *Id.* at 45.
360 *Id.* at 47.
361 *Id.* at 54.
362 *Id.*
363 *Id.* at 57.
364 87 Cong. Rec. 44, 46–47 (1941).
365 See Peter Enrich, *Leaving Equality Behind: New Directions in School Finance Reform*, 48 Vand. L. Rev. 101, 105–10 (1995).
366 *Id., see generally* Leandro v. State of North Carolina, 488 S.E.2d 249 (N.C. 1997); *see also* Brigham v. State of Vermont, 692 A.2d 384 (Vt. 1997).
367 San Antonio Indep. Sch. Dist. v. Rodriguez, 411 U.S. 1 (1973).
368 Daniel S. Greenspahn, *A Constitutional Right to Learn: The Uncertain Allure of Making a Federal Case out of Education*, 59 S.C. L. Rev. 755 (2008)
369 Louis Henkin, Gerald L. Neuman, Diane F. Orentlicher, David W. Leebron, Human Rights 1159 (1999).
370 *Id.*

Chapter 2

1 Yvonne Watterson, Documented Dreams: A Testimony of The Plight of a Generation of Young Latinos Caught in a Social Dilemma (2008).
2 *See* Rachel Ida Buff, *The Underground Railroad: Undocumented Immigrant Students and Public Universities* in Immigrant Rights in the Shadow of Citizenship 301 (Rachel Ida Buff ed. 2008).
3 *See* UCLA Center for Labor Research and Education, Underground Undergrads: UCLA Undocumented Immigrant Students Speak Out (Gabriela Madera et al. eds., 2008) [*hereinafter* Underground Undergrads].
4 Kevin R. Johnson & Bill Ong Hing, *The Immigrant Rights Marches of 2006 and the Prospect for a New Civil Rights Movement*, 42 Harv. Civ. Rts-Civ. Lib.L. Rev. 99 (2007).
5 Peter Carlson, *Stinky the Robot, Four Kids and a Brief Whiff of Success*, Wash. Post March 29, 2005 at C1, *available at* http://www.washingtonpost.com/wp-dyn/articles/A8429-2005Mar28.html.
6 *Id.*
7 *Id.*
8 *Id.*
9 Mel Melendez, *Ingenuity Brightens Future; Doors Finally Open for 4 Phoenix Migrant Youths after Beating MIT in Robotics Competition*, Arizona Republic, April 23, 2005 p 1A.
10 *Id.*
11 *Id.*
12 Richard Ruelas, *For Carl Hayden Robotics Team, Beating Immigration Is Tougher Than Beating the Competition*, Arizona Republic, July 31, 2008, *available at* http://www.azcentral.com/arizonarepublic/arizonaliving/articles/2008/07/31/20080731robotkids0731.html.
13 *Id.*
14 *Id.*
15 Yvonne Wingett and Matthew Benson, *Migrant Law Blocks Benefits: Prop 300 Denying College Aid, and Child-care*, Arizona Republic, August 2, 2007.

16 Nina Bernstein, *New Allies Bolster Student in his Immigration Struggle*, N.Y. TIMES, May 2, 2006, *available at* http://www.nytimes.com/2006/05/02/nyregion/02deport.html?_r=2&oref=slogin.

17 *Id.*

18 News Release, Congressman Charles B. Rangel, AMADOULY GRANTED VISA TO STUDY IN U.S., July 28, 2006, *available at* http://www.house.gov/list/press/ny15_rangel/CBRstatementAmadouLyVisa07282006.html.

19 Miriam Jordan, *Illegal at Princeton*, WALL ST. J., Apr. 15, 2006, at A1; *Princeton's 2006 Salutatorian Heads to Oxford, Still an Illegal Immigrant*, WALL ST. J., Sept. 14, 2006, at B1.

20 *Id.*

21 *Id.*

22 *Id.*

23 *Id.*

24 *Id.*

25 *Id.*

26 Diana Furchtgott-Roth, Op-Ed., *Give this Law an "A,"* N.Y. SUN, May 18, 2007, at 10.

27 Email of Dan-El Padilla to María Pabón López, October 9, 2008.

28 Richard Ruelas, *see supra* note 12. http://www.azcentral.com/arizonarepublic/arizonaliving/articles/2008/07/31/20080731robotkids0731.html.

29 Tim Padgett, *Can Two Kids Alter Immigration Law?* TIME, August 2, 2007.

30 *Id.*

31 *Id.*

32 *Id.*

33 *Id.*

34 Phuong Ly, *The Outsider*, WASH. POST, February 22, 2009 at W 10.

35 Tim Padgett, *see supra* note 29.

36 Juan Gomez—Once Facing Deportation, Now Going on To College, August 21, 2008, DreamActivist.org, *available at* http://dreamactivist.org/2008/08/21/juan-gomez-once-facing-deportation-grad-off-to-college.

37 *Id.*

38 Bartsch gains stay, PUTNAM SENTINEL, August 3, 2007, *available at*: http://putnamsentinel.com/main.asp?SectionID=1&SubSectionID=1&ArticleID=1225.

39 *See* Chris Vogel, *The Dream Act Might Be Dead, But These Kids' Hopes Are Not*, HOUS. PRESS, June 19, 2008.

40 Gale Holland, *Having Degree of Anxiety; Undocumented Graduates See a Mixed Future*, L.A. TIMES, July 8, 2008, at B1.

41 Jeffrey S. Passel & D'Vera Cohn, *A Portrait of Unauthorized Immigrants in the United States.*, Pew Hispanic Center. April 14, 2009, at ii.

42 Jeanne Batalova and Michael Fix, *New Estimates of Unauthorized Youth Eligible for Legal Status under the DREAM Act*, Migration Policy Institute Immigration Backgrounder Oct. 2006, No.1, *available at* http://www.migrationpolicy.org/pubs/Backgrounder1_Dream_Act.pdf.

43 *Id.*

44 Jeffrey S. Passel, *Further Demographic Information relating to DREAM Act*. Urban Institute, October 21, 2003, *available at* http://www.nilc.org/immlaw-policy/DREAM/DREAM_Demographics.pdf.

45 Roberto Gonzales, *Wasted Talent and Broken Dreams: The Lost Potential of Undocumented Students*, 5 IN FOCUS, Issue 13, Oct. 2007 (Immigration Policy Center, 2007), *available at* http://www.immigrationpolicy.org/index.php?content=f071001.

46 *Id.*

47 *Id.*

48 Youngro Lee, *To Dream or Not to Dream*, 16 Cornell J.L. & Pub. Pol'y 231, 235 (2006).

49 Katie Annand, *Still Waiting for the DREAM: the Injustice of Punishing Undocumented Immigrant Students*, 59 Hastings L.J. 683, 695 (2008). *See also* Thomas R. Ruge & Angela D. Iza, *Higher Education for Undocumented Students: the Case for Open Admission and In-State Tuition Rates for Students without Lawful Immigration Status*, 15 Ind. Int'l & Comp. L. Rev. 257 (2005).

50 The College Board a Supplement to Education Pays 2004: The Benefits of Higher Education for Individuals and Society, p 2 (citing U.S. Census Bureau Annual Social and Economic Supplement. Current Population Reports. http://ferret.bls.census.gov/macro/032004/perinc/new03_000.htm.)   (http://www.collegeboard.com/prod_downloads/press/cost05/education_pays_05.pdf).

51 U.S. Bureau of Labor Statistics (2005). *Labor Force Statistics from the Current Population Survey.* http://www.bls.gov/webapps/legacy/cpsatab4.htm.

52 As of April 2009, the national unemployment rate of college graduates (4.4 percent) had doubled in the previous year, but was significantly less than those with some college (7.4 percent), high school only (9.3 percent) or less than high school (14.8 percent). *See* The Labor Picture in April 2009, N.Y.Times, May 7, 2009, *available at* http://www.nytimes.com/interactive/2009/05/07/business/20090508-labor-picture-graphic.html.

53 Miriam Jordan, *Illegal at Princeton* Wall St. April 15, 2006 p A1(statement of Ira Melman).

54 Enrico Moretti, *Estimating the social return to higher education: Evidence from longitudinal and repeated cross-section data.* 121 J. Econometrics 175–212 (2004).

55 U.S. Census Bureau, *Voting and Registration in the Election of November 2004.*, *available at* http://www.census.gov/population/www/socdemo/voting/cps2004.html.

56 The College Board, *Education Pays Update 7* (2005), *available at* http://www.collegeboard.com/prod_downloads/press/cost05/education_pays_05.pdf.

57 *Id.*

58 Ruge and Iza, *supra* note 49 at 261(citing U.S. Census Bureau, *Profile of the Foreign-Born Population in the United States:* 2000 36 (2001), *available at* http://www.census.gov/prod/2002pubs/p23-206.pdf.

59 The Economic Benefits of the DREAM Act and the Student Adjustment Act, National Immigration Law Center, February 2005, *available at:* http://www.nilc.org/immlawpolicy/DREAM/Econ_Bens_DREAM&Stdnt_Adjst_0205.pdf.

60 *Plyler*, 457 U.S. at 228.

61 *See* Vicky Salinas, *You Can Be Whatever You Want to Be When You Grow Up, Unless Your Parents Brought You to this Country Illegally: The Struggle to Grant In-State Tuition to Undocumented Immigrant Students*, 43 Hous. L. Rev. 847, 873 (2006).

62 Kathleen Connolly, *In Search of the American Dream: An Examination of Undocumented Students, In-State Tuition and the DREAM Act*, 55 Cath. U.L. Rev. 193, 217 (2005).

63 Alejandra Rincon, Undocumented Immigrants and Higher Education: Si se puede! (2008).

64 Section 505 of the Illegal Immigration Reform and Immigrant Responsibility Act of 1996 (IIRIRA), codified at 8 U.S.C. § 1623 (2005); Personal Responsibility and

Work Opportunity Reconciliation Act of 1996 (PRWORA) codified at 8 U.S.C. § 1621(2005) generally prohibit undocumented students from receiving federal aid.

65 Gale Holland, *Having Degree of Anxiety; Undocumented Graduates See a Mixed Future*, L.A. TIMES, July 8, 2008, at B1.

66 *See* Amanda Cole, *N.C. Community Colleges Ban Illegal Immigrants,* TARTAN ONLINE, August 25, 2008, *available at* http://www.thetartan.org/2008/8/25/ news/immigrants. There are three very narrow exceptions to the ban: high school students who are enrolled concurrently in college under particular programs; students enrolled in non degree programs, for example, GED; and students who can prove they are "qualified aliens" under immigration law. *See* North Carolina Community College System, Study on the Admission of Undocumented Students into the North Carolina Community College System at 2 (April 19, 2009, *available at* http://www.wral.com/asset/news/state/2009/ 04/16/4963055/NCCCS_Final_Report.swf).

67 Gale Holland, *Having Degree of Anxiety; Undocumented Graduates See a Mixed Future*, L.A. TIMES, July 8, 2008, at B1.

68 UCLA Registrar's Office, *Fees Graduate and Undergraduate Annual 2007–08*, *available at* http://www.admissions.ucla.edu/prospect/budget.htm, last visited at Sept. 5, 2008.

69 Plyler v. Doe, 457 U.S. 202, 222, n.22 (1982).

70 Jennifer L. Maki, *The Three R's: Reading, Riting, and Rewarding Illegal Immigrants: How Higher Education Has Acquiesced in the Illegal Presence of Undocumented Aliens in the United States*, 13 WM. & MARY BILL RTS. J. 1341 (2005).

71 *Id.*

72 8 U.S.C. § 1621 (2000).

73 8 U.S.C. § 1823 (2000).

74 Beth Peters & Marshall Fitz, *To Repeal or Not To Repeal: The Federal Prohibition On In-State Tuition For Undocumented Immigrants Revisited*, IMMIGR. DAILY, Oct. 4, 2002, *available at* www.ilw.com/lawyers/articules/2002,1004-peters.shtm#610.

75 Kris W. Kobach, *Immigration Nullification: In-state Tuition and Lawmakers who Disregard the Law*, 10 N.Y.U. J. LEGIS. & PUB. POL'Y 473 (2007).

76 Michael Olivas, *Lawmakers Gone Wild? College Residency and the Response to Professor Kobach*, 61 SMU L. REV. 99, 119–25 (2008).

77 *Id.*

78 *Id.*

79 *Id.*

80 *Id.*

81 Ruge and Iza, *supra* note 49 at 261.

82 Michael Olivas, *A Rebuttal to FAIR: States Can Enact Residency Statutes for the Undocumented*, 7 Bender's Immigr Bull. 652 (2002).

83 Letter of Jim Pendergraph to Thomas Ziko, July 9, 2008, *available at* http://www.nilc.org/immlawpolicy/DREAM/DHS-letter-re-undoc-students-2008-07-9.pdf.

84 Martinez v. Regents of the Univ. of California, 83 Cal. Rptr. 3d 518, 523 (Cal. App. 2008).

85 ICE Letter to Jim Hackenberg, Esq. on May 9, 2008, Student and Exchange Visitor Program, *available at* www.ice.gov and at https://salsa.democracyinaction.org/o/371/images/ICE%20Statement%20on%20Enrollment%20of%20Undocumented.pdf.

86 *Id.*

87 *Id.*

88 *Id.*

89 Letter of Jim Pendergraph to Thomas Ziko, *supra* note 83.

90 *Id.*

91 *Id.*

92 Memorandum from Alison P. Landry, Assistant Attorney General, to Presidents, Chancellor, Rectors, Registrars, Admissions Directors, Domicile Officers and Foreign Student Advisors (INS Designated School Officials) and the Executive Director of the State Council for Higher Education in Virginia (Sept. 5, 2002), *available at* http://www.steinreport.com/va_colleges_11152002.htm.

93 Letter of J.B. Kelly to Shante Martin, July 24, 2008, *available at* http://www.newsobserver.com/content/media/2008/7/25/20080725_immigrationdoc.pdf.

94 Day v. Sebelius, 376 F. Supp. 2d 1022 (D. Kan. July 5, 2005) *aff'd* 500 F.3d 1127 (10th Cir. 2007); Equal Access Educ. v. Merten, 305 F. Supp. 2d 585 (E.D. Va. 2004); Martinez v. Regents, 83 Cal. Rptr. 3d 518 (Cal. App. 2008).

95 305 F. Supp. 2d 585 (E.D. Va. 2004).

96 *Id.* at 585.

97 *See* Equal Access Educ. v. Merten, 305 F. Supp. 2d 585 (E.D. Va. 2004).

98 *Id.* at 607.

99 *Id.* at 608.

100 *Id.* at 591.

101 *Id.*

102 *Id.*

103 *See* Doe v. Merten, 219 F.R.D. 387 (E.D. Va. 2004).

104 *See Equal Access Educ.*, 305 F. Supp. 2d at 592 n.3.

105 *Id.* at 614.

106 Equal Access Educ. v. Merten, 325 F. Supp. 2d 655 (E.D. Va. 2004); *see also* Kendra Nichols, *Federal Judge Dismisses Illegal Immigrants' Lawsuit Against Virginia's Public Colleges*, CHRON. OF HIGHER EDUC., July 16, 2004, at A24.

107 Equal Access Educ., 305 F. Supp. 2d at 609.

108 *Id.* at 610.

109 Day v. Sibelius, 376 F. Supp. 2d 1022 (D. Kan 2005).

110 *Id.*

111 Day v. Sibelius, 376 F. Supp. 2d 1022 (D. Kan 2005), *aff'd* Day v. Bond, 500 F. 3d. 1127 (10th Cir. 2007).

112 Day v. Bond, 500 F. 3d. 1127 (10th Cir. 2007).

113 Day v. Bond, 128 S. Ct. 2987 (2008).

114 *See* Martinez v. Regents, 83 Cal. Rptr. 3d 518, 524 (Cal. App. 2008).

115 Martinez v. Regents, 2006 WL 2974303 (Cal. Sup. Ct. October 4, 2006), *rev'd* Martinez v. Regents, 83 Cal. Rptr. 3d 518 (Cal. App. 2008).

116 Martinez v. Regents, 83 Cal. Rptr. 3d 518, 533 (Cal. App. 2008).

117 *Id.* at 531.

118 Martinez v. Regents, 87 Cal. Rptr. 3d 198 (Cal. 2008).

119 Plyler, 457 U.S. at 202.

120 *Plyler* 457 U.S. 242 (Burger, C.J. dissenting) ("We trespass on the assigned function of the political branches under our structure of limited and separated powers when we assume a policymaking role as the Court does today.").

121 UNDERGROUND UNDERGRADS, *supra* note 3 at 15–16.

122 Andorra Bruno and Jeffrey Kuenzi, *Unauthorized Alien Students: Issues and*

Legislation, CRS Report for Congress RL 31365 (Washington, DC: Congressional Research Service, December 17, 2003).

123 *Id.*

124 *Id.*

125 S. 1545 (Hatch) Development, Relief, and Education for Alien Minors Act of 2003. Reported by Judiciary Committee on November 25, 2003; S. Rept. 108–224 filed on February 9, 2004.

126 *Id.*

127 Andorra Bruno et al., *CRS Report: Immigration Legislation and Issues in the 108th Congress*, updated June 22, 2004, *available at* http://opencrs.cdt.org/document/RL32169/2004-06-22.

128 *Id.*

129 *Id.* at 10.

130 *Id.*

131 Andorra Bruno, *Unauthorized Alien Students: Issues and "DREAM Act" Legislation* at 4, CRS Report RL33863, January 30, 2007 *available at* http://assets.opencrs.com/rpts/RL33863_20070130.pdf.

132 *Id.*

133 *Id.*

134 *Id.*

135 *Id.* at 2.

136 *See* Subtitle C, Section 623 of the Comprehensive Immigration Reform Act of 2006, S. 2611, *available at* http://thomas.loc.gov/cgi-bin/bdquery/z?d109:SN02611:@@@L&summ2=m&.

137 *See* Subtitle C, Section 624 of the Comprehensive Immigration Reform Act of 2006, S. 2611, *available at* http://thomas.loc.gov/cgi-bin/bdquery/z?d109:SN02611:@@@L&summ2=m&.

138 *Id.*

139 *Id.*

140 Julia Preston, *In Increments, Senate Revisits Immigration Bill* N.Y. Times August 3, 2007, *available at* http://www.nytimes.com/2007/08/03/washington/03immig.html.

141 For detailed entries regarding S. 2205, *see e.g.* http://www.thomas.gov/cgi-bin/bdquery/D?d110:10:./temp/~bd9aVc::l/bss/110search.htmll.

142 Julia Preston, *Bill for Immigrant Students Fails Test Vote in Senate* N.Y. Times, October 25, 2007, *available at* http://www.nytimes.com/2007/10/25/washington/25immig.html?scp=1&sq=Test%20immigrants&st=cse.

143 See Library of Congress, Thomas, http://thomas.loc.gov/cgi-bin/bdquery/z?d111:SN00729:@@@X.

144 A webcast of her testimony is *available at* http://judiciary.senate.gov/hearings/hearing.cfm?id=3803.

145 Julia Preston, *supra* note 142.

146 Rick Maze, *Bill Would Grant Citizenship for Service*, Army Times, July 16, 2007, *available at* http://www.armytimes.com/news/2007/07/military_servicecitizenship_070716w/.

147 *See* Testimony of Marie Nazareth Gonzalez, Student Jefferson City Missouri, Hearing on Comprehensive Immigration Reform: The Future of Undocumented Students, May 18, 2007; *see also* Martine Mwanj Kalaw and Tam Tran, Written statements are *available at* http://judiciary.house.gov/media/pdfs/Gonzalez070518.pdf http://judiciary.house.gov/media/pdfs/Kalaw070518.pdf http://judiciary.house.gov/media/pdfs/Tran070518.pdf.

148 Julia Preston, *In Increments, Senate Revisits Immigration Bill* N.Y. Times August 3, 2007, *available at* http://www.nytimes.com/2007/08/03/washington/03immig.html.

149 Plyler v. Doe, 457 U.S. 202, n.11 (citing Wong Wing v. United States, 163 U.S. 228,. 242–43 (1896).

150 Dave Michaels, *DREAM Act, Affecting Children of Illegal Immigrants, Fails Senate Test Vote,* Dallas Morn. News, October 25, 2007, *available at* http://www.dallasnews.com/sharedcontent/dws/news/texassouthwest/stories/102507dnnatdreamact.1a216ca67.html.

151 Fernando Suarez Del Solar, *On the DREAM Act and the U.S. Military, An Open Letter to Latino and Latina Students and All Leaders of Immigrant Rights Organizations,* InMotion Magazine, August 5, 2007, *available at* http://www.inmotionmagazine.com/opin/fss_dream.html.

152 Congressional Budget Office Cost Estimate January 20, 2004, S. 2075, *available at* http://www.cbo.gov/showdoc.cfm?index=4981&sequence=0&from=6

153 *Id.*

154 *Id.*

155 Immigration Policy Center, Dreams *Deferred: The Costs of Ignoring Undocumented Students,* October 18, 2007, *available at* www.immigrationpolicy.org.

156 Wisconsin v. Yoder, 406 U.S. 205, 221–22 (1972), the U.S. Supreme Court noted that "as Thomas Jefferson pointed out early in our history, that some degree of education is necessary to prepare citizens to participate effectively and intelligently in our open political system if we are to preserve freedom and independence. Further, education prepares individuals to be self-reliant and self-sufficient participants in society." *See also* Romero, *Postsecondary School Education Benefits for Undocumented Immigrants: Promises and Pitfalls,* 27 N.C. J. Int'l & Com. Reg. 393, 410–11 (2002).

157 Regents University of California v. Bradford, 22 Cal. App. 3d 972, 276 Cal. Rptr. 197 (Cal. Ct. App. 1990).

158 *Id.* at 981.

159 *Id.*

160 *Id.*

161 *Id.*

162 Richard Delgado & Jean Stefancic, Critical Race Theory: An Introduction 5 (2001).

163 Regents University of California v. Bradford, 22 Cal. App. 3d 972, 276 Cal. Rptr. 197 (Cal. Ct. App. 1990) at 981 (see discussion on 1986 Immigration Reform and Control Act).

164 League of United American Citizens v. Wilson, 997 F. Supp. 1244 (C.D. Cal. 1997).

165 *Id.* at 1255.

166 *Id.* at 1256, 1261.

167 National Conference of State Legislatures, *In-State Tuition and Unauthorized Immigration Status,* July 26, 2006, *available at* http://www.ncsl.org/programs/immig/immig_InStateTuition0706.htm.

168 Kirk Semple, *In New Jersey, Uncertainty for Measures Offering In-State Tuition to Illegal Immigrants Face a Fight,* N.Y. Times, April 20, 2009 at A 20.

169 Jennifer Robinson, Center for Public Policy & Administration, the University of Utah: *Policy Brief, In-State Tuition for Undocumented Students in Utah Policy Brief,* Feb. 13, 2007, *available at* http://www.cppa.utah.edu/publications/higher_ed/Policy_Brief_2_13_07_In-state_Tuition.pdf.

170 *Id.*

171 H.B. 1403, 77th Leg., Reg. Sess. (Tex. 2001), codified at Tex. Educ. Code Ann. § 54.051, 54.052, 54.0551, 54.057, 54.060.

172 Ruge and Iza, *supra* note 49.

173 For a more detailed discussion, *see* Maki, *supra* note 70 at 1361.

174 S.B. 1528, 79th Leg., Reg. Sess. (Tex. 2005), codified at Tex. Educ. Code Ann. § 54.051, 54.052, 54.0551, 54.057, 54.060. See also, Texas Higher Education Coordinating Board, Summary of Higher Education legislation, 79th Texas Legislature, December 2006, *available at* http://www.thecb.state.tx.us/reports/PDF/0857.PDF, last visited August 8, 2008.

175 Juan Castillo, *Lawmakers Revisit Tuition Discounts for Illegal Immigrants*, Austin Am.-Statesman. April 20, 2007, *available at* http://www.statesman.com/news/content/region/legislature/stories/04/20/20immigtuition.html.

176 *Id.*

177 *Id.*

178 *Id.*

179 *Id.*

180 *Id.*

181 AB 540, Cal. Educ. Code § 68130.5 (2001). Assembly Bill Number: 540, Chapter 814, available at the Immigrant Legal Resource Center website http://www.ilrc.org/ab540bill.pdf. *See also* Underground Undergrads, 5–8.

182 *Id. See also* Robinson, *supra* note 169; Jessica Salsbury, *Evading "Residence": Undocumented Students, Higher Education, and the States*, 53 Am. U. L. Rev. 459, 472–80 (2003).

183 *Id. See also* Underground Undergrads, *supra* note 3 at 5–12.

184 *See* text accompanying notes 116–18.

185 Salsbury, *supra* note 182 at 473.

186 *See* Underground Undergrads, *supra* note 3 at 5–12.

187 *Id.*

188 *Id.* at 7.

189 *Id. See Schwarzenegger vetoes the DREAM Act*, Oct. 14, 2007, *available at* http://www.ktvu.com/news/14338741/detail.html?rss=fran&psp=news.

190 *See* Jennifer Robinson, *supra* note 169.

191 Michael A. Olivas, *Immigration-Related State Statutes and Local Ordinances: Preemption, Prejudice, and the Proper Role for Enforcement*, 12 Bender's Immigr. Bull. 901, 909 (July 15, 2007). The ten states are: California, A.B. 540, 2002–02 Leg. Reg. Sess. (Cal. 2001) (codified at Cal. Educ. Code § 68130.5 (Deering 2007)); Illinois, H.B. 60, 93rd Gen. Assemb., Reg. Sess. (Ill. 2003) (codified in various sections of 110 Ill. Comp. Stat. Ann. (LexisNexis 2007)); Kansas, H.B. 2145, 2003–2004 Leg., Reg. Sess. (Kan. 2004) codified at Kan. Stat ann. §76-731a (2006); Nebraska, L.B. 239, 99th Leg., 1st Sess. (Neb. 2006) (codified at neb. Rev. Stat. Ann. §85–502 (LexisNexis 2006)) (overriding governor's veto); New Mexico, S.B. 582, 47th leg., Reg. Sess. (N.M. 2005) (codified at N.M. Stat. Ann. § 21–1–4.6 (LexisNexis 2007)); New York, S.B. 7784, 225th leg., 2001 Sess. (N.Y. 2002) (codified at N.Y. EDUC. LAW §355(2)(h)(8)(Consol. 2007)); Oklahoma, S.B. 596, 49th Leg., 1st Reg. Sess. (Okla. 2003) (codified at OKLA. STAT. ANN. TIT. 70, § 3242 (West 2006)); Texas, H.B. 1403, 77th Leg., Reg. Sess. (Tex. 2001) (codified as amended by S.B. 1528, 79th Leg. Sess. (Tex. 2005) in various sections of Tex. Educ. Code Ann. Ch. 54 (Vernon 2007)); Utah, H.B. 144, 54th Leg., (Utah 2002) (codified at Utah Code Ann. § 53B-8-106 (2006)); Washington, H.B. 1079, 58th Leg., 2003

Reg. Sess. (Wash. 2003) (codified at Wash. Rev. Code Ann. § 28b.15.012 (LexisNexis 2007)).

192 Jennifer L. Frum, *Postsecondary Educational Access for Undocumented Students: Opportunities and Constraints*, 3 Amer. Academic 81 (Jan. 2007), *available at* http://www.aft.org/pubs-reports/american_academic/issues/january07/Frum. pdf.

193 S.B. 492.

194 H.B. 1023.

195 National Conference of State Legislatures, *Immigrant Policy Project, Overview of State Legislation Related to Immigrants and Immigration, January 1-June 30, 2008*, at 1, (July 24, 2008), *available at* http://www.ncsl.org/programs/ immig/immigreportjuly2008.htm.

196 National Coalition of Latino Clergy v. Henry, 2007 WL 4390650, CIV-07–613–GKF-FHM (N.D. Okla. December 12, 2007).

197 *Id.* at *8.

198 *Id.*

199 National Conference of State Legislatures, *Immigrant Policy Project, supra* note 195.

200 National Conference of State Legislatures, *Immigrant Policy Project, Overview of State Legislation Related to Immigrants and Immigration, January–March 2008*, at 3, Apr. 24, 2008, *available at* http://www.ncsl.org/programs/immig/immigre-portapril2008.htm.

201 *Id.*

202 National Conference of State Legislatures, *supra* note 195.

203 Sara Hebel, *In Rural America, Few People Harvest 4–Year Degrees*, Chron. High. Ed. November 3, 2006 at 22.

204 *Id.*

205 Tanya Broder, *State and Local Policies on Immigrant Access to Services: Promoting Immigration or Isolation*, National Immigration Law Center, May 2007, *available at* http://www.nilc.org/immspbs/sf_benefits/statelocalimmpolicies06-07_2007-05-24.pdf.

206 H.B. 39, 23d Leg., Reg. Sess. (Alaska 2003) (signed into law on Jan. 21, 2003).

207 Yvonne Wingett and Matthew Benson, *Migrant Law Blocks Benefits: Prop 300 Denying College Aid, Child Care*, Ariz. Republic August 2, 2007, *available at* http://www.azcentral.com/arizonarepublic/news/articles/0802program-eligibility 0802.html.

208 Arizona Joint Legislative Budget Committee- Monthly Fiscal High-lights 7 (July 2007), *available at* http://www.azleg.gov/jlbc/mfh-july-07.pdf.

209 *Id.*

210 *Id.*

211 *Id.*

212 *Id.*

213 *Id.*

214 State to Investigate *Whether Arizona State U. Broke Law on Aid to Illegal Immigrants*, Chron. Higher Ed. September 12, 2007, *available at* http:// chronicle.com/news/article/3015/state-to-investigate-whether-arizona-state-u-broke-law-on-aid-to-illegal-immigrants.

215 *Id.*

216 E.C. v. Obergfell, CV-0359–DFH-WTL (S.D. Ind. March 2, 2006).

217 *Id.*

218 Priscilla Huang, *Which Babies Are Real Americans?* February 20, 2007, *available at* http://www.commondreams.org/views07/0220-29.htm.
219 *Id.*
220 Mexican American Students' Alliance, Promoting Higher Education, home-page http://www.geocities.com/masanyus1/.
221 *Id.*
222 *CUNY Undocumented Students Organize To Stay In College*, Inmotion, *available at* http://www.inmotionmagazine.com/hrcr/nyund.html.
223 U.S. Const. Amend. I.
224 Reno v. American-Arab Anti-Discrimination Committee, 525 U.S. 471, 488 (1999); *see also* Jeanne Butterfield *Do Immigrants Have First Amendment Rights? Revisiting the Los Angeles Eight Case*, Middle East Report, Fall 1999.
225 525 U.S. 471 (1999).
226 *See* Maryam Kamali Miyamoto, *The First Amendment After Reno v. American-Arab Anti-Discrimination Commmittee: A Different Bill of Rights for Aliens?* 35 Harv C.R.-C.L. Rev. 183, 205 (2000).
227 *See* Gerald Neuman, *Terrorism, Selective Deportation and the First Amendment after Reno v. AADC*, 14 Geo. Immigr. L.J. 313, 314 (2000).
228 *See generally* R. George Wright *Undocumented Speakers and Freedom of Speech: A Relatively Unconstroversial Approach* (forthcoming).
229 *See* Michael J. Wishnie, *Immigrants and the Right to Petition*, 78 N.Y.U. L.Rev. 667, 715 (2003).
230 *Id.* at 687 (Indigenous colonial documents also codified the right to petition, beginning with the Body of Liberties adopted by the Massachusetts Bay Colony in 1641, which explicitly guaranteed the right to noncitizens: "Every man whether Inhabitant or forreiner, free or not free shall have libertie to come to any publique Court, Councell, or Towne meeting ... to present any necessary motion, complaint, petition, Bill or information ...".) (*citing* A Coppie of the Liberties of the Massachusetts Collonie in New England (1641), reprinted in 1 Documents on Fundamental Human Rights: The Anglo-American Tradition 122, 124 (Zechariah Chafee, Jr. ed., 1963)).
231 *Id.* at 714.
232 494 U.S. 259 (1990).
233 *Id.* at 265.
234 *Id.* at 271.
235 *See* 457 U.S. 202 (1982).
236 *See* Tinker v. Des Moines Indep. Cmty. Sch. Dist., 393 U.S. 503, 506 (1969); *see also* Morse v. Frederick, 127 S. Ct. 2618, 2625 (2007).
237 *Tinker*, 393 U.S. at 513.
238 *Id.* at 515.
239 Bethel School District v. Fraser, 478 U.S. 675, 685 (holding that lewd speech expressed during a school assembly was different than the political speech expressed in *Tinker* and subject to discipline); *see also Morse*, 127 S. Ct. 2618, 2622 ([w]e hold that schools may take steps to safeguard those entrusted to their care from speech that can reasonably be regarded as encouraging illegal drug use.).
240 Dunn v. Tyler Indep. Sch. Dist., 460 F.2d 137, 143 (5th Cir. 1972) (holding a school's policy against walking out was not overly broad or unconstitutional).
241 *Id.*
242 *Id.* at 143.

243 Jean Merl and Richard Winton, *Somber Note to an Upbeat Protest Rally; Organizers Dedicate L.A. Immigrant Rights March to a Boy whose Family Blames his Suicide on Fear Allegedly Instilled by a School Official*, L.A. TIMES, April 16, 2006, at B 3.

244 Morse v. Frederick, 127 S. Ct. 2618 (2007).

245 Richard Garnett, *Can There Really Be "Free Speech" in Public Schools?* 12 LEWIS & CLARK L. REV. 45 (2008)

246 Morse v. Frederick, 127 S. Ct. 2618 (2007).

247 *Id.*

248 Alan Maass, *Another Young Victim of the Stigmatization of Immigrants: The Suicide of Anthony Soltero*, April 12, 2006, COUNTERPUNCH, *available at* http://www.heal-online.org/soltero.pdf.

249 *Id.*

250 *Id.*

251 *Student's Suicide May Have Impact on Immigration Talks: Eighth-Grader Allegedly Killed Himself After Being Threatened for Protesting* available on *The Associated Press*, Apr. 14, 2006.

252 *Id.*

253 *Id.*

254 *See* Maass, *supra* note 248.

255 Garnett, *supra* note 245 at 107.

256 *See generally* VICTOR ROMERO, ALIENATED: IMMIGRANT RIGHTS, THE CONSTITUTION AND EQUALITY IN AMERICA 92–93 (2005).

Chapter 3

1 According to the Tempe Union High School District website (http://www. tuhsd.k12.az.us), East Valley Institute of Technology ("EVIT") is a regional public vocational school that serves students from ten school districts in Arizona's East Valley. Students enrolled at the school spend approximately half their school day at their home high school, where they receive instruction in the core content areas. Students are then bused to EVIT for their remaining half of their school day. EVIT offers a technical program in a variety of interest areas and is open to all 10th, 11th and 12th grade students who are residents of the ten participating districts. Busing is provided to and from EVIT by the student's home school district.

2 Mel Melendez, *Molera Backs District on Its Spanish Ban*, ARIZ. REPUBLIC, August 20, 2002, at 1B.

3 Mel Melendez, *No-Spanish Rule Vexes Students*, ARIZ. REPUBLIC, October 16, 2003, at 1B.

4 *Id.*

5 An interesting observation is that such an argument placed English-dominant children in the role of victim for not knowing Spanish. The irony of this argument is the implied reversal of power dynamics in favor of the English-speaking students.

6 *See generally* MICHAEL LIPSKY, STREET-LEVEL BUREAUCRACY: DILEMMAS OF THE INDIVIDUAL IN PUBLIC SERVICES (1980). (The notion of street-level bureaucracy suggests that decisionmakers often "interpret" state and federal policies to suit local conditions. In this regard, it highlights the fact that teachers and administrators can exercise substantial discretion in deciding how to interpret and implement policy.)

7 Justin Juozapavicius, *Feds Probe Tech School on English-Only Stance*, ARIZ. REPUBLIC, February 18, 2004 at 1B.

8 Efforts to investigate how the issue was resolved have not yielded conclusive results. All records from the Office of Civil Rights detailing the resolution and corrective action agreement have been removed from the OCR website. It appears that the Arizona State Attorney General's Office intervened in the matter, and ruled that the teacher's actions were inappropriate. They based their decision on the fact that the law stipulates what language can be used by the teacher for *instruction*, but does not stipulate what language a student can use in the school.

9 The other three English immersion initiatives put to popular vote were California's Proposition 227, Massachusetts' Question 2, and Colorado's Amendment 31. These initiatives were successful in every state except Colorado, where Amendment 31 was defeated at the polls. Interestingly, a recent legislation note by the editors of the *Harvard Law Review* suggests that the Colorado amendment was defeated because of an advertising campaign which tapped into voters' fears of white children being held back in school by Hispanic children. *See Education—English Immersion—Colorado Voters Reject an English Immersion Ballot Inititiative–Amendment 31: English Language Education, in Legislative Council of the Colorado General Assembly, 2002 Ballot Information Booklet 18–20, 69–74*, 16 HARV. L. REV. 2709, 2712–13 (2003).

10 *See* Kevin R. Johnson, *A Handicapped, Not "Sleeping" Giant: The Devastating Impact of the Initiative Process on Latina/o Immigrant Communities*, 96 CAL. L. REV. 1259 (2008).

11 Lisa B. Ross, *Learning the Language: An Examination of the use of Voter Initiatives to Make Language Education Policy*, 82 N.Y.U. L. REV. 1510 (2007).

12 MARIA E. BRISK, BILINGUAL EDUCATION: FROM COMPENSATORY TO QUALITY SCHOOLING (2006).

13 Proposition 203 did not apply to students who attended schools protected under tribal sovereignty or federal law. However, it did apply to students who spoke a tribal language, but attended a publicly funded state school.

14 Lisa B. Ross, *supra* note 11.

15 *Id.*

16 ANN C. WILLIG, A Meta-analysis of Selected Studies on the Effectiveness of Bilingual Education, 55, 269–317 (1985).

17 *See generally* Gilbert N. Garcia, *Lessons from Research: What is the Length of Time it Takes Limited English Proficient Students to Acquire English and Succeed in an All-English Classroom?* REV. EDUC. RES. ISSUE BRICF, National Clearinghouse for Bilingual Education (2000).

18 *See generally* JUAN F. PEREA, IMMIGRANTS OUT: IMMIGRANTS OUT!: THE NEW NATIVISM AND THE ANTI-IMMIGRANT IMPULSE IN THE UNITED STATES (1996).

19 *Id.*

20 *See* Ross, *supra* note 14.

21 *See generally* James Crawford, "Hold your Tongue," in RICHARD DELGADO & JEAN STEFANCIC, THE LATINO/A CONDITION (1998).

22 *See generally* Meyer v. Nebraska, 262 U.S. 390 (1923).

23 OFFICE OF CIVIL RIGHTS TITLE VI POLICY ON LANGUAGE MINORITY STUDENTS, 1970, *available at* http://www.ed.gov/about/offices/list/ocr/eeolep/index.html.

24 Lau v. Nichols, 414 U.S. 563 (1974).

25 *Id.*

26 20 U.S.C. § 1703 (1974).

27 *Castaneda v. Pickard*, 648 F.2d 989 (5th Cir. 1981).
28 Rachel F. Moran, *The Politics of Discretion: Federal Intervention in Bilingual Education.* 76 CAL. L. REV. 1249–1352 (1988).
29 Richard Ruiz, *From Language as Problem to Language as Asset: The Promise and Limitations of Lau.* Paper presented at the Annual Conference of the American Educational Research Association, San Diego, CA, 2004.
30 Richard Ruiz, *Orientations in Language Planning*, 8 NABE: THE JOURNAL FOR THE NATIONAL ASSOCIATION FOR BILINGUAL EDUCATION 15 (1984).
31 *Id.*
32 Patricia Gandara and Russell W. Rumberger, *Immigration, Language, and Education: How Does Language Policy Structure Opportunity?*, 111 TCHRS. C. REC. 750 (March 2009).

Chapter 4

1 Public Law 107–110 The No Child Left Behind Act of 2001, codified at 20 U.S.C. and 25 U.S.C.
2 20 U.S.C. § 6301 (2000 & 2004 Supp.)
3 *Id.*
4 20 U.S.C. § 6311(a).
5 20 U.S.C. § 6311(b)(1)(A).
6 20 U.S.C. § 6311(b).
7 20 U.S.C. § 6311(b)(2).
8 20 U.S.C. § 6311(b).
9 20 U.S.C. § 6311(b)(1)(D)(i).
10 20 U.S.C. § 6311(b)(1)(C).
11 20 U.S.C. § 6311(b)(1)(D)(ii).
12 *Id.*
13 20 U.S.C. § 6311 (b)(2)(E).
14 20 U.S.C. § 6311 (b)(3)(C).
15 *Id.*
16 20 U.S.C. § 6319 (a)(2)(A).
17 President George W. Bush, televised address, *The No Child Left Behind Act Is Improving Education*, June 10, 2003.
18 U.S. Department of Education, *Building on Results: A Blueprint for Strengthening The No Child Left Behind Act*, Washington, D.C., January 2007.
19 *Id.* at 2.
20 Sandra Feldman, President, American Federation of Teachers, Address: *Getting Testy*, June 2, 2001, *available at* http://www.aft.org/presscenter/speeches-columns/wws/2001/0601.htm.
21 *See generally* DEBORAH MEIER, ALFIE KOHN, LINDA DARLING-HAMMOND, THEODORE SIZER, AND GEORGE WOOD, MANY CHILDREN LEFT BEHIND: HOW THE NO CHILD LEFT BEHIND ACT IS DAMAGING OUR CHILDREN AND OUR SCHOOLS (2004).
22 Monty Neill, *Low Expectation and Less Learning: the Problem with No Child Left Behind*, 67 SOCIAL EDUCATION 281 (September 2003).
23 *Id.*
24 *See generally* MEIER, *supra* note 21.
25 Matthew Miltich, *Teaching and Learning Are Personal*, Viewpoint, 20 NEA TODAY 7 (March 2002).

26 Jonathan Kozol, The Shame of the Nation: The Restoration of Apartheid Schooling in America (2005).

27 *Id.*

28 *Id.*

29 Bethany Li, *From Bilingual Education to OELALEAALEPS: How the No Child Left Behind Act Has Undermined English Language Learners' Access to a Meaningful Education*, 14 Geo. J. Poverty Law & Pol'y 539 (2007).

30 Sam Dillon, "*No Child Law Is Not Closing a Racial Gap*," N.Y. Times, April 29, 2009 at A1.

31 B.D. Rampey, G.S. Dion, and P.L. Donahue, *NAEP 2008 Trends in Academic Progress* (NCES 2009–479). National Center for Education Statistics, Institute of Education Sciences, U.S. Department of Education (2009).

32 *Id.*

33 *See generally* Angelina KewalRamani, Lauren Gilbertson, Mary Ann Fox, and Stephen Provasnik, *Status and Trends in the Education of Racial and Ethnic Minorities* (NCES 2007–039). National Center for Education Statistics, Institute of Education Sciences, U.S. Department of Education (2007).

34 James E. Ryan, *The Perverse Incentives of the No Child Left Behind Act*, 79 N.Y.U. L. Rev. 932, 940 (2004).

35 Pepi Leistyna, *Corporate Testing: Standards, Profits, and the Demise of the Public Sphere*, 34 Tchr Educ. Q. 2, (March 22, 2007).

36 Francisco Vara-Orta, *Texas Under Fire over Pupils' English Skills*, Austin Am.-Statesman, July 8, 2006, at A01.

37 Randy Capps et al., *Promise or Peril: Immigrants, LEP Students, and the No Child Left Behind Act*, The Urban Institute (2005).

38 David Hayes-Bautista et al., *No Longer a Minority: Latinos and social policy in California.* UCLA Chicano Studies Research Center (1992).

39 Clemencia Cosentino de Cohen, Nicole Deterding, and Beatriz Chu Clewell, *Profile of US Elementary Schools: LEP Concentration and School Capacity*, The Urban Institute, 2005.

40 Randy Capps et al., *Immigration and the No Child Left Behind Act: The New Demography of America's Schools*, The Urban Institute (2005).

41 Robert R. Aponte & Marcelo E. Siles, *Latinos in the Heartland: The Browning of the Midwest* (JSRI Research Report No. 5, Julian Samora Research Institute, 1994).

42 Clemencia Cosentino de Cohen, *Who's Left Behind?: Immigrant Children in High and Low-LEP Schools*, Washington, DC: The Urban Institute, 2005.

43 Capps, *Immigration, supra* note 37.

44 Clemencia Cosentino de Cohen, *Who's Left Behind, supra* note 42.

45 *Id.*

46 *See generally* Stanton Wortham, Enrique G. Murillo & Edmund T. Hamman, Education in the New Latino Diaspora: Policy and the Politics of Identity (2001).

47 NCLB requires schools and districts to report progress by the following subgroups: (1) Native American, (2) Asian, (3) Latino, (4) African American, (5) White, (6) Limited English Proficient, (7) Special Education, and (8) Free and Reduced Lunch. Some states may include other subgroups such as migrant students or non-responders. A subgroup is formed when a minimum number of students in a school meet a particular categorical designation. The minimum threshold is operationally defined by each state. Student scores in each subgroup are then used to calculate AYP for the subgroup.

48 Capps et al., *Promise or Peril?, supra* note 37.

49 *Id.*

50 *See generally* WORTHAM, ET. AL., *supra* note 46.

51 *See* US Department of Education website: http://www.ed.gov/nclb/methods/ teachers/hqtflexibility.html.

52 In some states, ESL teachers do not have to meet the highly qualified designation because they do not teach in one of the "core" subject areas as defined by the state and/or NCLB.

53 *See* Cosentino de Cohen, *Who's Left Behind?, supra* note 42.

54 Christine H. Rossell, *The Flawed Requirements for Limited English Proficient Children of the No Child Left Behind Act,* 186 J. OF ED., 29–40 (2005).

55 U.S. Department of Education Fact Sheet, *New No Child Left Behind Regulations: Flexibility and Accountability for Limited Proficiency Student,* September 11, 2006, *available at:* http://www.ed.gov/admins/lead/account/lepfactsheet. pdf.

56 There is much debate about standardized tests being not valid or reliable measures for English Language Learners. Critics argue that ELL students perform poorly on such tests because they largely measure language competency and not content knowledge. This is true for all standardized tests—not just those in English/Language Arts. *See, e.g.* Marilyn S. Thompson, et al *¿Éxito en California? A validity critique of language program evaluations and analysis of English learner test scores.* 10 ED. POL'Y ANALYSIS (January 25, 2002), *available at:* http://epaa.asu.edu/epaa/v10n7.

57 US Department of Education Fact Sheet, *New No Child Left Behind Regulations: Flexibility and Accountability For Limited Proficient Students,* September 11, 2006, *available at:* http://www.ed.gov/admins/lead/account/lepfactsheet.pdf

58 *See* Rossell, *supra* note 54.

59 *Id.*

60 Randy Capps et al., *Paying the Price: The Impact of Immigration Raids on America's Children,* National Council of La Raza (2007).

61 For a summary table of the school sanctions by state, *see* National Center for Education Statistics, State Education Reforms, Table 1.4 "Types of school sanctions by state 2005–06, *available at:* http://nces.ed.gov/programs/statere form/ tab1_4.asp.

Chapter 5

1 Grutter v. Bollinger, 539 U.S. 306 (2003).

2 Parents Involved in Community Schools v. Seattle School District No. 1, 551 U.S. 701, 127 S. Ct. 2738 (2007).

3 Ian Haney López, *Colorblind to the Reality of Race in America,* 53 CHRON. HIGH. EDUC. 3 (November 2006).

4 *Id.*

5 *Id.*

6 Plessy v. Ferguson, 163 U.S. 537, 559 (1896) (Harlan, J. dissenting).

7 López, *supra* note 3.

8 Plessy, 163 U.S. at 559 (Harlan, J. dissenting).

9 *Id.* at 557 (Harlan, J. dissenting).

10 *See* López, *supra* note 3.

11 Mark Mather, *U.S. Racial/Ethnic and Regional Poverty Rates Converge, but Kids*

Are Still Left Behind, Population Reference Bureau (August 2007), *available at* http://www.prb.org/Articles/2007/USRacialEthnicAndRegionalPoverty.aspx.

12 *Id.*

13 Jack Balkin and Reva Siegel, *Principles, Practices and Social Movements*, 154 U. Pa. L. Rev. 927, n.48 (showing the use of Brown's legacy to advance arguments for the Racial Privacy Initiative).

14 *Id.*

15 Peggy McIntosh, *White Privilege and Male Privilege: A Personal Account of Coming to See Correspondences Through Work in Women's Studies* (1988).

16 López, *supra* note 7 at 3.

17 *Id.*

18 Regents of the University of California v. Bakke, 438 U.S. 265 (1978).

19 Maurice Dyson, *Multiracial Identity, Monoracial Authenticity & Racial Privacy: Towards an Adequate Theory of Multiracial Resistance*, 9 Mich. J. Race & L. 387 (2004).

20 Richa Amar, *Unequal Protection and the Racial Privacy Initiative*, 52 UCLA L. Rev. 1279, 1281 (2005).

21 Dyson, *supra* note 19 at 387.

22 Chris Chambers Goodman, *Redacting Race in the Quest for Colorblind Justice: How Racial Privacy Legislation Subverts Antidiscrimination Laws*, 88 Marquette L. Rev. 299, 300 (2004).

23 *Id.*

24 Amar, *supra* note 20 at 1283.

25 U.S. Const. Amend. XIV § 1. The Equal Protection Clause states that "No State shall make or enforce any law which shall abridge the privileges or immunities of citizens of the United States; nor shall any State deprive any person of life, liberty, or property, without due process of law; nor deny to any person within its jurisdiction the equal protection of the laws." *Id.*

26 J. Nowak & R. Rotunda, Treatise on Constitutional Law–Substance and Procedure, Section 18.8(a) (4th ed. 2007–8).

27 Amar, *supra* note 20 at 1293.

28 Korematsu v. United States, 323 U.S. 214 (1944).

29 Washington v. Seattle Sch. Dist. 458 U.S. 457, 471 (1982) (*citing* Pers. Adm'r of Mass. v. Feeney, 442 U.S. 256, 279 (1979).

30 *See* Amar No. 1 *supra* note 20 at 1301.

31 *Id.*

32 *Id.* at 1293.

33 *Id* at 1294; *see also,* Hunter v. Erickson, 393 U.S. 385 (1969).

34 Hunter v. Erickson, 393 U.S. at 391–93 (1969).

35 *Id.* at 392.

36 *Id.*

37 *Id.* at 391.

38 *Id.*

39 Goodman, *supra* note 22 at 351.

40 *Id.* at 322.

41 458 U.S. 457 (1982).

42 *Id.* at 474.

43 946 F. Supp. 1480 (N.D. Cal. 1996).

44 Cal. Const. art. I, 31(a).

45 946 F. Supp. at 1505–6.

46 *Id.* at 1520.

47 122 F.3d 692 (9th Cir. 1997).
48 Gary Phillips, *Initiative on Racial Privacy Will Thwart Bias Remedies*, L.A. DAILY J., August 18, 2003, at 6.
49 *Id.*
50 Law No. 78–17 of 1978, Journal Officiel de la République Française [J.O.] [Official Gazette of France], Jan. 6, 1978, secs. 1–8 (amended Aug. 6, 2004), *cited in* David B. Oppenheimer, *Why France Needs to Collect Data on Racial Identity*, 31 HASTINGS INT'L & COMP. L. REV. 735 (2008).
51 *Id.*
52 RICHARD ROTHSTEIN, CLASS AND SCHOOLS 15 (2004).
53 National Center for Education Statistics, Condition of Education 2003, Table 22–1, *available at* http://nces.ed.gov/pubs2003/2003067_App1.pdf.
54 Education Trust, Latino Achievement in America 1, (2003), *available at* http://www2.edtrust.org/edtrust/latino+achievement+in+america.
55 Educational Policy Institute, Media Release, New Study Reveals Scale of Education Gap between Latino and White Students, June 23, 2004, *available at* http://web.mit.edu/mites/www/about/latino_youth_press_release.pdf.
56 Richard Michaelson, Michelle Probert, Van Sweringen, Marc Wolf, *The Classification of Race, Ethnicity, Color or National Origin (CRECNO) Initiative: A Guide to the Projected Impacts on Californians*, Institute of Governmental Studies, Policy Papers, Paper 2003–1., *available at* http://repositories.cdlib.org/igs/igspp/pp2003-116–17, 2003.
57 *Id.* at 16.
58 Amar, *supra* note 20 at 1304.
59 Quotation and preceding list from Amar at 1304.
60 Parents Involved in Community Schools v. Seattle School District No. 1, 127 S. Ct. 2738, 2768 (2007).
61 Amar, *supra* note 20 at 1304.
62 Dyson, *supra* note 19 at 387.
63 Anita Allen, *Race, Face, and Rawls*, 72 FORDHAM L. REV. 1677, 1688 (2004).
64 Lior Jacob Strahilevitz, *Privacy versus Antidiscrimination*, 75 U. CHI. L. REV. 363, 371 (2008). Note that Strahilevitz makes this prescription regarding antidiscrimination lawsuits but its applicability for decisionmakers in other circumstances should be useful for undocumented students as well.
65 Ian F. Haney López, *The Social Construction of Race*, in CRITICAL RACE THEORY, THE CUTTING EDGE 165 (Richard Delgado and Jean Stefancic, eds., 2d ed., 2000).
66 TARA J. YOSSO, CRITICAL RACE COUNTERSTORIES ALONG THE CHICANA/CHICANO EDUCATIONAL PIPELINE 5 (2006).
67 RICHARD DELGADO & JEAN STEFANCIC, CRITICAL RACE THEORY: AN INTRODUCTION 16 (2001).
68 María Pabón López, *Reflections on Educating Latino and Latina Undocumented Children: Beyond* Plyler v. Doe, 35 SETON HALL L. REV. 1373 (2005).
69 Cheryl Harris, *Too Pure an Air: Somerset's Legacy from Anti-Slavery to Color Blindness*, 13 TEX. WESLEYAN L. REV. 439, 458 (2007).
70 *See* Allen, *supra* note 63 at 1696.
71 *Id.*
72 *Id.* at 1695.
73 Ruth Colker, *Anti-Subordination Above All: Sex, Race, and Equal Protection*, 61 N.Y.U. L. REV. 1003, 1007–08 (1986).
74 *Id.* at n. 12.

75 *See* Robert Westley, *First Time Encounters: "Passing" Revisited and Demystification as a Critical Practice*, 18 YALE L. & POL'Y REV. 297, 305 (2000).

76 *See* Dyson, *supra* note 19 at 387.

77 *See e.g.* United States v. Esparza Mendoza, 265 F. Supp. 2d 1256 (N.D. Utah 2003).

78 Amy Miller, *APS Safe for Migrant Students*, ALBUQ. J., June 2, 2006, at A1.

79 Debra Dominguez, *3 Students Returning to Mexico*, ALBUQ. J., February 2, 2005 at B1.

80 *Id.*

81 *Id.*

82 *Id.*

83 Murillo v. Musegades, 809 F. Supp. 487, 486–95 (W.D. Tex. 1992).

84 *Id.* at 501.

85 Raam Wong, *ICE Picks up Dad at School District*, ALBUQ. J. March 29, 2007 at 1.

86 Richard Jacques, *ICE Deports Pregnant High School Student Following Traffic Ticket*, ROSWELL DAILY REC, December 12, 2007.

87 Daniel T. v. Bd. of County Comm. of Otero County, First Amended Complaint, Civ. No. 07-1044 WJ/WPL (D. N. Mex 2007).

88 Otero County Sheriff's Office, New Mexico Operational Procedure Regarding Inquiry into Immigration Status, *available at* http://www.maldef.org/pdf/Otero.County.Operational.Procedure.pdf.

89 *Id.*

90 Jose Luis Aguirre, *California Interfaith Leaders Urge Suspension of Immigration Raids*, CATH ONLINE, April 4, 2007, *available at* http://www.catholic.org/national/national_story.php?id=23652.

91 *See* Lyanne Melendez, *Peninsula Parents Worry over Immigration Raids*, February 7, 2007, *available at* http://abclocal.go.com/kgo/story?section=local&id=5013389.

92 *Id.*

93 *Id.*

94 Amanda Martinez, *Immigration Raids Startle Communities in Oakland and Berkeley*, New American Media, News Report, May 7, 2008, *available at* http://news.ncmonline.com/news/view_article.html?article_id=9abc2b98739 510819087a8c2144d9c20.

95 *Id.*

96 *Id.*

97 Jill Tucker, Jaxon Van Derbeken, *ICE Raids on Homes Panic Schools, Politicians*, SAN FRANCISCO CHRON, May 7, 2008, *available at* http://www.sfgate.com/cgi-bin/article.cgi?f=/c/a/2008/05/06/BA8B10HRUS.DTL.

98 *See* Martinez, *supra* note 94.

99 Jill Tucker, Jaxon Van Derbeken, *supra* note 97.

100 *See* Martinez, *supra* note 94.

101 *Id.*

102 *Id.*

103 *Id.*

104 *Id.*

105 *Id.*

106 *See* Tucker, *supra* note 99.

107 Mary Ann Zehr, *Iowa Immigration Raid Called a "Man-Made Disaster,"* EDUC. WEEK, May 14, 2008.

108 Stephen Joel, *My Obligations during an Immigration Crackdown*, SCH. ADMINISTRATOR. November 2007.

109 Tim Walker, *Caught in the Crossfire, Schools in Oklahoma Grapple with New Laws Targeting Illegal Immigration*, NEA TODAY, January 2008.

110 Michael Norris, *Immigration Raid Leaves Schools Scrambling*, All Things Considered, National Public Radio, March 14, 2007, *available at* http://www.npr.org/templates/story/story.php?storyId=8904393 (last visited August 9, 2007).

111 *Id.*

112 Mary Ann Zehr, *With Immigrants, District Balance Safety, Legalities*, EDUC. WEEK, published online September 10, 2007.

113 *Id.*

114 *See* Murillo v. Musegades, 809 F. Supp. 487, 496 (W.D. Tex. 1992) ("[t]he El Paso Border Patrol does not comply with the policy issued by A.H. Giugi, District Director of the INS Service El Paso District, which states 'that all law enforcement activities at all levels and types of schools is prohibited unless prior approval has been granted as provided ... .'").

115 United States v. López-Mendoza, 468 U.S. 1032, 1051 (1984).

116 Wong Sun v. United States, 371 U.S. 471 (1963).

117 United States v. López-Mendoza, 468 U.S. 1032, 1041 (1984).

118 *Id.*

119 *Id.* ("[o]ur conclusions concerning the exclusionary rule's value might change, if there developed good reason to believe that Fourth Amendment violations by INS officers were widespread."); *see also id.* at 1041 (explaining that it was adopting the cost-benefit framework of United States v. Janis, 428 U.S. 433 (1976)).

120 U.S. CONST. amend. IV.

121 494 U.S. 259 (1990).

122 *Id.* at 264.

123 *Id.* at 266.

124 *Id.* at 265.

125 *Id.* at 271.

126 *Id.*

127 Verdugo-Urquidez, 494 U.S. at 279 (Brennan, J. dissenting).

128 *Id.* at 284 (Brennan, J. dissenting) (citing MADISON REPORT ON THE VIRGINIA RESOLUTIONS (1800), *reprinted in* 4 ELLIOT'S DEBATES 556 (2d ed. 1836)).

129 *Id.* at 287 (Brennan, J. dissenting).

130 *Id.* at 286–87 (Brennan, J. dissenting).

131 *Id.* at 271–73.

132 2005 WL 629487 (W.D.N.Y. 2005) (unpublished opinion by Magistrate Foschio).

133 Verdugo-Urquidez, 494 U.S. at 278. *See also*, Martinez-Aguero, 459 F.3d at 624–25 ("If, however, we take at face value the fact that Justice Kennedy joined the opinion of the Court, there are five votes for the proposition that 'aliens receive constitutional protections when they have come within the territory of the United States and developed substantial connections with the country.'").

134 United States v. López-Mendoza, 468 U.S. 1032, 1051 (1984). It is worth noting that the rationale for removing the exclusionary rule from use in deportation proceedings comes from language analogizing illegal immigrants to drugs and hazardous waste: "Presumably no one would argue that the exclusionary rule should be invoked to prevent an agency from ordering corrective action at a leaking hazardous waste dump if the evidence underlying the order had been improperly obtained, or to compel police to return contraband explosives or drugs to their owner if the contraband had been unlawfully seized." *Id.* at 1054. *See* also Raquel E. Aldana, *Of Katz and Aliens: Privacy Expectations and the*

Immigration Raids, 41 U.C. Davis L. Rev. 1089–90 (2008) (discussing such analogy by Justice O'Connor in López-Mendoza case).

135 Verdugo, 494 U.S. at 276.

136 *Id.*

137 *Id.*

138 Victor C. Romero, Alienated: Immigrant Rights, the Constitution and Equality in America 78 (2005).

139 *Id.*

140 *Id.* at 81–82.

141 *Id.* at 83.

142 *Id.* at 82.

143 *See* Martinez-Aguero v. Gonzalez, 459 F.3d 618, 625 (5th Cir. 2006) (Court countenanced noncitizen's argument that "her regular and lawful entry of the U.S. pursuant to a valid border-crossing card and her acquiescence in the U.S. system of immigration constitute her voluntary acceptance of societal obligations, rising to the level of 'substantial connections'"); United States v. Tehrani, 826 F. Supp. 789, 793 (D. Vt. 1993) (temporary tourist visas qualified as "substantial connections").

144 United States v. Iribe, 11 F.3d 153 (10th Cir. 1993); United States v. Medina Ortega, 2000 WL 1469314 (D. Kan. 2000).

145 United States v. Esparza Mendoza, 265 F. Supp. 2d 1254, 1256 (N.D. Utah 2003).

146 *Id.* at 1271.

147 *Id.*

148 386 F.3d. 953, 960.

149 *Id.* at 955.

150 Angie Welling, *Court Dilutes Verdict on Immigration*, Deseret Morn. News, October 15, 2004.

151 *Id.*

152 *Id.*

153 *Id.*

154 United States v. Guitterez, No. CR 96-40075 SBA, 1997 U.S. Dist. LEXIS 16446, at *16 (N.D. Cal. Oct. 14, 1997).

155 United States v. Guitterez, 983 F. Supp. 905, 917 (N.D. Cal. 1998), *rev'd on other grounds*, 203 F. 3d 833 (9th Cir. 1999).

156 2005 WL 3334758 (N.D. Utah 2005).

157 *Id.* at *6.

158 *Id.* at *1.

159 *Id.* at *5.

160 2005 WL 629487 (W.D.N.Y. 2005) (unpublished opinion by Magistrate Foschio).

161 520 F.3d 569 (6th Circ. 2008).

162 *Id.* at 571.

163 Travis Loller, *Court Says Illegal Immigrant's Rights Violated*, Associated Press, March 22, 2008.

164 520 F.3d at 572.

165 *Id.* at 577.

166 553 F Supp. 2d 1259 (D. Kan. 2008).

167 *Id.*

168 *Id.* at 1272.

169 983 F. Supp. 905, 912–13 (N.D. Cal. 1998), *rev'd on other grounds*, 203 F.3d 833 (9th Cir. 1999).

170   2005 WL 388589, at *16–17 (W.D. Tex.2005).
171   18 F. Supp. 2d 38, 60 & n.17 (D.D.C.1998).
172   United States v. Mendenhall, 446 U.S. 544, 554 (1980).
173   United States v. Delgado, 466 U.S. 210, 216 (1984) (INS questioning of workers for a brief time inside the factory after warrant was served was not a seizure).
174   *Reexamining the Constitutionality of INS Workplace Raids after the Immigration and Reform Act of 1986*, 100 Harv. L. Rev. 1979 (1987).
175   *See infra* text accompanying notes 293–303.
176   United States v. Mendoza, 559 F. Supp. 842, 847 (W.D. Tex. 1982) (tips by police that illegal aliens were in bars earlier in the month was insufficient to constitute a reasonable suspicion) (citing United States v. Cortez, 449 U.S. 411 (1981); *see also* United States v. Brignoni-Ponce, 422 U.S. 873, 884, 95 S Ct. at 2581 (1975) ("A roving patrol may stop a vehicle for brief investigation as to the citizenship of the occupants, where the intrusion is modest, based on specific articulable facts that reasonably warrant suspicion that the vehicles contain aliens who may be illegally in the country.").
177   United States v. Brignoni Ponce, 422 U.S. 873, 885 (1975).
178   Farm Labor Org. Comm. v. Ohio State Highway Patrol, 991 F. Supp. 895, 901 (N.D. Ohio 1997).
179   *Id.* at 904.
180   *Id.*
181   Matter of King and Yang, 16 I. & N. Dec. 502 (1978) ("The respondents' Oriental appearance, combined with the past history of illegal alien employment at that particular restaurant, and the anonymous tip, clearly would give rise to a reasonable suspicion of alienage sufficient to justify the very limited invasion of privacy engendered by a nondetentional questioning.").
182   Texas Civil Rights Project Newsclip, Email Warns of Illegal Immigration Crackdowns in Classrooms (Apr. 26, 2006), http:// www.texascivilrightsproject.org/newspub/clip_060426_email_warns.html.
183   *Id.*
184   *Id.*
185   Katie Humphrey, *Parents without ID Denied Access to Del Valle Schools, New Policy Protects Students, District Says*, Austin Am.-Statesman, April 8, 2007, at B1.
186   Katie Humphrey, *Del Valle Schools Change Rules on ID*, Austin Am. Statesman, May 23, 2007, at B1.
187   John Willshire Carrera, Immigrant Students: Their Legal Right of Access to Public Schools 14–15 (National Coalition of Advocates for Students, 1989).
188   Katz v. United States, 389 U.S. 347, 353 (1976).
189   *Id.* at 361.
190   Matthew B. Kurek, U.S. v. Guitterez: *A Functional Approach to a Vexing Issue*, 30 U. Tol. l. Rev. 359, 379 (1999).
191   *See* Aldana, *supra* note 134 at 1089.
192   Julia Preston, *U.S. Set to Begin a Vast Expansion of DNA Sampling*, N.Y. Times, Feb. 5, 2007.
193   United States v. Montoya de Hernandez, 473 U.S. 531, 537 (1985).
194   *Id.*
195   *See* 8 C.F.R. 287.1(a)(1) and (2) (2008).
196   413 U.S. 266, 273 (1973).
197   United States v. Brignoni-Ponce, 422 U.S. 873 (1975).
198   *Id.* at 886–87.

199 *See e.g.,* United States v. Matlock, 415 U.S. 164 (1974).
200 Boyd v. United States 115 U.S. 616 (1886).
201 Mapp v. Ohio, 367 U.S. 643, 648 (1961).
202 *Id.*
203 468 U.S. 1032 (1984).
204 *Id.* at 1038.
205 *Id.* at 1051 (citation omitted).
206 22 F.3d 1441 (9th Cir. 1994).
207 *Id.* at 1442.
208 Orhorhaghe v. I.N.S., 38 F.3d 488, 497 (9th Cir. 1994).
209 *Id.* at 498.
210 342 U.S. 165 (1951).
211 *Id.* at 175.
212 Stella Jane Elias, *Good Reason to Believe: Widespread Constitutional Violations in the Course of Immigration Enforcement and the Case for Revisiting López Mendoza,* 2008 Wis. L. Rev. 1109.
213 Plyler v. Doe, 457 U.S. 202, 221 (1982).
214 *See* Murillo v. Musegades, 809 F. Supp. 487 at 498 ("[t]he public interest is served when students and their teachers are free from undue interference from law enforcement officers.").
215 López-Mendoza, 468 U.S. at 1045.
216 Matthew B. Kurek, United States v. Guitterez: *A Functional Approach to a Vexing Issue,* 30 U. Tol. L. Rev. 359, 367 (1999).
217 Fong Yue Ting v. United States 149 US 698 (1893).
218 Legarda v. Valdez, 1 Phil. Rep. 146 (1902).
219 I.N.S v. López-Mendoza, 468 U.S. 1032 (1984).
220 *Id.* at 047, note 44, *cited in* Aldana, 41 U.C. Davis L. Rev. 1081, 1089–90 (2008).
221 Verdugo, 494 U.S. at 274; *but see* United States v. Baboolal, 2006 U.S. Dist. LEXIS 40645 ("the defendant has not been present physically within the U.S. since 2003. When he has been physically within the United States, it has been for brief periods of time and for activities such as vacationing, shopping, or picking up family from the airport. These connections do not fit into the category of substantial.").
222 United States v. Verdugo-Urquidez, 494 U.S. 259, 265 (1990).
223 *See* New Jersey v. T.L.O., 469 U.S. 325, 337 (1985).
224 *Id.* at 341–42.
225 *Id.* at 337.
226 *Id.* at 340.
227 *Id.* at 341.
228 *Id.* at 336.
229 469 U.S. 325, 342 (1985).
230 *See* Bd. of Educ. v. Earls, 536 U.S. 822, 838 (2002), Veronica School District 47J v. Acton, 515 U.S. 646, 665 (1995).
231 3–9 Educ. Law § 9.08[9][b] (James A. Rapp, ed. 1984 & 2008 Supp.) (citing M.J v. State, 399 So. 2d 996, 998 (Fla. Dist. Ct. App. 1981); F.P. v. State, 528 So. 2d 1253 (Fla. Ct. App. 1988)).
232 Colorado v. P.E.A, 754 P.2d 382, 385 (Colo. 1988).
233 *Id.*
234 *Id. (citing* Lawrence F. Rossow & Jacqueline A. Stefkovich, Search and Seizure in the Public Schools 77 (3d ed. 2006)).
235 3–9 Educ. Law § 9.08[9][b] (James A. Rapp, ed. 1984 & 2008 Supp.) (citing Milligan v. City of Slidell, 226 F.3d 652–55 (5th Cir. 2000)).

236 *Id.*
237 *Id.* (citing Cason v. Cook, 810 F.2d 188 (8th Cir. 1987).
238 *Id.*
239 Blackie's House of Beef v. Castillo, 659 F.2d 1211, 1222 (D.C. Cir. 1981).
240 8 U.S.C. § 1357 (2000).
241 *Id.*
242 Blackie's House of Beef v. Castillo, 659 F.2d 1211, 1222 (D.C. Cir. 1981).
243 *Id.* at 1226.
244 Molders v. Local Union No. 164, 799 F.2d 547, 552 (9th Cir. 1986).
245 *Id.* at 552.
246 443 U.S. 622 (1979).
247 *Id.* at 625.
248 *Id.* at 646; *see also* DOUGLAS ABRAMS & SARAH RAMSEY CHILDREN AND THE LAW 74 (2000) (explaining the mature minor doctrine).
249 *Bellotti,* 443 U.S. at 651.
250 *Id.* at 633.
251 *Id.* at 635.
252 *Id.* at 637.
253 *Id.* at 639, *see also id.* at 639 n.18 ("The Court's opinions discussed in the text above—*Pierce, Yoder, Prince* and *Ginsberg*—all have contributed to a line of decisions suggesting the existence of a constitutional parental right against undue, adverse interference by the State.").
254 *Bellotti,* 443 U.S. at 638.
255 *Plyler,* 457 U.S. at 238 (citing *Trimble v. Gordon,* 430 U.S. 762, 770 (1977)).
256 *Id.* at 241.
257 3–9 EDUC. LAW § 9.08[9][b] (James A. Rapp, ed. 1984 & 2008 Supp.)
258 *See* Aldana, *supra* note 134 at 1089.
259 *See* Randy Capps, Rosa Maria Castaneda, Ajay Chaudry, Robert Santos, *Paying the Price: The Impact of Immigration Raids on America's Children,* National Council of La Raza & The Urban Institute (2007).
260 *See* Standard 2, Council for Chief State School Officers, Interstate School Leaders Licensure Consortium ("ISLLC"), Standards for School Leaders.
261 *See* Standard 2, National Association for Secondary School Principals, Draft of Revised SLLC Standards, August 10, 2007.
262 403 U.S. 388 (1971).
263 *See* Sosa v. Alvarez-Machain, 542 U.S. 692, 736 (2004) (Discussing in dicta that a *Bivens* action would be preferable for an alien than an Alien Tort Claims Act action in this instance).
264 403 U.S. at 389–90.
265 *Id.* at 396.
266 *Id.* at 397.
267 *Id.*
268 *Id.*
269 CHARLES GORDON, STANLEY MAILMAN & STEPHEN YALE-LOEHR, IMMIGRATION LAW AND PROCEDURE § 109.02[3] Matthew Bender and Co. (updated 2007).
270 *Id.* at § 109.01.
271 *See* Martinez-Aguero v. Gonzalez, 459 F.3d 618, 625 (5th Cir. 2006).
272 *Id.* at 620.
273 *Id.*
274 *Id.*

275 *See supra* text accompanying notes 115–19, 134, 214–16, and 219–220.

276 Siegert v. Gilley, 500 U.S. 226 (1987).

277 United States v. Nichols, 21 F.3d 1016, 1018 (10th Cir. 1994) (citations omitted).

278 360 U.S. 423 (1959).

279 *Id.* at 425–26.

280 *Id.*

281 *Id.*

282 *Id.* at 439.

283 United States v. Levin, 973 F.2d 463, 466 (6th Cir. 1992) (explaining Raley. v. Ohio).

284 *Id*; *see also*, United States v. Laub, 385 U.S. 474; United States v. Pennsylvania Indus. Chem. Corp., 411 U.S. 655, Cox v. Louisiana, 379 U.S. 559.

285 184 F.3d 1160, 1167 (10th Cir. 1999).

286 *Id.*

287 *See* United States v. Etheridge, 932 F.2d 318, 321 (4th Cir. 1991) (holding that advice from a state court judge to a felon, that he could hunt with a gun, was not a defense to felony possession charges because "the government that advises and government that prosecutes is not the same."); *see also* Model Penal Code § 2.04(3)(b)(iv)(requiring an "official interpretation of the public officer or body charged by law with responsibility for the interpretation, administration, or enforcement of the law defining the defense").

288 *See generally*, "Public School Attendance of Undocumented Students," *available at*: www.doe.in.gov/lmmp/pdf/pamphlet.pdf (last visited May 14, 2009).

289 John Willshire Carrera, *Immigrant Students, Their Legal Right to Access Public Schools, A Guide for Advocates and Educators*, 39, (National Coalition for Advocates for Students) 1992 (ERIC Document Reproduction Service No. ED 381 588.

290 *See generally* Aldana, *supra* note 134.

291 *Id.*

292 *See* Juliet Stumpf, *The Crimmigration Crisis: Immigrants, Crime and Sovereign Power*, 56 Am. U. L. Rev. 367 (2008).

293 Devon Carbado, *(E)racing the Fourth Amendment*, 100 Mich. L. Rev. 946, 968 (2002).

294 *Id.* at 994.

295 *Id.* at 971.

296 *Id.*

297 *Id.*

298 *Id.* at 965.

299 466 U.S. 210, (1984).

300 *Id.*

301 *Id.* at 216.

302 Carbado *supra* note 293 at 998.

303 *See* text accompanying notes 73–75 *supra*.

Conclusion

1 Plyler v. Doe, 457 U.S. 202, 226 (1982).

2 See Sam Dillon, *"No Child Law" is not Closing Racial Achievement Gap*, N.Y. Times, April 29, 2009.

3 *See* Brian Alexander, *Amid Flu Outbreak Racism Goes Viral*, May 1, 2009, *available at* http://www.msnbc.msn.com/id/30467300/from/ET/. The outbursts

have included such offensive language as "no contact anywhere with an illegal alien" or "This disgusting blight is because MEXICANS ARE PIGS!" *Id.*

4 Ediberto Roman, *The Alien Invasion*, 45 Houston L. Rev. 841 (2008).

5 *Sheriffs Want to Test Immigration Ruling*, East Valley Trib., April 29, 2009, *available at* http://www.eastvalleytribune.com/story/138491.

6 347 U.S. 483 (1954).

7 *See* Derrick Bell, Silent Covenants: *Brown v. Board of Education* and the Unfulfilled Hopes for Racial Reform 67 (2004).

8 Admittedly, this view may change over time with a greater acceptance by the United States populace of the undocumented worker. As the number of retiring Americans increases, and there is a realization that the Social Security benefits available for them would be larger, or they could retire earlier with new entrants into the Social Security system who bring the fruits of their labor into the system, acceptance of undocumented workers may grow.

9 *See generally* Lani Guinier & Gerald Torres, The Miner's Canary (2002).

10 *Id., see also, About the Miner's Canary, available at:* http://www.minerscanary.org/about.shtm (last visited May 1, 2009).

Index

9 780415 957946